The Law of Negligence

To my children

The Law of Negligence

Francis McManus

EDINBURGH
University Press

Edinburgh University Press is one of the leading university presses in the UK. Publishing new research in the arts and humanities, EUP connects people and ideas to inspire creative thinking, open new perspectives and shape the world we live in. For more information, visit www.edinburghuniversitypress.com.

Edinburgh University Press Ltd
13 Infirmary Street, Edinburgh EH1 1LT

Typeset in Adobe Caslon Pro
by Deanta Global Publishing Services, Chennai, India
Printed and bound in the UK using 100% renewable electricity by
CPI Group (UK) Ltd

A CIP record for this book is available from the British Library

ISBN 978 1 3995 3541 0 (hardback)
ISBN 978 1 3995 3543 4 (webready PDF)
ISBN 978 1 3995 3544 1 (epub)

EU Authorised Representative:
Easy Access System Europe
Mustamäe tee 50, 10621 Tallinn, Estonia
gpsr.requests@easproject.com

MIX
Paper | Supporting responsible forestry
FSC
www.fsc.org
FSC® C013604

This book is printed using paper from well-managed forests, recycling and other controlled sources

Contents

Acknowledgements

I would like to thank the library staff of Stirling University, Edinburgh University, the National Library of Scotland, and the Institute of Advanced Legal Studies, London for their help.

I would also like to thank the anonymous peer-reviewers for their helpful comments.

Finally, I must thank the staff of Edinburgh University Press for their help in the publication of this book.

The law is considered correct as of the 31st March 2025. However, it has been possible to take account of some later developments.

Francis McManus
Livingston

Table of Cases

National Cases

European Court of Human Rights

Table of Legislation

Statutes

International Documents

Introduction

The law of negligence represents the most rapidly expanding and challenging areas of the law of delict. In *The Law of Negligence* the author discusses negligence in relation to the modern law in Scotland. Scottish courts have tended to follow English decisions in this area of law. However, the author has indicated where the Scottish courts have not done so. The law is currently at an interesting juncture, with the courts continuing to redefine the boundaries of the duty of care since the landmark decision of *Donoghue v Stevenson* in 1932. Indeed, the law is in a constant state of flux. Negligence actions brought against public authorities, including hospital authorities, the police and local authorities, represent a particularly fertile ground of litigation. Therefore, a book concentrating on the law of negligence seems timely. The book is aimed at academics, advanced law students and also practitioners.

CHAPTER 1

The development of the concept of duty of care during the nineteenth century, until the landmark House of Lords case of *Donoghue* v *Stevenson*,[1] is discussed. The chapter then discusses the application of Lord Atkin's 'neighbour principle', which was enunciated in that case, which considerably expanded the boundaries of the duty of care. The neighbour principle reached its high-water mark in the House of Lords case of *Home Office v Dorset Yacht Co*[2] where the House displayed willingness to apply the neighbour principle, unless there was justification for its exclusion. However, such a sanguine approach to the neighbour principle did not survive the decade. The change in judicial attitude was heralded by the House of Lords case of *Anns v Merton LBC*[3] where Lord Wilberforce, in refining Lord Atkin's 'neighbour principle', in terms of the duty of care, introduced the two-staged test. The application of that test is discussed. However, the two-stage test was short-lived. The chapter then traces the judicial retreat from *Anns*, up to the decision of the House of Lords in *Caparo v Dickman*[4] where that retreat was completed. In that case, the House instituted the so-called tripartite test, in terms of the duty of care. The chapter then discusses the

---

1 1932 SC (HL) 31.
2 [1970] AC 1004.
3 [1977] AC 728.
4 [1990] 2 AC 605.

application of the tripartite test, up to the Supreme Court case of *Robinson v Chief Constable of West Yorkshire*[5] where the court reinterpreted the tripartite test. In effect, the court advocated a more conservative approach to the development of the concept of the duty of care. The chapter discusses the case law post-*Robinson*. The chapter then examines the concept of the duty of care in relation to liability for omissions. The chapter then focusses on liability for omissions in certain discrete areas, including the well-litigated area of liability of public authorities.

CHAPTER 2

The chapter discusses the concept of duty of care in relation to liability for negligent misstatements. Here, the courts have been required to adopt a more nuanced approach to the development of duty of care. The chapter discusses the landmark case of *Hedley Byrne v Heller*[6] which, in effect, represents 'ground zero' in relation to the development of the law of liability for negligent misstatements. The chapter then goes on to discuss how the law was reformulated in the House of Lords case of *Caparo v Dickman* (above). Subsequent case law, including the Supreme Court case of *Steel v NRAM*,[7] is discussed.

CHAPTER 3

The chapter discusses liability for loss which is not based on any physical injury to the pursuer or his property. In short, the courts have been unwilling to allow claims for economic loss, fearing that to allow such claims would encourage a multiplicity of claims. The chapter discusses the leading cases, both in the United Kingdom and Commonwealth, relating to pure economic loss. The chapter includes discussion of economic loss concerning defective buildings.

CHAPTER 4

The chapter discusses liability for negligently caused psychiatric harm. The chapter traces the development of the law from the nineteenth century. The chapter includes discussion of liability for harm caused to primary and secondary victims of nervous shock. Leading cases, including *Page v Smith* [1996] AC 155 and *Alcock v Chief Constable of South Yorkshire* [1991] 1 AC 310, are discussed. The chapter includes discussion of the recent Supreme Court case of *Paul v Royal Wolverhampton NHS Trust* [2024] UKSC 1.

CHAPTER 5

The chapter discusses breach of the duty of care. The criterion of the reasonable man is discussed, in terms of the standard of care the law demands of the defender.

[5] [2018] UKSC 4.
[6] [1964] AC 463.
[7] [2018] SC (UKSC) 141.

Leading cases, including *Wilsher v Essex Area Health Authority*[8] and *Darnley v Croydon Health Services NHS Trust*,[9] are discussed. The chapter discusses how the standard of care is determined, including discussion of the relevance of custom and practice. Here, the author discusses the test laid down in *Bolam v Friern Hospital Management Committee*.[10] The leading cases, including *Bolitho v City and Hackney Health Authority*[11] and *Montgomery v Lanarkshire Health Board*,[12] are discussed. The chapter concludes with a discussion of the *res ipsa loquitur* rule.

CHAPTER 6

The chapter discusses factual causation in relation to the harm caused by the defender's negligent conduct. The 'but for' and 'material contribution' tests are discussed. As far as the former is concerned, the House of Lords case of *Chester v Afshar*[13] is discussed in detail. As far as the material contribution test is concerned the chapter discusses the leading cases, including *Wardlaw v Bonnington Castings Ltd*.[14] The chapter goes on to discuss how the material contribution test was developed and expanded in *McGhee v National Coal Board*,[15] *Fairchild v Glenhaven Funeral Services Ltd*,[16] *Barker v Corus Ltd*[17] and *Sienkiewicz v Greif*.[18] Subsequent case law, including *Henaghan v Manchester Dry Docks Ltd*,[19] *Williams v Bermuda Hospitals Board*,[20] *John v Central Manchester and Manchester Children's Hospitals NHS Foundation Trust*,[21] *Thorley v Sandwell and West Birmingham Hospitals*,[22] *Holmes v Poeton Holdings Ltd*[23] and *Chetwynd v Tunmore*,[24] is discussed. The chapter then goes on to discuss the relevance of supervening events in terms of factual causation. The chapter then discusses factual causation in terms of loss of chance. Among the cases discussed are *Hotson v East Berkshire Area Health Authority*,[25] *Allied Maples Group Ltd v Simmons and Simmons*[26] and *Perry v Raleys Solicitors*.[27]

---

8 [1987] QB 730.
9 [2019] AC 831.
10 [1957] 1 WLR 582.
11 [1998] AC 232.
12 [2015] UKSC 11.
13 [2005] 1 AC 134.
14 [1956] SC (HL) 26.
15 [1973] SC (HL) 37.
16 [2003] 1 AC 32.
17 [2006] 2 AC 572.
18 [2011] 2 WLR 523.
19 [2016] 1 WLR 2036.
20 [2016] 2 WLR 774.
21 [2016] 4 WLR 54.
22 [2021] EWHC 2604.
23 [2023] EWCA Civ 1377.
24 [2016] EWHC 156.
25 [1987] AC 750.
26 [1995] 1 WLR 1602.
27 [2020] AC 352.

CHAPTER 7

The chapter discusses whether the harm which the pursuer sustains is too remote to allow the pursuer to recover. The now discredited 'directness' test as enunciated in *Re Polemis*[28] is discussed. The chapter then discusses the *Wagon Mound*[29] in which the Privy Council decided that one should employ the foreseeability test to determine if harm which the pursuer suffered was too remote. The chapter goes on to discuss the refinement of the foreseeability test in *Hughes v Lord Advocate*.[30] The chapter continues with the author discussing cases where the court requires to decide the degree of foreseeability, which is required of the defender, for liability to lie. The chapter also includes discussion as to whether the pursuer can recover damages if the relevant accident is of a greater magnitude than could reasonably have been foreseen. The chapter then discusses the application of the so-called 'thin skull' rule, including its application in relation to the pursuer's impecuniosity. The chapter goes on to discuss 'breaking the chain of causation' and how the courts have determined whether the causal chain between the defender's negligent act and the harm which the pursuer has sustained has been broken.

CHAPTER 8

The chapter discusses the defences in delict, which are most relevant in negligence actions. The chapter commences with a discussion of the law relating to contributory negligence. The defence has generated a plethora of case law. The most important cases are discussed. The chapter includes a discussion of how the defence of contributory negligence has been invoked in specific situations, such as road traffic and workplace accidents.

The defence of illegality is discussed. Leading cases, including *Day v Womble Bond Dickinson (UK) Ltd*,[31] *Stoffel v Grondona*,[32] *Patel v Mirza*[33] and the recent case of *Lewis-Ranwell v G4S Health Services Ltd*,[34] are discussed.

The chapter includes discussion of the defence of *volenti*. In addition to discussing the leading cases, the defence is discussed in relation to particular areas of activity.

The chapter concludes with a discussion of the defence of *res judicata*.

[28] [1921] 2 KB 560.
[29] [1961] AC 388.
[30] 1963 SC (HL) 31.
[31] [2020] EWCA Civ 447.
[32] [2021] AC 540.
[33] [2017] AC 467.
[34] [2024] EWCA Civ 138.

Chapter 1

The Duty of Care

INTRODUCTION

In this chapter the emergence of the concept of the duty of care, in terms of the law of negligence in the nineteenth century, is discussed. The chapter then traces the development of the concept of duty of care, up to the landmark case of *Donoghue v Stevenson* (1932).[1] The author goes on to consider subsequent case law, including the leading case of *Home Office v Dorset Yacht Co Ltd* (1970),[2] and the reformulation of Lord Atkin's neighbourhood principle by the House of Lords, in *Anns v Merton LBC* (1977).[3] The author then discusses the House of Lords decision in *Caparo v Dickman*, which overruled *Anns* and introduced the tripartite test in the development of the duty of care, and also established the principle that the law should develop incrementally, that is, on a case-by-case basis. The chapter concludes with a discussion of the Supreme Court case of *Robinson v Chief Constable of West Yorkshire*, which reformulated the tripartite test in *Caparo*, and then goes on to discuss subsequent case law.

THE EMERGENCE OF THE DUTY OF CARE IN NEGLIGENCE

England

The start of the nineteenth century saw a significant number of negligence cases being brought before the English courts.[4] According to Winfield, the rise in the number of cases was attributable to the 'rise ... in industrial machinery. Early railroad trains, in particular, were notable neither for speed nor safety. They killed any object, from a Minister of State to a wandering cow, and this naturally reacted on the law.'[5] The English courts explicitly recognised the concept of duty by 1837. For example, in *Vaughan v Menlove*[6] the defendant negligently constructed a hay rick, near the boundary of his premises. The rick caught fire, by way of spontaneous combustion, and burnt down the claimant's house, which was situated nearby. In holding the

---

1 [1932] AC 562.
2 [1970] AC 1004.
3 [1978] AC 728.
4 J Plunkett *The Duty of Care in Negligence* (Hart, 2018) at 13.
5 P Winfield 'The History of Negligence in the Law of Torts' (1926) 42 LQR 184 at 195.
6 (1837) 3 Bing NC 468; 132 ER 490.

defendant liable, Vaughan J held that everyone takes upon himself the duty of so dealing with his own property as not to injure the property of others.[7] Again, in *Langridge v Levy*[8] the defendant had sold a gun to the father of the plaintiff, the former warranting that the gun was in a safe condition, which it was not. The father gave the gun to his son, the plaintiff, who discharged the gun and was injured. The court rejected the plaintiff's argument that the defendant owed the plaintiff a duty, on the basis that that would lead to an

> indefinite extent of liability ... [and] would be authority for an action against the vendors, even of such instruments and articles as are dangerous in themselves, at the suit of any person whomsoever into whose hands they may happen to pass, and who should be injured thereby.[9]

The concept of duty featured again in the celebrated case of *Winterbottom v Wright*.[10] In that case, the defendant contracted with the Postmaster General to provide a mail coach to convey mail bags. The plaintiff was employed to drive the coach. The defendant had agreed with the Postmaster General that the coach should be kept in a safe condition for the duration of the contract. However, the defendant failed to keep the coach in a safe condition, the upshot of which was that the plaintiff was thrown from his seat and was injured. The plaintiff argued that the defendant owed him a duty to keep the coach in a safe condition. However, the court held that no such duty existed. Lord Abinger, after stating that there was no privity of contract between the parties, added that unless one confined the operation of such contracts to the parties who entered into them, 'the most absurd and outrageous consequences ... to which I can see no limit, would ensue'.[11]

Plunkett states that by the middle of the nineteenth century, the idea of duty was being used to explain liability in cases of both relationship and non-relationship negligence alike.[12] However, the concept of duty was still only being used in an ad hoc manner to bolster claims, rather than because it was required. The author goes on to argue that despite the language of duty being used in 'relationship negligence' (that is to say, in circumstances where there was a prior relationship between the parties such as bailor/bailee, employer/employee) it was not until the second half of the century that judges began to insist that a duty of care was a *necessary* ingredient in cases of negligence.[13] For example, in *Marfell v The South Wales Railway Co*[14] the defendants were owners of a railway and also of a tramway which for some distance ran by the side of the railway and was separated from the railway by a hedge or fence (which also belonged to the railway) down to the point where the tramway crossed the railway. The plaintiff's servant was proceeding along the railway with certain horses and trucks when one of the horses, alarmed by the noise of an approaching train, swerved

[7] Ibid 477, 494.
[8] (1837) 2 M & W 519; 150 ER 863.
[9] Ibid 530, 868.
[10] (1842) 10 M & W 109; 152 ER 402.
[11] Ibid 114, 405.
[12] Plunkett n 4 at 15.
[13] Ibid at 16.
[14] (1860) 8 C.B. NS 525, 141 ER 1271.

onto the railway and was knocked down and killed. The plaintiff brought an action against the railway company, charging it with omitting to use reasonable or proper means to prevent their engines and carriages doing damage, or injury, to persons lawfully being upon and using the tramway. It was held that the plaintiff was entitled to recover. Earle CJ[15] stated:

> The undefined latitude and meaning in which the word 'negligence' has been used, appears to me to have introduced the evil of uncertain law to a pernicious extent; and I think it essential to ascertain that there was a legal duty, and a breach thereof, before a party is made liable by reason of negligence.[16]

However, Plunkett observes that there was absent any clear conceptual unity among the duty cases.[17] No general principles had been established. The law was developed in an empirical manner, decisions that in certain circumstances there was a duty and that in others there was none.[18] However, the law relating to duty was beginning to take shape, as the century progressed. In the leading Court of Appeal case of *Heaven v Pender*[19] Brett MR, in attempting to establish a general principle, whereby one could determine whether the defendant owed the plaintiff a duty of care, introduced the concept of foreseeability. In that case, the defendant, a dock owner, supplied and put up staging outside a ship in his dock, under a contract with the shipowner. The plaintiff was a workman who was employed by a ship painter, who had contracted with the shipowner to paint the outside of the ship. In order to do the painting, the plaintiff went onto and used the staging. One of the ropes by which the staging was slung was defective, the upshot of which was that the plaintiff fell into the dock and was injured. The court held the defendant liable. Brett MR stated:

> When two drivers or two ships are approaching each other, such a relation arises between them when they are approaching each other in such a manner that, unless they use ordinary skill to avoid it, there will be a danger of an injurious collision between them. This relation is established in such circumstances between them, not only if it be proved that they actually know and think of this danger, but whether such proof be made or not … In the case of a railway company carrying a passenger, with whom it has not entered into the contract of carriage, the law implies the duty because it must be obvious that, unless ordinary care and skill be used, the personal safety of the passenger must be endangered … [Whenever] one person is by circumstances placed in such a position with regard to another that everyone with common sense who did think would at once recognise that if he did not at once use reasonable care and skill in his own conduct with regard to these circumstances, he would cause danger of injury to the person or property of the other, a duty arises to use ordinary care and skill to avoid such danger.[20]

---

15 Dissenting.
16 Ibid at 534, 1275.
17 Plunkett n 4 at 22.
18 H Street *The Law of Torts* (2nd edn) (Butterworths, 1959) at 105.
19 (1883) 11 QB 503.
20 Ibid at 509.

Lord Esher (formerly Brett MR) had an opportunity to reformulate the duty test in the Court of Appeal case of *Le Levre v Gould*.[21] In that case, the mortgagees of the interest of a builder, under a building agreement, advanced money to him from time to time, on the faith of certificates given by a surveyor, to the effect that certain specified stages had been reached. The surveyor was not appointed by the mortgagees, and there was no contractual relationship between him and them. The statements were negligently prepared. The court held that the surveyor did not owe the mortgagees a duty of care. Lord Esher stated:

> If one man is near to another, or is near to the property of another, a duty lies upon him not to do that which may cause a personal injury to the other or may injure his property.[22]

Therefore, Lord Esher was prepared to accept that whereas it was necessary that the defendant should foresee that his act would harm the plaintiff, the court would impose a duty of care on the former to the latter, only if the harm consisted of harm to the plaintiff's person or property. Lord Esher went on to further confine the scope of the duty of care to certain discrete situations, thereby reverting to the traditional multifarious approach to the application of the duty, in the Court of Appeal case of *Lane v Cox*.[23] In that case, the defendant was the owner of a house which he let unfurnished to a weekly tenant. The plaintiff was a workman who was employed to move some furniture. While so employed, he was injured because of the defective state of a staircase in the house. There was evidence that at the time the house was let, the staircase was in an unsafe condition. The plaintiff brought an action to recover damages for the injury which he had sustained. The court held that the landlord did not owe the plaintiff a duty of care. Lord Esher MR stated:

> There are many circumstances that may give rise [to a duty of care] for instance, in the case of two persons using a highway, and similarly there is a duty to an adjoining owner or occupier.[24]

In short, Lord Esher refrained from employing a more generalised test to determine whether the landlord owed the workman a duty of care. Plunkett observes that by the end of the nineteenth century, after Brett MR's brief flirtation with the idea of a generalised test, the law again returned to the single instances approach to the duty of care.[25]

In his retrospective, but at the same time incisive, conspectus of the stance taken by the courts in negligence cases, Asquith LJ, in the Court of Appeal case of *Candler v Crane Christmas and Co*,[26]stated that Lord Atkin had observed in the landmark case of *Donoghue v Stevenson* in 1932, that the law governing the duty A owed to B, in the absence of fraud, contract or fiduciary relationship, had been built up piecemeal. Asquith LJ continued:

[21] [1893] 1 QB 491.
[22] Ibid at 497.
[23] [1897] 1 QB 415. See Plunkett, n4 at 24.
[24] [1897] 1 QB 415 at 417.
[25] Plunkett n 4 at 25.
[26] [1951] 2 KB 164 at 188.

> Certain classes owed duties of care to certain other classes; road users to other road users; bailees to other persons entrusting property to them; doctors and surgeons (and originally barbers) to persons entrusting their bodies to them; occupiers of premises to persons whom they invite or permit to come on the premises; and so on. These categories attracting the duty had been added to and subtracted from time to time. But no attempt had been made in the past, to rationalise them; to find a common denominator between road users; bailees; surgeons, occupiers; and so on, which would explain why they should be bound to a duty of care and some other classes who might be expected equally to be so bound, should be exempt – no attempt, that is, save that of Lord Esher MR (from which his colleagues associated themselves) in *Heaven v Pender*.

Baker argues that well into the nineteenth century, liability for negligence was regarded only as an explanation for the cases already recognised, and not as a basis for potentially wider claims.[27] Writing specifically of the duty of care in 1935, Buckland somewhat caustically observed that:

> the duty to take care … is an unnecessary fifth wheel on the coach, incapable of sound analysis and possibly productive of injustice. The distinctions which have grown up in our law as to the duties of an occupier towards trespassers, licensees, invitees etc resting as it seems on an ascending scale of duty, do not seem very rational.[28]

Scotland

In the seventh edition of *Bell's Principles*,[29] which was published in 1876, Guthrie stated that negligence was a 'quasi delict' in the law of Scotland. He went on to state that certain categories of individuals, such as shipowners, keepers of dangerous animals, public officers, could be liable for any harm caused by the defenders' 'negligence' or 'carelessness', respectively. Employers were liable for the 'faults' or 'gross negligence' of employees, or those under his command.[30] However, the author refrained from using the concept of duty, in terms of defining the basis of the defender's potential liability. However, Guthrie Smith included a brief section on the duty of care in his second edition of *Damages* which was published in 1889.[31] The learned author described duty of care in a broad, general sense, as 'failure to take care … in the conduct of himself and the management of his property, to prevent harm to others'.[32]

The concept of duty, in relation to negligence actions, was explicitly recognised by the Scottish courts by the turn of the nineteenth century.[33] Black argues that less than a decade after *Heaven v Pender*, the doctrine of 'directional' duty of care (that is to say, judicial recognition that the defender owed the pursuer a duty of care, in terms

27 J H Baker *An Introduction to English Legal History* (3rd edn) (Butterworths, 1990) at 470.

28 W Buckland 'The Duty to Take Care' (1935) 51 LQR 637 at 639.

29 *Bells Principles of the Law of Scotland* (ed W Guthrie) (7th edn) (T and T Clark, 1876) at para. 553.

30 Ibid at para. 554.

31 J Guthrie Smith *The Law on Damages: A Treatise on the Reparation of Injuries, as Administered in Scotland* (1889).

32 J Guthrie Smith *The Law of Damages* (2nd edn) (T and T Clark, 1889) at 22.

33 See for example *Owners of Islay v Patience* (1892) 20 R 224 at 227; *Kemp and Dougall v Darngavil Coal Co* 1909 SC 1314 at 1319; *Clelland v Robb* 1911 SC 253 at 256.

of the former's negligent conduct) was making a tentative appearance in Scotland.[34] Writing in 1912, Guthrie stated that the duty to take care, a duty imposed by law, may exist along with or independently of contractual relation.[35] Pillans argues that duty was used as a device to limit claims.[36] The author goes on to observe that at the same time, in doing so, the courts preferred to employ the doctrine of privity of contract over liability in negligence.[37] In 1916 in the leading New York case of *MacPherson v Buick Motor Co*[38] Judge Cardozo decided that a manufacturer's duty to take care for the safety of his products extended to the ultimate consumer, irrespective of contractual status. Reid argues that, in contrast, in Scotland, even after *Heaven v Pender*, the case law was conflicting, drawing complex distinctions to block the extension of duty to manufactures of defective products.[39] The law certainly remained unsettled and lacked a firm juridical basis. The scene was therefore set for the House of Lords to rationalise the law in *Donoghue*.

DONOGHUE V STEVENSON

The facts in the House of Lords case of *Donoghue v Stevenson* were simple. The pursuer went to a café in Paisley. She was accompanied by a friend, who bought the pursuer a bottle of ginger beer, which had been manufactured by the defender. The pursuer's friend also bought her some ice cream. The bottle was made of dark opaque glass. The pursuer, therefore, could not observe the contents of the bottle. Therefore, the pursuer had no reason to suspect that the bottle contained anything other than pure ginger beer. The café proprietor poured some ginger beer into the glass which contained the ice cream. The pursuer drank some of the contents of the glass. Her friend then poured the remainder of the contents of the bottle into the glass. The pursuer saw a decomposing snail floating from the bottle. The pursuer claimed that she suffered nervous shock and severe gastro-enteritis as a consequence. There was, of course, no contract between Mrs Donoghue and the defender. Therefore, the House was required to determine whether the defender owed the pursuer a duty of care, in terms of the law of negligence. By a majority of 3 to 2, the House held in her favour. The leading judgment was given by Lord Atkin. His Lordship stated:

[34] R Black 'A Historical Survey of Delictual Liability in Scotland for Personal Injuries and Death' (1975) 8 CILSA 318 at 322.

[35] *Greens Encyclopaedia of Scots Law* (2nd edn) (W Green, 1912) at 512.

[36] B Pillans *Delict: Law and Policy* (5th edn) (W Green, 2014) at 254.

[37] The author cites the Inner House case of *Mullen v Barr and Co* 1929 SC 461 as an example of this approach. In that case, an action was brought against a firm of ginger beer manufacturers on behalf of two children who had been injured through drinking a bottle of ginger beer manufactured by the defenders. The bottle contained a decaying mouse. The bottle had been purchased from a retailer. The pursuers alleged that the defenders owed them a duty of care. The court held that the defenders did not owe the pursuers a duty of care. After stating that there was no privity of contract between the pursuers and the defenders, Lord Anderson stated (at 479) that 'where the goods of the defenders are widely distributed throughout Scotland, it would seem little short of outrageous to make them responsible to members of the public for the contents of every bottle which issues from their works'.

[38] 217 NY 382.

[39] E Reid *The Law of Delict in Scotland* (Edinburgh University Press, 2022) at 24.

> The rule that you are to love your neighbour becomes in law you must not injure your neighbour; and the lawyer's question, Who is my neighbour? receives a restricted reply. You must take reasonable care to avoid acts or omissions which you can reasonably foresee would be likely to injure your neighbour. Who, then, in law, is my neighbour? The answer seems to be persons who are so closely and directly affected by my act, that I ought reasonably to have them in contemplation as being so affected, when I am directing my mind to the acts or omissions which are called into question.

Lord Atkin, thereby, established the 'neighbour principle' in the law of negligence, which has become known as the 'broad rule' in *Donoghue*. One's neighbour was simply someone whom one could reasonably foresee could be injured by one's negligent conduct. However, Lord Atkin's dictum was not the ratio of *Donoghue*.[40] Nor was the neighbour principle, founded on the concept of foreseeability, intended by Lord Atkin to apply to all situations in which the pursuer had sustained injury.[41] Indeed, Lord Atkin was fully aware that there were certain areas where the law had resolutely set its face against deciding that the defender owed the pursuer a duty of care. For example, it had been established by 1932 that, with certain exceptions, the courts would not recognise claims in respect of pure economic loss, or liability for pure omissions. Lord Atkin did not intend his neighbour principle, founded on the concept of foreseeability, to apply to these situations. Rather, the 'foreseeability' test was to be enlisted by the courts, in order to determine whether the defender owed the pursuer a duty of care in a novel situation. Never again was the law of negligence to be so rigidly hide-bound within the then existing categories of duty of care. Indeed, the Atkinian 'foreseeability test' ostensibly provided the judiciary with ample scope for creativity.

By way of conclusion on *Donoghue*, the decision firmly established, firstly, that the manufacturer of a product owed a duty of care to the ultimate consumer[42] of the product in relation to the safety of the product. Contractual liability was completely irrelevant to the existence of liability in tort or delict.[43] This has become known as the 'narrow' rule in *Donoghue*. Secondly, the case firmly 'knocked on the head' the notion that the duty of care was solely owed by certain categories of persons to others and permitted a more expansive approach to the duty of care, in terms of the law of negligence.

However, whilst *Donoghue* is now regarded as somewhat revolutionary, in terms of the development of the law of negligence, its significance was not immediately recognised, either by certain academic writers or indeed by the courts.[44] As far as the former were concerned, Street (writing in 1959) observed that 'if the court views the

---

[40] Street *n 18* at 106; C Whiting (ed) *Street on Torts* (15th edn) (OUP, 2021) at 33.

[41] See for example *Haseldine v C. A. Daw and Son Ltd* [1941] 2KB 343 at 362 (per Scott LJ).

[42] The terms 'manufacturer', 'product' and 'ultimate consumer' have been expanded since 1932. See F McManus et al *Delict* (3rd edn) (Edinburgh University Press, 2021) Ch 18.

[43] T Ellis Lewis (ed) *Winfield on Tort* (6th edn) (Sweet and Maxwell, 1954) at 482.

[44] Clerk and Lindsell argue that the foreseeability and proximity test only was the means by which the ratio in *Donoghue* was determined and not the ratio itself which was confined to the liability of a manufacturer of goods towards ultimate consumers. The authors go on to argue that the courts were not bound to apply the Atkin test and for some years remained reluctant to utilise it; *Clerk and Lindsell on Torts* (24th edn) para. 7-18.

plaintiff's case favourably, it may accept the dictum of Lord Atkin as binding, and apply it directly, or alternatively apply some other general test of foreseeability'.[45] Lindsay Duncan (writing in 1959) confined a discussion of *Donoghue* under the rubric 'Liability of Manufacturer to the Public', and refrained from according any discussion to the application of the broad rule in that case.[46]

As far as the courts were concerned, Lord Atkin's dictum was being applied shortly after *Donoghue* was decided. For example, in *Cunard v Antifyre Ltd*[47] the plaintiff who was in her kitchen, which was situated beneath a roof which was occupied by the defendant, was injured when a heavy piece of guttering on the roof fell through the kitchen's glass roof into the kitchen. The defendants were required to keep their premises in repair, by the terms of their lease. In holding the defendants liable for the plaintiff's injury, Talbot J, after referring to Lord Atkin's dictum, stated:

> It seems clear that the persons having control of this guttering, if they had directed themselves to the omission, of which they had been accused, to take reasonable care that it should not fall, must have had the occupier of kitchen, and any person lawfully in the kitchen, on which if it did fall it must fall, 'reasonably in contemplation' as 'closely and directly' affected by the omission.[48]

However, the universal judicial endorsement of the 'broad rule' in *Donoghue* was not immediate. For example, in the House of Lords case of *Brackenborough v Spalding UDC*[49] (decided in 1942) the defendant conducted a market. A steer, which belonged to a local farmer, escaped from a pen which was operated by the defendant and careered through the town. The steer collided with a member of the public, who was on the highway. He was killed. The plaintiff's widow sued the defendant, claiming that it was under a duty to provide a pen which was reasonably secure. The question which the House of Lords was required to answer was whether the defendant owed a duty of care to the deceased, in this novel situation? The House unanimously answered this question in the negative. In so deciding, Viscount Simon LC stated that there was 'no authority on the point'.[50] However, he refrained from referring to Lord Atkin's broad rule in *Donoghue*. Lord MacMillan, in turn, was unable to find 'any legal basis for the duty which is sought to lay on the respondents'.[51] Street argued that *Brackenborough* was an example of a situation where the court wished to deny a duty, deciding that it was not bound by the dictum of Lord Atkin, or else ignored it altogether, and showed that the alleged duty fell outside the existing categories and stressed the lack of precedent.[52]

---

45 Street n 18 at 107.

46 J Lindsay Duncan (ed) *Glegg on Reparation*) (W Green, 1955) at 36–7 (incl).

47 [1933] 1 KB 551.

48 Ibid at 560.

49 [1942] AC 310.

50 Ibid 317/318.

51 Ibid at 319.

52 Street n 18 at 107. See also the House of Lords case of *Carmarthenshire County Council v Lewis* [1953] AC 549. In that case the plaintiff's husband was driving a lorry at the time, when he swerved his lorry in order to avoid striking a child who had 'escaped' from a nursery operated by the defendant.

One reason that Lord Atkin's neighbour principle, based on the concept of foreseeability, failed to achieve immediate endorsement by the courts was that it was deemed, at times, too broad to provide a firm basis for the court to conclude whether the defender owed the pursuer a duty of care. For example, in the Court of Appeal case of *Deyong v Shenburn*[53] the plaintiff, who was an actor, left his personal clothing in his dressing room, in the defendant's theatre, during rehearsal. Some of his clothing was stolen, due to the careless supervision of the room by the defendant. The court held that the defendant did not owe the plaintiff a duty of care. Du Parcq LJ, after stating that Lord Atkin's neighbour principle was too wide to be applied in the instant case, stated:

> It is not true to say that whenever a man finds himself in such a position that unless he does a certain act, another person may suffer, then it is duty in the one case to be careful to do the act. Any such proposition is much too wide. There has to be a breach of a duty which the law recognises, and to ascertain what the law recognises, regard must be had to the decisions of the courts.[54]

However, Lord Atkin's neighbour principle was firmly established in the law of negligence by 1970,[55] when the principle attained its high-water mark in the House of Lords case of *Home Office v Dorset Yacht Co Ltd*.[56] In that case, a party of borstal trainees were working on Brownsea Island in Poole Harbour, under the supervision and control of three borstal officers. During the night, seven of the trainees escaped

---

The House (by a majority) held the defendant liable in terms of the law of negligence. However, their Lordships made no reference to Lord Atkin's dictum in *Donoghue*.

[53] [1946] KB 227.

[54] Ibid at 233.

[55] See for example *Beaumont v Surrey CC* (1968) 66 LGR 580. In that case, a teacher discarded a long piece of elastic in an open bin in a classroom. The elastic was used in horseplay between pupils after she left the classroom. The claimant lost an eye. The education authority was held liable on the basis that the injury in question was foreseeable. For a discussion of a teacher's duty of care see L Barnes '"Trips, Slips and Bangs": Pupil Injury Claims and the Teacher's Duty of Care' 2009 JR 189. See also the Court of Appeal case of *Clay v A.J. Crump and Sons Ltd* [1964] 1 QB 533. In that case, the owner of a site, on which there were situated some old buildings, appointed an architect to plan and supervise its redevelopment. Demolition contractors were instructed to clear the site in accordance with the architect's plan. The plan indicated that a wall which was standing on the site was to be demolished before any building work was commenced. At the building owner's request, the demolition contractors left the wall standing after the architect had sanctioned that course of action during a telephone conversation with the demolition contractors, if it were safe to do so. However, the architect never inspected the wall which was in a dangerous condition. This would have been apparent to anyone making a proper inspection. The wall collapsed and injured a labourer who was working on the site. The court applied the broad rule in *Donoghue* and held that the architect owed the labourer a duty of care.

See also the Court of Appeal case of *Ministry of Housing v Sharp* [1970] 2 QB 233. In that case, the claimant suffered financial loss as a result of the negligence of the clerk of a local land charges registry, who negligently issued a 'clear certificate' to the purchaser of land, over which the claimant had a land charge in its favour. The certificate had failed to mention the charge, the result of which, under the Land Charges Act 1925, the purchaser was absolved from the obligation to financially compensate the claimant. Lord Denning MR stated (at 269) that the defendant owed a duty of care to any person whom he knew, or ought to have known, would be injuriously affected by a mistake (such as the claimant).

[56] [1970] AC 1004.

because of the negligence of the officers. The trainees boarded a yacht which they had found nearby. They set the yacht in motion and collided with the claimants' yacht, which was moored nearby. They then boarded the claimants' yacht. Much damage was done to that yacht by the collision and also by the subsequent conduct of the trainees. The House held that the defendant owed the claimants a duty of care. Lord Reid stated:

> Lord Atkin's speech should, I think be regarded as a statement of principle. It is not to be treated as if it were a statutory definition. It will require qualification in new circumstances. But I think that the time has come when we can and should say that it ought to apply, unless there is some justification or valid explanation for its exclusion.[57]

Lord Reid's generous approach to the duty of care is well illustrated in the Court of Appeal case of *Dutton v Bognor Regis UDC*.[58] In that case, a builder, developing a housing estate, applied to the defendant local authority to build a house on a plot of land on the estate. Approval was given in terms of the then extant building byelaws, made under the Public Health Act 1936, subject to a condition that the foundations and drains must first be examined by the surveyor before being covered up. The foundations were examined by a building inspector who approved them. The foundations were then covered up with concrete. After the building works had been completed, the house was purchased by C, who shortly after sold the house to the plaintiff. Soon after she had moved in, serious defects developed in the internal structure of the house. It was discovered that the house had been built on an old rubbish tip. This ought to have been detected at the relevant time. The plaintiff brought an action against both the builder and the defendant. She settled her claim against the builder.

Lord Denning MR, in deciding that the defendant local authority owed the plaintiff a duty of care, applied the test laid down by Lord Atkin in *Donoghue*.[59] Lord Denning MR stated that the inspector 'ought to have had subsequent purchasers in mind when he was examining the building foundations. He ought to have realised that if he was negligent, they might suffer damage.'[60]

[57] Ibid at 1027.

[58] [1972] 1 QB 373. Over-ruled by *Murphy v Brentwood DC* [1991] 1 AC 398. See also *SCM (United Kingdom) Ltd v W J Whittall and Son Ltd* [1971] 1 QB 337. In that case, the defendants were building contractors. They were rebuilding a boundary wall. A workman damaged an electric cable (which was owned by the electricity board) which supplied electricity to several factories in the neighbourhood. The plaintiffs alleged that the electricity supply to their typewriter factory had been cut off, the upshot of which was that this had resulted in damage to materials and machines, and consequent loss of production. The Court of Appeal held that the defendants owed the plaintiffs a duty of care and were therefore liable. Lord Denning MR stated (at 343) that 'they (the defendants) knew that if they damaged the cable, the current would be cut off, and damage would be suffered by factory owners. Those simple facts put them under a duty to take care not to injure the cable: and this was a duty which they owed to all the factory owners in the vicinity. It comes straight within the principle laid down by Lord Atkin in *Donoghue v Stevenson*'.

[59] Ibid at 396.

[60] See also the House of Lords case of *Junior Books Ltd v Veitchi and Co Ltd* [1983] 1 AC 520. In that case, the defenders Veitchi Ltd, who were specialist subcontractors, laid a floor in a factory which was being constructed for the pursuers, Junior Books Ltd. There was no contractual relationship between the pursuers and the defenders. It was alleged that the floor had been negligently laid and had required

In *Dorset Yacht*, Lord Reid had implicitly advocated a two-stage test, in relation to the duty of care. That is to say, that if one could foresee that one's actions would harm one's neighbour, a duty of care would be owed to the pursuer, unless there was some justification (or policy ground) for its exclusion. However, Lord Reid's dictum was formally endorsed and refined by the House some eight years later in *Anns v Merton LBC*[61] which we will now discuss.

ANNS V MERTON LBC

In *Anns v Merton LBC* the claimants were lessees under long leases of flats which had been built under plans passed by a local authority, whose legal duties and obligations had passed to Merton LBC. The block in which the flats were situated had been built on foundations which were of an inadequate depth, in terms of the relevant building byelaws. However, the defendant local authority had failed to notice this during the course of their inspections. As a result of this, there was structural movement in the block in which the claimants' premises were situated. Cracks began to appear on the walls of the building and there was also sloping of floors. The claimants sued the local authority. The basic question which the House was required to answer was whether the defendant owed the claimants a duty of care, in terms of the law of negligence. Lord Wilberforce stated:

> [The] position has now been reached that in order to establish that a duty of care arises in a particular situation, it is not necessary to bring the facts of that situation within those of previous situations in which duty of care has been held to exist. Rather, the question is to be approached in two stages. First, one has to ask whether, as between the alleged wrongdoer and the person who has suffered damage, there is a sufficient relationship of proximity or neighbourhood such that, in the reasonable contemplation of the former, carelessness on his part may be likely to cause damage to the latter – in which case a prima facie duty of care arises. Secondly, if the first question is answered affirmatively, it is necessary to consider whether there are any considerations which ought to negative or reduce or limit the scope of the duty, or the class of person to whom it is owed, or the damage to which a breach of it may give rise.[62]

Thus, the so-called 'two-stage' approach to the duty of care was enunciated. By this approach, in order to ascertain whether a duty of care was owed by the defender to the pursuer, one was required to ascertain whether there was a sufficient relationship of proximity between the defender and the pursuer. The first stage incorporated Lord Atkin's 'neighbour' principle, that is, if the defender should have foreseen that his conduct would result in harm to the pursuer, then *prima facie* a duty of care would

replacement. The pursuers claimed that as a consequence of this, they had sustained financial loss resulting from *inter alia* having to replace the floor, remove machinery and also lost profits. The pursuers successfully sued the defendants, notwithstanding the loss in question ranked as pure economic loss. Lord Keith stated (at 535), 'There undoubtedly exists between the appellants and the respondents such proximity of relationship, within the well-known principle of *Donoghue v Stevenson*, as to give rise a duty of care owed by the former to the latter.'

61 [1977] AC 728.

62 Ibid at 751, 752.

arise. The second stage consisted of ascertaining whether there were any policy considerations which would militate against the imposition of a duty of care. One can readily see here that Lord Wilberforce's two-stage test offered the judiciary considerable scope for expanding the existing categories of duty of care, since the only apparent check on applying Lord Atkin's neighbour principle or test to the facts of any novel case were considerations of public policy.

A case which neatly illustrates the application of the two-stage test is the House of Lords case of *McLoughlin v O'Brian*.[63] In that case, the plaintiff's husband and three children were involved in a road accident after their car was in a collision with a lorry which was being driven negligently by the first defendant. Her husband sustained physical injury as a consequence of the accident, as did the children, one of whom died. At the time of the accident, the claimant was at home, about two miles away. The claimant was taken to visit her family in hospital. She sustained nervous shock on seeing her family and on being told that her daughter had been killed. However, case law had established that a plaintiff could not recover for harm sustained by nervous shock, where the injury to the relative occurred out of the sight and earshot of the relative. The only exception was in circumstances in which the plaintiff did not see the incident but had come across its immediate aftermath. The House held that the defendant owed the claimant a duty of care, in terms of the law of negligence. Lord Wilberforce, after deciding that there was sufficient proximity between the parties, went on, in effect, to consider the application of Lord Wilberforce's second limb of *Anns* to the facts of the case.[64] First, there were no grounds for accepting the argument that by admitting claims for nervous shock in the instant case, that would lead to a proliferation of claims. Second, Lord Wilberforce rejected the suggestion that an extension of liability would be unfair to defendants, in that it would impose damages which were out of all proportion to the negligent conduct in question. Third, to admit such 'aftermath' claims would not lead to evidentiary difficulties and tend to lengthen litigation.[65] The claimant, therefore, succeeded.[66]

The expansive approach to the duty of care heralded by *Anns* is also illustrated in *Ross v Caunters*[67] which concerned economic loss. In that case, the defendant solicitors prepared a will for a testator and sent it to him for execution. However, the former failed to warn the latter that the will should not be witnessed by the spouse of the beneficiary. When the testator signed the will one of the witnesses was the husband of a residuary beneficiary under the will. Section 15 of the Wills Act 1837 provided that where a beneficiary or spouse of a beneficiary witnessed a will, the gift to that beneficiary was void. The beneficiary claimed damages from the solicitors for negligence in respect of the loss of the benefits given to her by the will. The court

63 [1983] 1 AC 410.

64 Ibid at 421, 422.

65 Lord Scarman, however, expressed the view that policy considerations were a matter for Parliament, as opposed to the courts; Ibid at 430.

66 See also the Court of Appeal case of *Attia v British Gas plc* [1988] QB 304. In that case the court held that the law relating to nervous shock (psychiatric injury) could be extended to allow the claimant to recover damages on seeing her house burn, as a result of the defendant's negligence.

67 [1980] Ch 297.

held that the defendants owed the beneficiary a duty of care. In so deciding, the court held that the beneficiary was in the solicitors' direct contemplation as being someone likely to be injured by their failure to carry out the testator's instructions. There were no considerations to reduce or limit the scope of the solicitors' duty. Furthermore, it was immaterial that the beneficiary had not relied on the defendants' skill.

THE RETREAT FROM *ANNS*

The expansive approach to the duty of care, which was enunciated in *Anns*, and was described by Rougier J in *John Munroe Ltd v London Fire Authority*[68] as 'extreme', was relatively short-lived. Indeed, the judiciary were beginning to have some doubts about the utility of the 'two-stage' test in determining the duty of care. However, the reasons for such a change are easier to narrate than explain. The first sign of such a change came in the House of Lords case of *Governors of the Peabody Donation Fund v Sir Lindsay Parkinson and Co Ltd*.[69] In that case, the claimants owned land. The claimants' architects submitted plans on behalf of the claimants for the construction of houses on the land. The plans made provision for the construction of a flexible drainage system. However, the drainage system which was subsequently installed by the claimants' building contractors was of a rigid construction. The departure from the approved plans came to the knowledge of the local authority drainage inspector. However, he took no action. When the drains were tested, two years later, they were found to be unsatisfactory and were required to be reconstructed. This caused construction work to be delayed, which resulted in substantial financial loss to the claimants. The claimants claimed that the local authority owed them a duty of care to ensure that the drains were in conformity with the plans which had been approved. Therefore, the claimants claimed that the defendant was liable for the financial loss which the claimants had sustained. In deciding that the defendants did not owe the claimants a duty of care, Lord Keith, in effect, refused to treat the two-stage test in *Anns* as an inflexible rule, which was applicable in all situations. Rather, in His Lordship's view, it was necessary to ascertain whether a relationship of proximity, in the Atkinian sense, existed between the parties for a duty of care to arise.[70] However, the scope of that duty depended on all the circumstances of the case. Lord Keith then went on to state that in determining whether the defendant owed the claimant a duty of a particular scope, one should consider whether it was just and reasonable that it should be so.[71]

Whilst *Peabody* did not overrule the two-stage test which was enunciated in *Anns*, the principle was weakened. The momentum against *Anns* continued with the decision of the Privy Council in *Yuen Kun Yeu v Attorney General of Hong Kong*.[72] In that case, the claimants had deposited money with a deposit-taking registered company, which subsequently went into liquidation. The claimants lost the money

[68] [1997] QB 983 at 995.
[69] [1985] AC 210.
[70] Ibid at 240.
[71] Ibid at 241.
[72] [1988] AC 175.

which they had deposited. The Commissioner of Deposit-taking Companies had registered the company. The claimants brought an action for damages in negligence against the Attorney General of Hong Kong, representing the Commissioner, alleging that they had made the deposits in reliance upon the company's registration, and that the Commissioner either knew or ought to have known, had he taken reasonable care, that the company's affairs were being conducted fraudulently, and that he should not have registered the company, or alternatively, that he should have revoked its registration under his statutory powers. In short, the Privy Council was required to decide whether the defendant owed the claimants a duty of care, in terms of the law of negligence. The Board rejected the claimants' claim. In so deciding, the Board concurred with the reasoning of Brennan J in the High Court of Australia case of *Council of the Shire of Sutherland v Heyman*[73] where he advocated that in contrast to the two-stage approach, which was enunciated in *Anns*, it was preferable that the law should develop categories of negligence incrementally and by analogy, with established categories, rather than by a massive extension of a *prima facie* duty of care, restrained only by indefinable considerations which ought to negative or to reduce or limit the scope of the duty, or the class of person to whom it was owed. Lord Keith in *Yuen Kun Yeu* expressed the view that the two-stage test, which was formulated by Lord Wilberforce in *Anns*, had been elevated to a degree of importance that was greater than it merited.[74]

CAPARO V DICKMAN

The courts, therefore, were experiencing a degree of discomfort in applying Lord Wilberforce's two-stage test, in order to determine whether the defender owed the pursuer a duty of care. Indeed, the reluctance to apply the test and the move away from *Anns* seemed inexorable. The retreat from *Anns* was completed with the decision of the House of Lords in *Caparo v Dickman*.[75] In that case, the claimants were shareholders in a company. Relying on a negligently prepared audit and report, the claimants purchased further shares in the company, and then made an unsuccessful takeover bid. The claimants lost money. However, the House held that no duty of care was owed by the defendants to the claimants. Lord Bridge stated:

> What emerges is that in addition to the foreseeability of damage, necessary ingredients in any situation, giving rise to a duty of care, are that there should exist between the party owing the duty, and party to whom it is owed, a relationship characterised by the law as one of 'proximity' or 'neighbourhood,' and that the situation should be one in which the courts considers it fair just and reasonable, that the law should impose a duty of a given scope, upon one party, for the benefit of the other. But it is implicit in the passages referred to, the concepts of proximity and fairness, embodied in these additional ingredients, are not susceptible to any such precise definition, as would be necessary to give them utility as any practical tests, but amount in effect, to little more than convenient labels to attach to the features of specific situations which, on a detailed examination of all the circumstances,

[73] (1985) 59 ALJR 564 at 588.

[74] [1988] AC 175 at 191.

[75] [1990] 2 AC 605.

> the law recognises pragmatically as giving rise to a duty of care of a given scope. Whilst recognising, of course, the importance of the underlying general principles common to the whole field of negligence, I think that the law has now moved in the direction of attaching greater significance to the more traditional categorisation of distinct and recognisable situations, as guides to the existence the scope and the limits of the varied duties of care the law imposes.[76]

Another important factor which influenced the House's decision was that the provisions of the Companies Act 1985 (in relation to the preparation of the audit of a public company) imposed a duty on the defendant auditors to make a report to enable shareholders to exercise their class rights in a general meeting, and that such a duty did not extend to the provision of information to assist shareholders in making decisions on future investments in the company.

The House, in addition to establishing a tripartite test to establish whether the defendant owed the pursuer a duty of care, decided that an extension to the existing categories, in which it had been held that a duty of care existed, should be in conformity with public policy.[77]

Therefore, in *Caparo*, the House of Lords held that in order to establish whether the defendant owed the claimant a duty of care it required to be shown that:

1. the loss in question is reasonably foreseeable;
2. there is a relationship of proximity between the parties;
3. it is fair, just and reasonable that a duty of care be imposed; and
4. the imposition of a duty of care is in conformity with (or not contrary to) public policy.

However, these requirements are not hermetically sealed. There is, indeed, an overlap between each category.[78] There is a pronounced overlap between categories 3 and 4 which, in the author's view, are amorphous and, in theory at least, confer fairly wide latitude on the judge to expand the existing categories of negligence.

However, importantly, superimposed on the above requirements, the first three of which have become known as the 'tripartite test', is the requirement that any extension to the duty of care requires to be incremental, with the court expanding the ambit of the duty of care, if the facts of the case before it are either four-square, or are analogous with a previously decided case.

Each component of the *Caparo* decision is now discussed in turn.

Foreseeability

In *Donoghue* (above)[79] Lord Atkin employed the concept of reasonable foreseeability when deciding if the defender owed the pursuer a duty of care. In the House of

[76] Ibid at 617–18.

[77] Ibid at 642 (per Lord Oliver).

[78] Ibid at 633 (per Lord Oliver). See also *Michael v Chief Constable of South Wales Police* [2015] AC 1732 at 1776 (per Lord Kerr).

[79] See p.10.

Lords case of *Rothwell v Chemical and Insulating Co Ltd*[80] Lord Hoffman stated that the test for foreseeability will vary according to firstly, the precise description of what should have been foreseen, and secondly, the degree of probability which makes it foreseeable.[81] However, the concept of foreseeability, as a tool to determine whether the defender owes the pursuer a duty of care, requires to be assessed objectively, in terms of the type of harm which is the subject matter of the case before the court. For example, whereas it may be foreseeable that if I drive negligently, I may physically injure a fellow road user, the fact that bystanders at the roadside may sustain nervous shock, in witnessing the accident, might not. This scenario also illustrates the point that what the defender must reasonably foresee is the class of potential individuals which may be harmed by his negligent conduct, as opposed to the particular individual who is actually harmed.[82] The House of Lords case of *Haley v London Electricity Board*[83] illustrates this point. In that case, the defendants' employees had excavated a trench in a pavement. They had placed a long-handled hammer across the pavement, in order to guard the trench and prevent persons walking along the pavement. The plaintiff was blind. He failed to notice the hammer. He tripped and fell. The accident rendered him deaf. The House held, in effect, that the defendants had owed a duty of care to blind persons, as a class, to take reasonable care to ensure that they were reasonably safe. The plaintiff, therefore, recovered.[84]

Proximity

In *Caparo* Lord Bridge described the concepts of proximity and fairness as not susceptible to any precise definition, as would be necessary to give them utility as practical tests, but amounted to little more than convenient labels to attach to the features of different specific situations which, on a detailed examination of all the circumstances, the law recognised pragmatically as giving rise to a duty of care of a given scope.[85] In turn, Lord Oliver stated that the concept of proximity was no more than a label which embraced not a definable concept, but merely a description of circumstances from which, pragmatically, the court concluded that a duty of care existed.[86] Several years later, in the House of Lords case of *Alcock v Chief Constable of South Yorkshire Police*[87] Lord Oliver went on to state that the concept of proximity was an artificial

[80] [2008] 1 AC 281 at 295.

[81] In the House of Lords case of *Bourhill v Young* [1943] AC 92 at 104, Lord MacMillan stated that 'there is no absolute standard of what is reasonable and probable. It must depend on circumstances and must always be a question of degree.'

[82] *Farrugia v Great Western Railway* [1947] 2 All ER 565.

[83] [1965] AC 778.

[84] See also the House of Lords case of *Glasgow Corporation v Taylor* [1922] 1 AC 44. In that case, the pursuer's son died after consuming a poisonous berry, which he had picked from a shrub in the defender's botanic garden. The berries were of such an appearance that they would have been attractive to children. The House held that the defender owed a duty of care to children to warn them of the danger of picking berries from that shrub or to prevent them from doing so.

[85] [1990] 2 AC 605 at 618.

[86] Ibid at 633. J Goodkamp and D Nolan *Winfield and Jolowicz Tort* (20th edn) (2020, Sweet and Maxwell) at 5-025 describe the concept of proximity as 'essentially empty and, hence, meaningless.

[87] [1992] 1 AC 310 at 411.

one, which depended more upon the court's perception of what is the reasonable area for the imposition of liability, than upon any logical process of analogical deduction. In other words, according to Lord Oliver, 'proximity' was, to all intents and purposes, simply a label which the court uses to describe a relationship between the defender and the pursuer, in a situation where the court considered it appropriate to impose a duty of care. In short, the concept of proximity, on its own, provided little guidance as to whether the court should impose a duty of care.

Indeed, the concept of proximity is a nebulous concept which is fiendishly difficult to define. The concepts of foreseeability and proximity overlap each other to some extent.[88] However, they are separate concepts. This point was emphasised in the Inner House case of *Thomson v Scottish Ministers*[89] where Lord Carloway stated that whilst the concepts of foreseeability and proximity were not entirely distinct, they ranked as distinct concepts in the tripartite test. The distinction between the two concepts was applied in *Glasgow City Council v First Glasgow (No 1) Ltd.*[90] In that case, a bin lorry, which was owned and operated by a local authority, crashed in the centre of Glasgow, causing death and injury to a large number of pedestrians, after the driver of the vehicle, Clarke, had lost consciousness at the wheel. His former employer had allegedly given a reference to the local authority, which did not mention a previous incident in which Clarke had lost consciousness while driving a bus. The local authority sought to recover £860,000 plus expenses which had been paid in settlement to the family of the deceased who had been struck by the bin lorry. The essential issue which the court was required to determine was whether the defenders (Clarke's previous employers) owed the deceased a duty of care. Lord Ericht held that whereas it was reasonably foreseeable that Clarke would injure pedestrians in the course of his employment, in the event of the reference failing to mention that risk, there was no proximity between the provider of the reference and the injured persons.[91] It followed that the reference giver did not owe the deceased a duty of care.

'Fair, just and reasonable' and 'Policy'

The concepts of 'fair', 'just' and 'reasonable' have tended to be construed conjunctively by the courts, in other words, as bearing the same meaning.[92] 'Policy', which MacCormick scathingly described as a 'hideously inexact word in legal discourse',[93] has simply ranked as a factor which is embedded in each of the trio.[94]

---

88 *Caparo v Dickman* above at 633 (per Lord Oliver).

89 2013 SC 628 at 642.

90 2020 SLT 75.

91 Ibid at 86–7, incl.

92 See for example *White v Jones* [1995] 2 AC 207 at 276 (per Lord Browne-Wilkinson). See also *Rathband v The Chief Constable of Northumbria Constabulary* [2016] EWHC 181 at [91] (per Mann J). See also *Seddon v Driver and Vehicle Licensing Agency* [2019] 1 WLR 4593 at 4608.

93 N MacCormick *Legal Reasoning and Legal Theory* (OUP, 1978) at 263.

94 In *N v Poole BC* [2020] AC 780 at [30] Lord Reed stated that the requirements that imposition of duty of care be fair, just and reasonable in practice led to evaluations in public policy which the courts were not well equipped to conduct in a convincing fashion.

However, occasionally, 'fairness', 'justice' and 'reasonableness' have been expressly treated separately from that of 'policy'. For example, in *Hughes v Turning Point Scotland*[95] Hughes (H) was an alcoholic. The defender, Turning Point Scotland (TPS), operated a facility which was known as Link Up. Link Up provided a service for people who were homeless, or sleeping rough, and experiencing a crisis, including one which derived from alcohol addiction. H had been an alcoholic for many years prior to his death. He was also prone to alcoholic-related seizures. He wished to use the facility which offered accommodation and assistance for withdrawal from alcohol. He attended Link Up. He was accompanied by his alcohol support worker. Following an initial assessment by a project worker, one afternoon, H was admitted to a bedroom in Link Up. H was found dead in his bed on the following evening of the same day. H's relatives brought an action against TPS, *inter alia*, on the basis that the latter owed H a duty of care.

However, Lord Clark held that it would not be fair, just and reasonable to impose a duty of care.[96] That was the case because TPS was a homeless charity, which sought to assist with alcohol detox, but only had limited staff and resources, and relied on volunteer medics. The judge, in treating policy as a separate head, stated that there was no evidence of any substance, which had been led, on behalf of the pursuer, to the effect that the defender could continue to provide its crucially important services, if it were to be subjected to such a duty; indeed, there was some evidence to the contrary.

In the author's view, the concepts of 'fair', 'just' and 'reasonable' can be criticised on the basis that they are vague in substance, and therefore incapable of providing a court with a useful tool in deciding whether the defender owes the pursuer a duty of care.

THE DEVELOPMENT OF THE *CAPARO* TRIPARTITE TEST BEFORE *ROBINSON V CHIEF CONSTABLE OF WEST YORKSHIRE*

The development of the *Caparo* tripartite test, up to the decision of the Supreme Court in *Robinson v Chief Constable of West Yorkshire*[97] (where the tripartite test was reinterpreted) is now discussed. Here, the author has simply selected some leading cases, as being illustrative of the approach of the courts to the application of the test. In other words, the author has not attempted to give an exhaustive account of the development of the test before the decision in *Robinson*. However, at this stage, it is important to bear in mind the dictum of Lord Oliver in *Caparo*, to the effect that the duty of care, in terms of the law of negligence, should not be viewed in the abstract but, rather, in terms of the particular *type* of damage which the pursuer sustains.[98]

[95] 2019 SLT 651.

[96] Ibid at [94].

[97] [2018] UKSC 4.

[98] [1990] 2 AC 605 at 651. See also *South Australian Management Corp v York Montague Ltd* [1997] AC 191. In that case defendants had provided negligent advice to commercial lenders about the value of property, in relation to which the claimants were considering lending money, by way of mortgages. In the light of such advice the claimants lent money. The borrowers defaulted. The properties had been over-valued by the defendants. However, the properties had fallen in value since the time of the loans. The House of Lords held that the defendants' duty of care extended only to giving accurate

The application of the tripartite test

Physical harm to property

In *Caparo* the House of Lords was required to determine whether auditors owed a duty of care to the shareholders of a company, in relation to the economic loss which the latter had sustained, by virtue of relying on an audit which the former had negligently prepared. However, the House was required to determine whether the learning in *Caparo* could be applied in relation to the physical damage which the claimant had sustained in *Marc Rich and Co v Bishop Rock Marine Co Ltd* (The Nicholas H).[99] In that case, the claimants, Marc Rich and Co, were cargo owners. They raised an action against, *inter alia*, a marine classification society, NKK. The facts of the case were that during a voyage, the *Nicholas H* developed a crack in her hull. It was feared that the crack presented a danger. The master of the ship therefore requested NKK to examine the ship. A surveyor did so, on behalf of NKK. The surveyor recommended that after temporary repairs were carried out, the vessel could continue on her voyage. A few days after leaving port, the vessel sank with the loss of the cargo.

The main question which the House was required to answer was whether NKK owed a duty of care to the claimants. As stated above, NKK was a classification society. It was a non-profit-making, non-governmental organisation, which was registered in Japan as a foundation, related to safeguarding life and property at sea. Its founding instrument described the purpose of NKK as being to 'promote the improvement and development of various matters relating to ships ... so as to safeguard the safety of life and ships at sea in the public interest'. The claimants submitted that given that they had sustained physical damage to the property in which they had propriety or possessory interest, the only requirement on their part, in order to establish the requisite duty of care, was proof of reasonable foreseeability of damage. However, the House rejected that claim.[100] Rather the question as to whether a duty of care existed depended on fairness, justice and reasonableness, in addition to foreseeability and proximity, regardless of the nature of the relevant harm (that is, whether the relevant harm ranked in terms of either physical harm or economic loss). The shipowner was primarily responsible for the vessel sailing in a seaworthy condition. However, the role of NKK was a subsidiary one. The carelessness of the NKK surveyor did not involve the direct infliction of physical damage.[101] Furthermore, there was no contract between the cargo owners and the NKK surveyor. Indeed, the cargo owners may not have been aware that the NKK had surveyed the vessel. The cargo owners had simply relied on the owners of the vessel to keep the vessel seaworthy and look after the cargo. Furthermore, the dealings between shipowners and cargo owners were based on a contractual structure – namely the Hague Rules and tonnage limitation,

information to the claimants, at the date of valuation. The scope of that duty did not extend to embracing the losses which were consequent on a fall in the market. See also *Hughes-Holland v BPE Solicitors* [2018] AC 599; *Ascetco plc v Grant Thornton* LLP [2020] EWCA Civ 1151. See also *Rihan v Ernst and Young Global Ltd* [2020] EWHC 901 at [460] (per Kerr J). For a discussion of *Rihan* see 2020 SLT 167. See also *Wokingham BC v Arshad* [2022] EWHC 2419.

99 [1996] AC 211.

100 Ibid at 236 (per Lord Steyn).

101 Ibid at 237.

on which the insurance of international trade depended.[102] If one were to recognise a duty of care by classification societies, that would have a substantial impact on international trade. In all the circumstances, the recognition of a duty would be unfair, unjust and unreasonable towards classification societies because they acted for the collective welfare. Furthermore, unlike shipowners, a classification society would not have the benefit of any limitation provisions.

Physical harm to the person

The Court of Appeal was required to decide if the *Caparo* tripartite test could be applied when the loss which the claimant had sustained consisted of physical harm to the person, in *Barrett v Ministry of Defence*.[103] In that case, an off-duty naval airman engaged in a bout of heavy drinking at a naval establishment. He became inebriated and then unconscious. He was later found dead, having choked on his own vomit. The claimant, the widow of the deceased, claimed damages against the Ministry of Defence, on the basis that it had failed to enforce its own standards of discipline, in order to protect the deceased airman from drinking himself to death. The court held that, up to the time it had assumed responsibility for the well-being of the deceased (by placing the deceased in his bunk and using the recovery position), the defendant did not owe the deceased a duty of care in law. The fact that it was foreseeable that the deceased would sustain harm if he drank too much was insufficient to ground liability on the part of the defendant. Rather, it was fair, just and reasonable for the law to leave a responsible adult to assume responsibility for his own actions, in consuming alcoholic drink. Beldam LJ stated: 'To dilute self-responsibility, and to blame one adult for another's lack of self-control, is neither just nor reasonable, and in the development of the law of negligence, an increment too far.'[104]

The tripartite test in *Caparo* was applied again, in terms of physical harm to the person, in the Court of Appeal case of *Everett v Comojo (UK) Ltd (t/a The Metropolitan)*.[105] The facts of the case were simple. The claimants visited a night club which was operated by the defendants. They were attacked and seriously injured by another guest. They claimed that the club had failed to take appropriate measures to prevent the assault from taking place. The court held that club owed the claimants a duty of care, in terms of the law of negligence. Smith LJ stated that the relationship between the management of the club and its guests was of sufficient proximity to justify the existence of a duty of care.[106] The management was in control of the premises. It could regulate who entered and it could refuse entry, as well as remove guests after entry. There was also an economic relationship between the nightclub and the guest. The judge held that these factors demonstrated sufficient proximity between the parties. Furthermore, given the relationship between the consumption of alcohol and violence, it was reasonably foreseeable that one guest might attack another.[107]

[102] Ibid at 239.
[103] [1995] 1 WLR 1217.
[104] Ibid at 1224.
[105] [2012] 1 WLR 150.
[106] Ibid at 158.
[107] Ibid at 158/159.

After stating that the common law duty of care was an extremely flexible concept, and was adaptable to the very wide range of circumstances to which it applied, the judge stated that it was fair, just and reasonable that it should govern the relationship between the managers of a hotel or nightclub and their guests, in relation to actions of third parties on the premises.[108]

Pure economic loss

In the House of Lords case of *White v Jones*[109] the House was required to decide if the defendant solicitors, who were acting for a testator, and had negligently failed to carry out his instructions in relation to the preparation of a will, owed a duty of care to intended beneficiaries, who had failed to receive money which the testator had desired they should, on his demise. The House (by a bare majority) held that the defendants owed the claimants a duty of care. The conceptual difficulties which the claimants faced, seemed formidable, if not insurmountable, in that:

1. it is well established that a solicitor, who acts on behalf of a client, normally owes a duty of care only to that client;
2. a claimant cannot normally recover in delict or tort for pure financial loss; and
3. if the claimants were allowed to recover in the instant case, the decision would open the floodgates to claims against solicitors by indeterminate classes of people, including those who were affected by *inter vivos* transactions.

Lord Goff, however, was prepared to sidestep these difficulties.[110] Uppermost in the mind of his Lordship was the injustice that would be done if the solicitors were not held liable to the beneficiaries. The *Hedley Byrne* principle could be extended by accepting the proposition that the assumption of responsibility by the solicitor to his client should be extended to an intended beneficiary whom the solicitor could foresee would be deprived of his intended legacy, in circumstances in which neither the testator nor his estate would have a remedy against the solicitor.

In turn, Lord Browne-Wilkinson, in deciding that the defendants owed the beneficiaries a duty of care, stated that his decision was based on an extension of the principle of an assumption of responsibility which was considered in *Hedley Byrne*.[111] His Lordship continued by stating that whereas the present case was not directly covered by the decided cases, 'it was legitimate to extend the law to the limited extent proposed, using the incremental approach, by way of an analogy, advocated in *Caparo Industries plc v Dickman*.'

However, the approach which was adopted by Lords Goff and Browne-Wilkinson to the ability of the court to extend the existing categories of duty of care incrementally in favour of the plaintiff beneficiaries, in the wake of *Caparo*, contrasts quite starkly with the dissenting judgment of Lord Keith who stated that 'there was no

[108] Ibid at 160.
[109] [1995] 2 AC 207.
[110] Ibid at 268.
[111] Ibid at 270.

decided case, the grounds of decision in which are capable of being extended incrementally, and by way of analogy, so as to admit of a remedy in tort being made available to the plaintiffs'.[112]

In the author's opinion, *White* neatly illustrates how judicial opinion may vary quite markedly, as to whether the facts of a decided case are analogous to the facts of a case which is being considered by the court. Indeed, in the House of Lords case of *Customs and Excise Commissioners v Barclays Bank plc*[113] Lord Bingham stated that the incremental test was of little value as a test, in itself, and was only helpful when used in combination with a test or principle which identified the legally significant features of a situation.[114]

Caparo reinterpreted

The concept of duty of care has been in a constant state of flux since its very inception. It therefore seemed, in the author's view, well within the range of human prevision that the tripartite test in *Caparo* would fall to be reconsidered and reformulated in due course. Faint signs that change was afoot were seen in the Supreme Court case of *Michael v Chief Constable of South Wales Police*[115] which will be considered in more detail later in the chapter.[116] Essentially, the case concerned the potential liability of a police authority for failing to prevent a woman from being murdered by her partner. Lord Toulson stated:

> The development of the law of negligence has been an incremental process, rather than giant steps. The established method of the court involves examining the decided cases, to see how far the law has gone, and where it has refrained from going. From that analysis, it looks to see whether there is an argument by analogy, for extending liability to a new situation, or whether an earlier limitation is no longer socially, or logically justifiable. In doing so, it pays regard to overall coherence. Often there will be a mixture of policy considerations to be taken into account.[117]

In the author's view, Lord Toulson's analysis is notable for its absence of any reference to the *Caparo* tripartite test in his emphasis on the law developing incrementally.

The important issue which the Supreme Court in *Robinson v Chief Constable of West Yorkshire*[118] was required to address was the relationship between the tripartite test and the analogous approach to the expansion of the duty of care. The facts of the case were simple. One afternoon, the claimant, Mrs Robinson, who was frail and elderly, was walking along a shopping street in the centre of Huddersfield. She was knocked over and injured by a group of men, who were struggling with one another. Two were sturdily built police officers. The other was a suspected drug-dealer, whom

---

112 Ibid at 251.

113 [2007] 1 AC 181 at para. [7].

114 In *Bryan v Malony* [1995] HCA 17 at [18], Toohey J stated that the 'very term "incremental" invites inquiry because what is incremental is to an extent in the eye of the beholder'.

115 [2015] AC 1732.

116 See p.50 below.

117 [2015] AC 1732 at para. [102].

118 [2018] UKSC 4; [2018] AC 736.

the police officers were attempting to arrest. The question which the court was required to answer was whether the officers owed a duty of care to the claimant. In the county court, the Recorder, founding on the decision in the House of Lords case of *Hill v Chief Constable of West Yorkshire*,[119] held that that case had conferred immunity on the police against claims in negligence. Furthermore, that immunity was not confined to cases of omission. Rather, it applied to the facts of the present case. On appeal, to the Court of Appeal,[120] Hallett LJ, who gave the leading judgment, in dismissing the claimant's appeal, held that the *Caparo* test applied to all claims in the modern law of negligence. Her Ladyship expressed the view that most claims against the police would fail, at the third stage of the *Caparo* test, on the grounds that it would not be fair, just and reasonable to impose a duty.[121] That was the case because the courts have concluded that the interests of the public would not be served by the courts imposing such a duty. The claimant appealed.

The main substantive issues which fell to be answered by the Supreme Court, in terms of the general application of the concept of the duty of care, were as follows:

1. Did the existence of a duty of care always depend on the application of the *Caparo* test to the facts of the particular case?
2. Did the police officers owe a duty of care to the claimant?

The leading judgment was given by Lord Reed.

As far as 1 was concerned, for his Lordship, the *Caparo* test did not apply to all claims in the modern law of negligence, and that, in consequence, the court would only impose a duty where it considered it fair, just and reasonable on the particular facts.[122] Lord Reed went on to state that such an approach represented a misunderstanding of the 'whole point' of *Caparo*, which was to repudiate the idea that there was a single test which could be applied in all cases, in order to determine whether a duty of care existed. For his Lordship the correct approach was one which was based on precedent, and on the development of the law incrementally, and by analogy, with established authorities. Lord Reed continued by stating that it was normally only in a novel type of case, where established principles did not provide an answer, that the courts needed to go beyond such principles to decide whether a duty of care should be recognised.[123] As far as the instant case was concerned, his Lordship stated that the police were generally under a duty to avoid causing personal injury, where such a duty would arise in accordance with the ordinary principles of negligence.[124]

Lord Mance, in delivering a concurring judgment, also concluded that it was unnecessary, in every case, to resort to the application of the tripartite test which was identified in *Caparo*.[125] However, his Lordship observed that when recognising and developing an established category (that is, where the tripartite test would be

[119] [1989] AC 53.
[120] [2014] EWCA Civ 15 at para. [40].
[121] Ibid at para. [46].
[122] [2018] UKSC 4 at para. [21].
[123] Ibid at para. [27].
[124] Ibid at para. [67].
[125] Ibid at para. [83]

redundant) the courts were not uninfluenced by policy considerations.[126] His Lordship went on to state that, whereas the courts were not a Law Commission, in making a decision as to whether a duty of care was owed, in particular circumstances, the courts were making policy choices, in which considerations such as proximity, fairness, justice and reasonableness must inhere. Lord Mance went on to observe that, in the instant case, there was, open to the law, a genuine policy choice as to whether or not to hold the police responsible, on a generalised basis, for direct physical intervention on the ground, causing an innocent passer-by physical injury, in the performance of their duties to investigate, prevent and arrest for suspected offending by some third person(s). In other words, one could view the facts of the case, in a broader context, as embracing the performance of the police, in the conduct of their general duties, and not simply as one in which a duty of care automatically fell to be imposed on the defendants, simply because their actions had caused physical injury to the claimant. In effect, Lord Mance's approach would, therefore, allow the courts to expand the law to a greater extent than that which was favoured by Lord Reed.

As far as 2 was concerned, Lord Reed held that it was not only reasonable but actually foreseen by the officers that the suspected drug-dealer was likely to resist arrest by attempting to escape.[127] The place where the officers decided to arrest the drug-dealer was a moderately busy shopping centre where pedestrians were passing in close proximity to the drug-dealer. It was, therefore, reasonably foreseeable that if the arrest was attempted at a time when pedestrians, especially physically vulnerable pedestrians, such as a frail and elderly woman, were in close proximity to the suspected drug-dealer, they might be knocked into and injured in the course of his attempting to escape.

Lord Reed concluded by deciding that the defendant was liable in damages to the claimant.[128]

Robinson, therefore, establishes the principle that the *Caparo* tripartite test is not of universal application when one considers whether the defender owes the pursuer a duty of care. That test has currency only in relation to cases which are novel. *Robinson*, therefore, gives judges more limited scope for creativity in the expansion of the duty of care. It has been argued that the incremental approach, in principle, brings enhanced certainty in this area of the law, on account of its anchoring the duty enquiry firmly in existing authority.[129] However, in the author's view, such certainty would depend on how conservative or restrictive an approach the courts adopt in determining whether the facts of the case are novel. It has already been argued above[130] that judicial opinion may vary markedly as to whether the facts of a case are analogous to an established category of cases. Whereas *Robinson* does elevate the importance of decided cases, in terms of the development of the duty of care, and certainly acts as a powerful brake

---

[126] Ibid at para. [84].

[127] Ibid at para. [74].

[128] Ibid at para. [81]. For a discussion of *Robinson* see G Cameron 'Negligence and the Duty of Care; the Demise of the *Caparo* Test; and Police Immunity Revisited: Robinson v Chief Constable of West Yorkshire' (2019) 23 Edin.LR 82.

[129] J Goudkamp and D Nolan *Winfield and Jolowicz Tort* (20th edn) (2020, Sweet and Maxwell) at 5-028.

[130] At p.26.

to the expansion of the law, the author would argue that since *Donoghue*, judges have shown a capacity for creativity in their approach to the expansion of the duty of care. How firmly judges perceive their ability to develop the law, as being firmly anchored to decided cases, can only be ascertained by considering case law. The author now discusses how the courts have applied the decision in *Robinson*.

Post Robinson

Shortly after *Robinson* was decided, the Supreme Court was required to apply the learning in that case in *Darnley v Croydon Health Services NHS Trust*.[131] Here, the claimant attended the accident and emergency department of the defendant's hospital, with a suspected head injury. A receptionist informed him that he faced a likely wait of four to five hours before being seen by a member of the medical staff. However, she did not inform him that he would be seen by a triage nurse within thirty minutes. The claimant waited for nineteen minutes and then went home, because he was feeling worse and was unwilling to wait for four to five hours, as indicated by the receptionist. The claimant did not inform the hospital staff that he was leaving. However, the receptionist on duty noticed that he had left. An hour later the claimant's condition deteriorated while he was at home. His family called for an ambulance. He was taken back to the hospital where a scan identified a large extradural haematoma. He underwent surgery to remove the haematoma. However, he was left with permanent brain damage. The claimant claimed damages in negligence against the defendant. The former alleged that the receptionist had been in breach of duty by failing to provide accurate information about waiting times. The agreed medical evidence was that if the claimant had received proper timeous medical treatment, that he would have made a near full recovery.

The Court of Appeal, by a majority, held that neither the receptionist nor the defendant owed any duty to the claimant to provide advice about waiting times. The court held *inter alia* that it was not fair, just and reasonable to impose on them a duty not to provide inaccurate information about waiting times. The claimant successfully appealed to the Supreme Court.

Lord Lloyd-Jones, with whom the remainder of the court agreed, following the judgment of Lord Reed in *Robinson*, stated that where the existence of a duty of care had been previously established, a consideration of justice and reasonableness had already been taken into account in arriving at the relevant principles.[132] His Lordship continued that it would only be in cases where the court was asked to go beyond the established categories of duty of care that it would be fair, just and reasonable to impose such a duty. Lord Lloyd-Jones went on to emphasise that the facts of the instant case fell squarely within an established category of duty of care. It had long been established that such a duty was owed by those who provide and run an accident and emergency department to persons who present themselves, complaining of illness or injury. Citing *Barnett v Chelsea and Kensington Hospital Management Committee*[133]

[131] [2018] 3 WLR 1153.
[132] Ibid at 1159.
[133] [1969] 1 QB 428.

Lord Lloyd-Jones stated that that duty was one to take reasonable care not to cause physical injury to the patient. Furthermore, in determining whether a duty of care was owed by the defendant, no distinction should be drawn between medically qualified and non-medical staff.[134] In the last analysis, the defendant had conferred on its non-medically qualified staff the role of being the first point of contact with persons seeking medical assistance and, as a result, the responsibility for providing accurate information as to its availability.

It should be observed, at this juncture, that *Darnley* neatly illustrates the point, which has previously been made, to the effect that judicial opinion may vary significantly as to whether the facts of a case fall within an established category. Whereas in the Court of Appeal, Jackson LJ considered that to hold the defendant liable would create a new head of liability for National Health Service (NHS) Trusts,[135] as stated above, Lord Lloyd-Jones held that the facts of the case fell within an existing category.

The approach to the application of the duty of care, in the light of *Robinson*, is further illustrated in the Supreme Court case of *James-Bowen v Commissioner of Police of the Metropolis*.[136] There, claimants were serving officers in the Metropolitan Police Service. They had taken part in the arrest and detention of BA, who was a suspected terrorist. The latter claimed that the claimants had assaulted and injured him in doing so. The claims were investigated in disciplinary proceedings and then dismissed. In 2005 the officers' identities were released into the public domain. The claimants and their families then received threats of serious violence from BA's supporters. In 2007, BA brought an action against the Commissioner of Police of the Metropolis (the defendant) on the basis that the latter was vicariously liable for the acts of the claimants. The officers were not part of the action, and the Commissioner did not bring contribution proceedings against them. At a conference in 2008, the claimants were allegedly assured by the defendant's legal team that their interests would be safeguarded, and that the claim would be vigorously defended. At a second conference the claimants were allegedly told that the legal team would no longer represent their interests, but solely those of the defendant. During the trial the defendant settled the claim, admitted liability and apologised for the officers' gratuitous violence. A press release was also issued, which the claimants considered was tantamount to endorsing their culpability. In 2010 they were charged and acquitted of causing actual bodily harm to BA. In 2013, the claimants began proceedings against the defendant, alleging *inter alia* negligence. The claimants asserted that the defendant owed them a duty of care, as their employer, to take reasonable care to safeguard their welfare, including their economic and professional welfare and reputational interests, in the conduct of BA's claim, and when considering and effecting any settlement of it.

The claimants' claim was rejected at first instance. On appeal to the Court of Appeal, it was held that it was at least arguable that the defendant owed the claimants a duty to safeguard their interests, including their economic and reputational

[134] [2018] 3 WLR 1153 at 1160.
[135] [2017] EWCA Civ 151 at para. 53.
[136] [2018] 1 WLR 4021.

interests, in relation to the former's conduct of the litigation. The defendant successfully appealed to the Supreme Court.

Lord Lloyd-Jones identified the facts of the case as novel.[137] Therefore, in the light of *Robinson*, the court was, first, required to employ an approach which was incremental and proceeded by analogy with previous decisions. His Lordship regarded the House of Lords case of *Calveley v Chief Constable of Merseyside Police*[138] as having an important bearing on the case.[139] In that case, police officers, against whom disciplinary proceedings had been taken, brought actions in negligence against their chief constables, on the basis that they were vicariously liable for the actions of the investigating officers. The police officers claimed that the investigating officers had failed to conduct the proceedings properly or expeditiously and claimed *inter alia* damages in respect of loss of overtime earnings during their suspension, and damages also for injury to reputation. The House of Lords held that no duty of care was owed to the claimants by the defendant.

Lord Lloyd-Jones, in applying the tripartite test, stated that in the instant case, it would not be fair, just or reasonable to impose on an employer a duty of care to defend legal proceedings, so as to protect the economic or reputational interests of his employee.[140] Furthermore, to impose such a duty would be contrary to public policy.

It has been already stated above that judicial opinion may vary as to whether the facts of a case which is before a court either falls into an established category or, on the other hand, are novel. *ABC v St George's Healthcare NHS Trust*[141] provides a good example of the court being required to consider whether the facts before it fell within an existing category. In that case, the claimant brought an action against three NHS trusts. She contended that the defendants had breached a duty of care that was owed to her, in terms of the law of negligence, and she also claimed that the defendants had acted contrary to her rights, under Art 8 of the European Convention on Human Rights (ECHR), in failing to alert her to the risk that she might have inherited Huntington's disease in time for her to terminate her pregnancy. The claimant sought damages for the continuation of her pregnancy, psychiatric damage and also consequential losses. The genetic risk to the claimant had been revealed to the defendants, through diagnosis of the claimant's father ('XX'). However, XX had declined to consent to the disclosure of the information to the claimant. The defendants' clinicians, in turn, decided that they would not override XX's decision.

The facts upon which the claimant's action were founded were both tragic and unusual. XX had killed the claimant's mother. XX was convicted of manslaughter, by reason of diminished responsibility, and was made subject of a restricted hospital order, in terms of the Mental Health Act 1983. XX was then detained in a clinic, which was run by the second defendant. Clinicians then formed the impression that XX might be suffering from Huntington's disease. However, XX refused to undergo genetic testing. He also made it clear that he did not want either the claimant or her

137 Ibid at 4032.
138 [1989] AC 1228.
139 Ibid 4034.
140 Ibid 4036.
141 [2020] EWHC 455.

sister to know that he was thought to have Huntington's disease. Both daughters were in their thirties at the time. Neither had started a family. The claimant became pregnant in 2009. That was about the time it emerged that XX probably had Huntington's disease. The claimant was a patient of the second defendant's family therapy team.

Yipp J found that the relationship between the claimant and the second defendant to be analogous to a situation in which a patient was undergoing a therapeutic intervention.[142] Therefore, the duty which was owed by hospital trusts to patients to deliver services competently applied to all patients who were undertaking family therapy. However, the judge added that simply because the claimant was a patient of the second defendant, that duty did not extend to the scope of duty which the claimant contended, namely the imparting of confidential information concerning her father's physical condition.[143] In short, the claimant's participation in the family therapy did not bring with it a right to receive other information about participants.[144]

Having decided that the second defendant did not owe a duty of care to the claimant, by way of imparting to her confidential information about her father's medical condition, the court then addressed the issue as to whether a duty of care was owed to the claimant, outwith that relationship. The judge stated that in certain circumstances the courts had been willing to recognise that a doctor, or a health authority, may owe a duty of care to those other than their patients.[145] That duty was capable of arising only if there was a relationship of proximity between the parties. The judge held that since the second defendant was in possession of the relevant facts concerning the claimant, the former was in a close proximate relationship with the latter.[146] Furthermore, it was actually foreseen that the claimant would suffer harm if the genetic risk she was exposed to was withheld.[147] After citing ECHR case law, to the effect that an individual has the right to have information about her health imparted to her, including information concerning reproductive autonomy, Yipp J concluded that it was fair, just and reasonable to impose a duty of care on the second defendant, to conduct a balancing exercise that consisted of weighing the claimant's right to be informed against XX's interest in preserving confidentiality.[148]

However, the judge held that notwithstanding the fact that the second defendant owed a duty of care to the claimant, her action failed because she had failed to establish a causal link between the negligent act of the second claimant and the harm which she had sustained, since she failed to prove that she would have terminated the pregnancy had the relevant risk been disclosed to her timeously.[149]

It is established law that a hospital does not owe a duty of care to a third party in relation to the manner in which it treats a patient. For example, in *Smith v University of Leicester NHS Trust*[150] a hospital trust was held not to owe a duty of care to a third

142 Ibid at para. [138].
143 Ibid at para. [139].
144 Ibid at para. [141].
145 Ibid at para. [170].
146 Ibid at para. [173].
147 Ibid at para. [174].
148 Ibid at para. [187]–[188] incl.
149 Ibid at para. [264].
150 [2016] EWHC 817.

party for negligently diagnosing a patient who was related to the claimant. In deciding that the facts in the instant case (that is, outwith the doctor/patient relationship) disclosed a novel situation, and were, therefore, amenable to the application of the *Caparo* tripartite test (rather than the application of established principles as enunciated in *Robinson*), the court took into account *inter alia* that the relevant confidential information affected the claimant, that she would suffer further harm if the relevant information was withheld from her, and also that the second defendant had actively considered the impact of that information, if it were disclosed to her.

However, it could be argued that such factors were insufficient to transform the facts of the case from a scenario where established principles should be held to apply to a situation in which the facts should be treated as novel. In the author's view the facts in *ABC* were most closely analogous to the facts in *Smith* (as indicated above). Furthermore, the facts in *ABC* were also analogous to those in the Court of Appeal case of *Goodwill v British Pregnancy Advisory Service*[151] in which the court held that the defendant did not owe the claimant a duty of care in respect of a failed vasectomy that had been performed on the claimant's partner, who had been informed that he no longer required to use contraceptives, the upshot of which was that the claimant had become pregnant. The court held that there was insufficient proximity between the parties to ground a duty of care on the part of the defendant to the claimant. Furthermore, the former had not assumed any responsibility towards the latter. One could, therefore, argue that Yipp J adopted a rather myopic approach in refusing to treat the facts in *ABC* as analogous to decided cases.[152]

DUTY OF CARE-LIABILITY FOR OMISSIONS

We now consider the extent, if any, to which the law imposes a duty of care in respect of omissions, sometimes referred to as 'pure omissions'.[153] In the House of Lords case of *Stoven v Wise*[154] Lord Hoffman stated that 'omissions, like economic loss, are notoriously a category of conduct, in which Lord Atkin's generalisation in *Donoghue v Stevenson* offers limited help'. Indeed, ascertaining the potential liability for omissions, on the part of the defender, the upshot of which is that the pursuer sustains injury, represents a grey area of law which is un-theorised and has taunted and teased the courts. One major difficulty which has contributed to this state of affairs is that it may be difficult, at the outset, to determine whether the defender's conduct ranks as an omission (or 'pure' omission), or on the other hand, is simply part of a chain of active conduct.[155] No one could seriously contend that a driver's failure to brake at a junction was an omission.[156] For example, in the Court of Appeal case of *Kelly*

[151] [1996] 1 WLR 1397.

[152] For a discussion of *ABC* see (2020) 154 Rep B. 3 and [2020] CLJ 214.

[153] *Smith v Littlewoods Organisation Ltd* [1987] AC 241 at 271 (per Lord Goff).

[154] [1996] AC 923 at 943.

[155] In the Privy Council case of AG of the *British Virgin Isles v Harwell* [2004] 1 WLR 1273 at para. [31] Lord Nicholls stated that the line separating liability for acts and liability for omissions was imprecisely drawn. Again, in *Began v Maran* [2022] EWHC 1846 at para. 38, Jay J described the distinction between an act and an omission as 'often rather fluid'.

[156] *Winfield and Jolowicz Tort* n 129 at 5-033.

v Metropolitan Company[157] the driver of a train failed to turn off the steam engine of a train, the upshot of which was that it ran into a wall at Baker Street Station. The plaintiff was injured. Rigby LJ stated that:

> the attempt to dissect the act of the defendant's servant, and to treat the mere omission to turn off steam as a nonfeasance within the meaning of the cases referred to, altogether fails ... The proper description of what was done is that it was a negligent act in so managing the train, as to allow it to come into contact with the dead end, and so cause the accident.[158]

Indeed, in *Donoghue v Stevenson* the failure on the part of the defender manufacturer to ensure that his lemonade was in pristine condition and 'snail-free' was not regarded by the House as an omission, but rather as an integral part of the defender's negligent act, in supplying the tainted drink to the consumer. In other words, the omission simply formed part of a chain of events, commencing with the manufacture of the lemonade, its being bottled, and then supplied to the consumer.

In the last analysis, the courts approach the question as to whether the conduct of the defender should be categorised as one of omission (or 'pure omission') or otherwise, intuitively, and address the issue on a case-by-case basis.

As far as the imposition of liability for omissions is concerned, the general rule is that there is no duty on the defender to take affirmative action in the law of negligence. That is to say, that the law does not impose liability for pure omissions.[159] In other words, subject to certain exceptions, I am under no duty to save my neighbour from harm. I can smugly watch him walk towards a dangerous cliff, without shouting a warning. I can idly stand by and watch a baby drown in a shallow pool of water, provided that I do not stand in a special relationship to the child.[160]

However, there are certain circumstances in which the law does impose a duty on the defender to take affirmative action to prevent harm. These situations are now considered.[161]

Occupiers of land duty to abate nuisances on land

Land may present a danger to neighbouring proprietors because of human conduct, or by virtue of an act of nature. The law imposes a duty of care on an occupier of land, in certain circumstances, not to allow his land to become a known source of danger to neighbouring proprietors. The nature and extent of that duty was considered in a trilogy of cases which we now discuss.

In *Sedleigh-Denfield v O'Callaghan*[162] a local authority trespassed on the land of the defendant, and then constructed a culvert on a ditch. One of the employees of the defendant knew of the existence of the culvert. Furthermore, the defendants had also used the culvert, in order to get rid of water from their own property. However, the

[157] [1895] 1 QB 944.

[158] Ibid at 947.

[159] *Smith v Littlewoods Organisation Ltd* [1987] AC 241 at 271 (per Lord Goff).

[160] L Eldridge *Modern Tort Law* (1941) at 12.

[161] For a useful discussion of liability for omissions in negligence, see S Steel 'Rationalising Omissions Liability in Negligence' (2019) 135 LQR 484.

[162] [1940] AC 880.

culvert was not properly constructed, the upshot of which was that it became blocked by detritus. A heavy thunderstorm caused the ditch to flood, and the claimant's land also became flooded. The House of Lords held the defendants liable in nuisance, by virtue of both continuing and adopting the nuisance in question. The defendants had continued the nuisance, by failing to take the necessary remedial action after the defendants had become aware (through their servant) of the existence of the nuisance. The nuisance had been adopted by the defendants, in their using the culvert for their own purposes.

After stating that the facts of the case had properly been treated as a nuisance, Lord Wright stated that the facts also had affinity with a claim for negligence, since the trouble arose from the negligent fitting of the grid on the culvert.[163] Importantly, in the present context, Lord Wright stated that, in the instant case, negligence was not an independent cause of action but was ancillary to the actual cause of action, which was nuisance.

The relationship between the law of nuisance and negligence came in for further discussion in the Privy Council case of *Goldman v Hargrave*.[164] In that case, a tall gum tree, which was 100 feet high, and was situated on the defendant's land, was struck by lightning. It caught fire. The defendant then cut the tree down the following day. However, he did not take further steps to stop the fire from spreading, preferring simply to let the fire burn itself out. Several days later, the weather changed. The wind became stronger, and the air temperature increased. This caused the fire to revive, and it spread over the plaintiff's land, which was damaged. The Privy Council held that the defendant was liable for the damage caused, on basis that he had failed to remove the nuisance from his land. Importantly, in the present context, in so deciding, the Board held that no distinction fell to be made between liability in terms of the law of negligence and liability in terms of the law of nuisance.[165]

However, in deciding whether the defendant had failed to reach the standard of care which the law demanded, the Board held that one was required to take into account the defendant's knowledge of the hazard, as well as his ability to foresee the consequences of not checking or removing it, and also his ability to abate the nuisance.[166] One was also required to take into account the defendant's individual circumstances. In other words, one should adopt a subjective approach. Therefore, less would be expected of the infirm than of the able bodied. One would also require to take into account the resources of the defendant. Again, one would expect less of an owner of smaller premises than of larger premises.

---

[163] Ibid at 903, 904.

[164] [1967] 1 AC 645.

[165] Lord Wilberforce stated (at [1967] 1 AC 645 at 656) that the question whether the facts of the case should be brought under the heading of nuisance or negligence was disputable. However, the present case rested on negligence and nothing else. In the House of Lords case of *Delaware Mansions Ltd v Westminster City Council* [2002] 1 AC 321 at 333, Lord Cooke expressed the view that in circumstances similar to those in the *Wagon Mound* and *Goldman v Hargrave* the label nuisance was treated as of no real significance. In that context, the concern of the common law was in working out the fair and just content and incidents of a neighbour's duty, rather than affixing a label, and inferring the extent of the duty from it. See also *Smith v Littlewoods Ltd* [1987] AC 241 at 274 (per Lord Goff).

[166] [1967] 1 AC 645 at 663.

The question which the Court of Appeal was required to determine in *Leakey v National Trust for Places of Historic Interest or Natural Beauty*[167] was whether the learning in *Goldman* represented that of the law of England. In *Leakey* the claimants owned houses, which were situated at the base of a steep conical hill, which rejoiced in the name of 'Burrow Mump'. Part of the hill which adjoined the claimants' land had become unstable. The condition of the hill was made known to the defendants by the claimants. However, no remedial work was undertaken by the former. A few weeks later, there was a substantial fall of earth and tree stumps from the hill, on to the claimants' land. The claimant brought an action in nuisance against the defendants.

The Court of Appeal held the defendants liable. In so deciding, the court refused to draw a distinction between an adverse state of affairs which had been foist on the defendants by man-made activities and those which had arisen by the operation of nature. Importantly, in the present context, Megaw LJ stated that the defendants had owed the claimants a duty of care.[168] His Lordship then went on to define the scope of that duty. He held that the learning in *Goldman* should be followed. Therefore, the duty on the defendant was to do only that which was reasonable in the circumstances, to prevent or minimise the known risk of damage or injury to one's neighbour, or to his property. In determining whether that duty had been breached, one should take into account the extent of the risk, what could reasonably be foreseen; the practicality of taking the necessary prophylactic action; the cost of the relevant works; and the available period of time the defendant had at his disposal to carry out the work, after he discovered the adverse state of affairs on his property.[169]

The above cases establish the general principle that an occupier of land is under a duty to abate a known source of danger (or 'hazard') on his land which either damages or has the potential to cause damage to a neighbouring proprietor of land.[170] However, that duty is a measured one. These cases also show that, whereas the above cases were framed in terms of the law of nuisance, the courts have held that in such circumstances, there is little substantive difference between the law of nuisance and the law of negligence. However, the relationship between nuisance and negligence in this context is not clear-cut.[171]

To what extent, if any, do the English and Commonwealth authorities, which are discussed above, represent the law of Scotland? There is, indeed, sparse authority on this point. However, in the Outer House case of *Gourock Rope Co Ltd v Greenock Corp*[172] a mill lead, which passed through a site which was owned by the defender local authority, also flowed through factory premises, which were owned by the pursuers. The mill lead became blocked by timber, or other materials, which fell into the lead as it passed through the ground, which was owned by the defender. Damage was

[167] [1980] QB 485.

[168] Ibid at 524.

[169] See also *Bybrook Barn Garden Centre Ltd v Kent County Council* [2001] Env LR 30 and *Ward v Coope* [2015] 1 WLR 4081.

[170] *Bockenfield Aerodrome Ltd v Clarehugh* [2022] 1 P. and C.R.17.

[171] See for example *Judge v Waugh* [2022] NU Ch 16 at [56] per McBride J. Murphy argues that *Sedleigh-Denfield*, *Goldman* and *Leakey* are better seen as negligence cases that call for a future corrective in relation to the standard of care; *The Law of Nuisance* (OUP, 2010) at 1.28.

[172] 1966 SLT 125.

done when the mill lead overflowed and flooded the factory. At the time the flooding took place, the site was occupied by an independent contractor. The pursuers sued the defender. The substantive question which the court was required to answer was whether the defender, as proprietor of the site, was liable for a nuisance which had been created, or caused by timber and suchlike, which either had fallen into the mill lead at the site or had been deposited by persons, other than the defender, or its servants. Lord Fraser held that since the defender had not been in occupation of the site, at the time the flooding occurred, that the defender would only be liable for the nuisance originating from the site, if it either had knowledge or the means of knowledge that the actual nuisance was likely to be committed by the contractors, or by other persons, in the course of works being carried out on the site.[173]

After tacitly accepting that *Sedleigh-Denfield* represented the law of Scotland, Lord Fraser held that foreseeability of the nuisance was an essential factor, before the defender could be held liable.[174] The judge went on to decide that since the defender could not have foreseen the debris falling into the mill lead, and being carried down to the pursuer's premises, the defender was not liable. The author would observe, however, that whereas in *Sedleigh-Denfield* the defendant actually occupied the land whence the nuisance arose, in *Gourock Rope Co* the site, as stated above, was occupied by an independent contractor at the time the flooding occurred. There is no subsequent Scottish authority on whether the owner (as opposed to the occupier) of land would be liable in terms of the law of nuisance, on facts similar to those in *Gourock*.

Finally, there is no Scottish authority as to whether the occupier of land, on which a hazard has occurred by an act of nature, would be liable to a neighbouring proprietor, for failure on the part of the occupier to remove the hazard, the upshot of which is that the hazard causes harm to the latter's premises. However, in the author's opinion the learning of the Court of Appeal in *Leakey* would be followed.

Special relationships

The law imposes an affirmative duty of care on someone who stands in a particular relationship with (and therefore exercises, or has the capacity to exercise, some form of control over) another person, or his immediate environment, to protect that person from harm, in certain circumstances. The relationship between parent and child;[175] employer and employee;[176] school authority and pupil;[177] religious organisation and child member;[178] occupier of land and visitor;[179] hospital authority and members of

---

173 Ibid at 127.

174 Ibid at 128.

175 *Hastie v Magistrates of Edinburgh* 1907 SC 1102; *Phipps v Rochester Corp* [1955] 1 QB 450 at 472; *Surtees v The Royal Borough of Kingston upon Thames* [1992] PIQR P101.

176 *Paris v Stepney BC* [1951] AC 367.

177 *Barnes v Hampshire CC* [1969] 1 WLR 1563. See also *Moddejonge v Huron County Board of Education* [1972] 2 OR 437 (school authority owed duty of care to student on a field trip); *Smith v Horizon Aero Sports Ltd* (1981) 19 CCLT 89 (BCSC) (parachute instructor owed duty of care to student).

178 *A v The Trustees of the Watchtower Bible and Tract Society* [2015] EWHC 1722.

179 *Glasgow Corp v Muir* [1943] AC 448; Occupiers Liability (Scotland) Act 1960.

the public presenting themselves at A&E departments;[180] hospital authority and patient;[181] and night club and guest, have been recognised by the courts as imposing an affirmative duty of care on the defender.[182] In the House of Lords case of *Reeves v Metropolitan Police Commissioner*[183] the House of Lords held that a prison authority owed a duty of care to a prisoner, who had previously manifest suicidal tendencies, to take adequate measures to prevent his suicide while he was in police custody. Similarly in *Thorne v Northern Group Hospital Management Committee*[184] it was held that as a general principle, a hospital authority was under a duty to avoid the possibility of injury, whether self-inflicted or otherwise, occurring to patients whom it knows, or ought to know, have a history of mental illness.[185] Again, in the Canadian Supreme Court case of *Jordan House Ltd v Menow*[186] the employees of the defendant hotel had served the plaintiff with drink, until he became patently drunk. He was subsequently ejected from the hotel on a dark, rainy night, in a state in which it was quite clear he could not look after himself. The plaintiff was wearing dark clothes, and therefore was not readily visible to motorists. He was hit by a car while he was crossing the road and was injured. It was held that the proprietors of the hotel owed an affirmative duty of care to a drunken customer, to the effect that he should not be turned out of the former's premises if it would be unsafe to do so.

In the Canadian Supreme Court case of *Horsley v MacLaren*[187] the defendant was the owner and operator of a boat, on which he was carrying invited guests. One of the guests fell overboard and drowned. It was held that, having brought his guests into a relationship with him, in their capacity as passengers of the boat, albeit as gratuitous passengers, the defendant was under a duty to take reasonable care for their safety. That duty existed, whether the passenger fell overboard accidentally or by reason of his own carelessness.[188]

In certain circumstances, the law will impose an affirmative duty on those who benefit, or stand to benefit, from a particular relationship. A carrier is therefore under an affirmative duty to locate and rescue a passenger who has fallen overboard.[189] Again, in the Court of Appeal case of *Everett v Comojo (UK) Ltd (t/a The Metropolitan)*[190] one of the reasons why the court felt justified in holding that the defendant club owed a duty to protect a guest from injury from assault by another patron, was that the club derived an economic advantage from the presence of the claimant on the premises.

---

180 *Barnett v Chelsea and Kensington Hospital Management Committee* [1969] 1 QB 428; *Darnley v Croydon Health Services NHS Trust* [2019] AC 831.

181 *Gorringe v Calderdale MBC* [2004] 1 WLR 1057 at 1068, 1069 (per Lord Hoffman).

182 *Everett v Comojo (UK) Ltd (t/a The Metropolitan)* [2012] 1 WLR 150.

183 [2000] 1 AC 360.

184 (1964) 108 SJ 484.

185 See also *Rabone v Pennine Care NHS Trust* [2012] 2 AC 72.

186 (1973) 38 DLR (3rd) 105.

187 [1972] SCR 441.

188 Ibid at [43].

189 *Davis v Stena Line Ltd* [2005] EWHC 420.

190 n 105 (above).

In the Canadian Supreme Court case of *Crocker v Sundance Northwest Resorts Ltd*[191] the defendant company operated a ski complex. A competitor was allowed to enter a race, despite the fact that he was visibly drunk. He was seriously injured. It was held that since the defendants derived economic advantage from the competition, the latter owed the former a duty of care.[192]

Control over potentially dangerous situations

In certain cases the law will impose an affirmative duty of care on the pursuer where he either exercises or has the capacity to exercise control over (1) an existing or (2) a potentially dangerous situation which could result in injury to the pursuer.

As far as (1) is concerned, in the Outer House case of *Gibson v Orr*[193] a bridge which carried a public road collapsed. The attention of the police was drawn to the danger which was posed to traffic. The police coned off the north side of the bridge, and then left a police vehicle, with its lights flashing on that side, so that it would be visible to vehicles approaching from the south side of the road. The police then left the scene of the accident, without having received confirmation that any warning or barrier had been placed on the south side of the bridge. Shortly after this, a car, which approached the bridge from the south side, fell into the river. The pursuer survived, but the other occupants of the car were killed. It was held that by virtue of the police having taken control of the hazard, they came under a duty of care to the pursuer.

However, Gibson requires to be reconsidered in the light of the Supreme Court case of *Tindall v Chief Constable of Thames Valley*.[194] The facts of the case were simple and straightforward. The claimant was the widow of Tindall ('T'). T had been driving along a road, early one morning. B had been driving in the opposite direction. B lost control of his car when the car encountered black ice on a stretch of the road. B's car collided with T's car. Both B and T were killed. About an hour earlier there had been another accident on the same stretch of the road. In the first accident, K had lost control of his car, which had rolled over and had ended up in a ditch. As a consequence, K had sustained injuries which were non-life-threatening. K had been taken to hospital. Before K was taken to hospital, and before the arrival of the police, K had made efforts to alert traffic to the danger. Police officers attended the scene of the accident twenty minutes after the first accident. They had removed some debris from the road. The police remained at the scene of the accident for twenty minutes. They had put up a 'Police Slow' sign by the carriageway. On leaving, the police removed the sign. The police left the road in the same condition as when they had arrived. Nobody remained to warn traffic. No warning signs remained, nor did the police take any action at the site, in order to ensure that traffic knew of the existence of the hazard, once the police had left. The claimant claimed that the police had been negligent in

191 (1988) 44 CCLT 192.

192 For a useful discussion of the duties of occupiers of licensed premises to their customers, see C Hare 'Am I My (Drunken) Neighbour's Keeper?' [2010] CLJ 16.

193 1999 SC 420.

194 [2024] 3 WLR 822.

leaving the scene of the accident, and therefore, that the police were liable in tort for the negligent conduct of the police.

At first instance, the judge refused to strike out the claimant's claim. The Chief Constable successfully appealed to the Court of Appeal. The Supreme Court dismissed the claimant's appeal against that decision.

The court rejected the claimant's claim that the police had owed the deceased a duty of care *inter alia* by having taken control of the scene of the accident.[195] The police had not taken control of the scene of the accident. The patch of ice which had caused first K and later B to lose control of their vehicles was at some distance from the scene where K's car had ended up in a ditch. The distance from that spot was some 184 metres from the spot where T was killed.

As far as (2) is concerned, in *Wilson v Chief Constable of Lothian and Borders Police*[196] the police were called to a domestic incident. The husband ('W') was found in an inebriated condition. W was removed in a police car, with the intention that W could be taken sufficiently far away that he could not return. However, he was not arrested. After causing a disturbance in the car, W was released in the early hours of the morning, on the outskirts of Edinburgh, in adverse weather conditions. W subsequently died of hypothermia. It was held that, by virtue of the control which the police exercised over W, they owed him a duty of care, in terms of the law of negligence.

Another interesting example of the courts being willing to impose an affirmative duty of care on the defender, who assumes, or enjoys, a position of control vis-à-vis the pursuer, can be seen in the Court of Appeal case of *Watson v British Boxing Board of Control*.[197] That case concerned liability for head injuries which were sustained by Michael Watson, who was a professional boxer, in his fight with Chris Eubank. The fight was regulated by the British Boxing Board of Control (BBBC). Watson claimed that the BBBC had failed to take adequate measures to ensure that he would receive immediate attention should he sustain injury during the fight. The court held that there was sufficient proximity between the parties to ground a duty of care in law.[198] The basis for the decision was that, since the BBBC had complete control over the contest, it was fair, just and reasonable to conclude that a duty of care existed. Lord Phillips MR, in deciding in favour of the claimant, set store by the following factors:

1. Watson was one of a defined number of boxing members of the BBBC.
2. A primary stated object of the BBBC was to look after its boxing members' physical safety.
3. The BBBC encouraged and supported its boxing members in the pursuit of an activity which involved inevitable physical injury.
4. The BBBC controlled every aspect of the activity, including the medical assistance which could be provided.

195 Ibid at [78].
196 1989 SLT 97.
197 [2001] QB 1134.
198 Ibid at 1162.

5. The BBBC had or had access to specialist expertise, in relation to the appropriate standards of medical care.
6. If Watson had no remedy against the BBBC he had no remedy at all.
7. Boxing members of the BBBC, including Watson, could reasonably rely on the BBBC to look after their safety.[199]

In *Everett*[200] the Court of Appeal held that the defendant night club owed one of its guests an affirmative duty of care to prevent the guest from being attacked by a fellow guest. The court held that there was sufficient proximity between the parties to ground a duty of care, on the basis that the management had complete control of the premises and could regulate who entered, refuse entry and also regulate who was to be removed after entry.[201]

Again, in the Privy Council case of *The Airport Authority v Western Air Ltd (The Bahamas)*[202] the Airport Authority ('AA') owned and operated an airport at Nassau. Western Air Ltd ('WA') was an airline operator which owned and operated commercial airlines. Early one morning one of its aircraft was stolen. It had been parked at the airport in a designated restricted zone. AA, as the statutory authority for the airport, had been required to control access to the zone. Access to the location where the aircraft was parked should have been controlled by a manned security booth. The court held that AA owed WA a duty of care. The court held that there was a relationship of proximity between the parties, on the basis that AA was the sole agency into whose care the safety of the aircraft fell. WA was, therefore, uniquely dependent on AA to safeguard its property.[203] Arguably, AA possessed a degree of control over its airport that was as great as or greater than either of the defendants in *Everett* or *Watson* above, in relation to their respective premises.[204]

Relationship between defender and wrongdoer

The defender may come under a duty of care to the pursuer if the former exercises some form of control over the immediate wrongdoer. For example, in *Donaldson v McNiven*[205] the defendant allowed his son, aged thirteen, to have an air rifle, on condition that it was never used outside the house, which was situated in a populous district. Without the defendant's knowledge, the son fired the gun outside the house and injured the plaintiff. The court held that it would have been negligent for a parent to allow his child to have an air rifle in a populous district, if the parent did not take adequate measures to restrict the use of the rifle to a place of safety. However, it was held that the defendant had taken adequate measures. The plaintiff therefore failed in his action.[206]

---

199 Ibid at 1162, 1163.
200 n 105 (above).
201 [2012] 1 WLR 150 at 158 (per Smith LJ).
202 [2020] UKPC 29.
203 Ibid at [42].
204 For a discussion of *The Airport Authority Ltd* see 2021 SLT 12.
205 [1952] 1 All ER 1213.
206 See, however, *Newton v Edgerley* [1959] 3 All ER 337 where it was held that on the facts, a father was liable in negligence for either allowing his twelve-year-old son (who was found to be young for

Again, in the House of Lords case of *Carmarthenshire CC v Lewis*[207] a four-year-old boy attending a nursery school strayed from the school on to a public highway. The plaintiff's husband, who was driving a lorry at the time, was killed after the lorry struck a telegraph post, in the husband's attempt to avoid him. The defendant local authority was held liable in negligence.

Another example of the courts imposing an affirmative duty on the defender who exercises control over the immediate wrongdoer, is demonstrated in the House of Lords case of *Home Office v Dorset Yacht Co Ltd*.[208] In that case, seven borstal boys who were working under the supervision of three officers on Brownsea Island, in Poole Harbour, left the island at night and boarded, cast adrift and damaged the plaintiffs' yacht, which was moored offshore. The plaintiffs brought an action for damages against the Home Office, alleging negligence. It was held that the defendant owed a duty of care to the owners of nearby yachts.[209] In other words, the duty was owed to those in close proximity to the place where the boys were being detained.

The learning in *Dorset Yacht* was applied in the Inner House case of *Thomson v Scottish Ministers*.[210] In that case, the deceased had been murdered by a prisoner while he was on short-term leave. However, the court held that since the prisoner posed no greater risk to the deceased than that to the general public, there was insufficient proximity between the parties to ground a duty of care.[211]

Thomson was followed in *A v B Ltd*.[212] The first defender, B Ltd, operated a residential care home. The second defender ('C') was a local authority. In spite of a report which had assessed him at 'high risk', B allowed a 16-year-old resident ('X') unsupervised leave. While on leave, X raped and sexually assaulted a child. The child's grandmother ('A') raised an action against both B and C. The key question which the court was required to answer was whether B and C owed the child a duty of care for the criminal acts of X. In rejecting the pursuer's claim, Lord Ericht held that X posed no greater a risk of harm to the victim than X posed to the general public.[213] The child members of the public whom X might come across during leave did not constitute a distinct class which gave rise to a duty of care.[214] A therefore failed in her action.

The extent to which a prison authority is responsible for an assault which is committed by a prisoner on a fellow prisoner was considered in the Outer House case of *Kaizer v Scottish Ministers*.[215] In that case, the pursuer was seriously injured in a racially motivated attack by a fellow prisoner. The prisoner who committed the assault had made a threat to the pursuer a week before the assault had taken place. The threat

his age), who injured another child, to be in possession of a gun in the presence of other children, or alternatively, without having given instructions to the son as to how to handle the gun when others were present.

207 [1955] AC 549.

208 [1970] AC 1004.

209 Ibid at 1034 (per Lord Morris).

210 2013 SC 628.

211 Ibid at [57].

212 2022 SLT 577.

213 Ibid at 582.

214 For a discussion of *A v B Ltd* see 2022 SLT 82.

215 [2017] CSOH 110.

had been reported to a prison officer, who should have reported this. However, he failed to do this. It was held that the defenders (who were responsible for the Scottish Prison Service) owed the pursuer a duty of care, which had been breached, since the assault had been reasonably foreseeable, if reasonable care was not taken.[216]

Assumption of responsibility

The defender may come under an affirmative duty to the pursuer if the defender assumes responsibility[217] to the pursuer who, in turn, relies on the defender, to the pursuer's detriment. The application of this principle is seen in the Court of Appeal case of *Swinney v Chief Constable of Northumbria Police Force*.[218] In that case, the first plaintiff had supplied information (which had been given in confidence) to a police officer, regarding the identity of the driver who had killed another police officer. The information had been stolen from a police vehicle and had come into the hands of the alleged driver. As a consequence, the first and second plaintiff (the first plaintiff's wife) were threatened with violence and arson. They had suffered psychiatric harm as a consequence. In a striking out action, it was held arguable that the police owed the plaintiffs a duty of care, on the basis that the former had assumed responsibility to the latter to preserve the confidentiality of the information, the disclosure of which had put the plaintiffs at a special risk of harm (in contrast to the risk which had been posed to the general public); the latter, in turn, had relied on the police to keep the information confidential.

In *Welsh v Chief Constable of Merseyside Police*[219] the plaintiff had appeared before a magistrates court, charged with two offences for theft. He was remanded on bail to appear before the court at a later date. The plaintiff was also due to appear before the Crown Court, in relation to several criminal matters. Before the case was called in the Crown Court, the plaintiff's counsel informed the police officer in charge of the case, counsel for the prosecution and a representative of the Crown Prosecution Service, that the plaintiff wanted the offences of theft with which he was being charged in the magistrates court, and to which he intended to plead guilty, to be taken into account when the plaintiff was being sentenced by the Crown Court. That was in fact done. The plaintiff failed to answer to his bail in the magistrates court, believing that the court had been informed that the offences had been taken into account in the Crown Court. The magistrates court was not aware of this fact and issued a warrant for his arrest. The plaintiff was arrested and taken into custody. The plaintiff then brought an action against the police and the Crown Prosecution Service ('CPS'), alleging that he had suffered loss, damage and distress, as a result of the defendants' negligent failure

[216] Ibid at [63]. By contrast, in *Leslie v Secretary of State for Scotland* 1999 Rep LR 39 the defender (who was responsible for the Scottish Prison Service) was not liable for an assault which had been perpetrated by a prisoner on a fellow prisoner, since the assault had not been reasonably foreseeable.

[217] In the Court of Appeal case of *Chief Constable of Northamptonshire Police v Woodcock* [2025] EWCA Civ 13 at [121] the court held that whether the defendant had assumed responsibility to the claimant was highly fact-specific.

[218] [1997] QB 464.

[219] [1993] 1 All ER 692.

to ensure that the magistrates court was informed that the offences, for which he had been bailed, had subsequently been taken into consideration by the Crown Court.

In a striking out action, the court held that on the assumed facts, the CPS had assumed responsibility to the plaintiff to advise the magistrates court that the plaintiff wished the relevant offences to be taken into account.[220] In turn, the plaintiff had relied on the CPS. Therefore, the latter owed the former a duty of care.

In order to ascertain whether the defender owes the pursuer a duty of care, by virtue of having assumed responsibility to the pursuer, one requires to ascertain the scope of that duty, by taking into account the type of harm which the pursuer has sustained. This point was neatly illustrated in the Court of Appeal case of *Calvert v William Hill Credit Ltd*.[221] The claimant was a compulsive gambler. He had opened a telephone account with the defendant bookmaker. At the time the defendant, together with other bookmakers, had offered problem gamblers who had accounts, and who made telephone bets with the bookmaker, the choice of making self-exclusion agreements, whereby following requests by the gambler, the bookmaker would close his account and not accept telephone bets from him for a period of six months. The claimant had asked the defendant to close his account for ever. However, two weeks later the claimant phoned the defendant. The defendant allowed the claimant to reopen his account. The latter proceeded to place bets and succeeded in winning more money than he lost. A month later he tried again to make a self-exclusion agreement with the defendant. However, the defendant's employee who took the call failed to implement the agreement, the upshot of which was that the claimant continued to place large telephone bets. The claimant lost over £2,000,000. The claimant brought an action in negligence against the defendant, claiming damages of nearly £1,800,000 on the basis that in allowing him to operate accounts with it, and to place bets while the self-exclusion agreement was in force, the defendant was in breach of its duty of care.

The court held that the defendant had not assumed responsibility to the claimant to prevent him from gambling.[222] The defendant had simply assumed responsibility not to allow the claimant to place telephone bets with them. The defendant had not assumed responsibility to prevent him from gambling in other ways, for example with other bookmakers, as in fact he had done. The scope of the defendant's duty was to help the claimant control his gambling. The defendant had not assumed responsibility to enable the claimant to gamble free from all risk.[223] In short, the scope of the defendant's duty of care did not extend to prevent the claimant from gambling.

The principle that the defender comes under a duty of care to the pursuer if the former assumes responsibility towards the latter also applies in relation to a situation where the pursuer has sustained physical injury or has been the victim of theft.[224] For

220 Ibid at 703.

221 [2009] Ch 330.

222 Ibid at 348.

223 Ibid at 349.

224 See for example *Airport Authority v Western Air Ltd.* [2020] UKPC 29. The airport authority was liable for theft of a plane parked in its premises. The latter had assumed responsibility to the former for safety of the plane. See 2021 SLT 12. See, however, *Great Lakes Reinsurance v RAV* [2024] UKPC 11.

example, in the Court of Appeal case of *Barrett v Ministry of Defence*[225] which was discussed above,[226] a serviceman collapsed after a bout of heavy drinking at a military base. He died after he had been taken to his bunk. It was held that whilst the defendant did not owe the deceased a duty of care to prevent him from drinking too much, it had assumed responsibility to the deceased thereafter.[227]

Again, in the Court of Appeal case of *Ministry of Defence v Radclyffe*[228] the claimant ('R') was a second lieutenant in the First Battalion of the Irish Guards. The battalion had organised an Adventure Training Exercise in Germany. Captain Jones ('J') was in charge of one group with R. One day, when there was no adventure training, some members of R's group decided to go to a reservoir to swim. Four guardsmen asked J if they could jump from a bridge into the reservoir. After having had the depth of the water checked, J authorised the guardsmen to jump, which they did, while J and R watched. J and R then joined the men and both jumped from the bridge together. No one had made R jump. However, J had put pressure on R to prove that the officers were as brave as the men. The following day R, and a group of soldiers, went mountain biking. They then decided to go to the lake to swim. Two of the guardsmen asked if they could go to the bridge and dive from it. R decided that it would be in order, since J had authorised people to jump from it on the previous day. R decided that he would demonstrate how to jump. However, he did so with his legs bent. He was seriously injured. The court held that J, by his own presence at the lake, and also because of his rank, had assumed responsibility to prevent his men from taking unreasonable risks, of which he was, or ought to have been aware.[229] Whereas the men were off duty when the accident took place, that did not mean that the military relationship had become irrelevant. J therefore owed R a duty of care. The defendant was therefore vicariously liable for J's negligence.

In the vast majority of cases where the court has imposed a duty of care on the defender, for his having assumed responsibility to the pursuer, the latter has relied on the defender. However, *Barrett* (above) indicates that the assumption of responsibility on the part of the defender is, on occasions, sufficient of itself to generate a duty of care.

The concept of assumption of responsibility will be further discussed below, in terms of the duty of care owed by public authorities and also in relation to liability for negligent statements.[230]

The owner and operator of a marina did not owe a duty of care to the lessee of a dock in the marina to prevent the theft of the lessee's yacht. The owner had not assumed responsibility to the lessee to take reasonable care to prevent theft of the vessel.

225 [1995] 1 WLR 1217 at 1225.

226 See page p.26.

227 In *Zelenko v Gimbel Bros* (1935) 287 NYS 134 the deceased fell ill in the defendant's store. She was taken to the store's infirmary and left there for six hours without medical care. She died. It was held that the defendant owed the deceased a duty of care, on the basis that it had assumed responsibility to provide the deceased with medical aid.

228 [2009] EWCA Civ 6345.

229 Ibid at [21].

230 See pp.47–74 incl. and Ch. 2 below.

DEFENDER CREATES A DANGEROUS SITUATION

The defender may come under an affirmative duty of care to take the necessary prophylactic action to protect the pursuer, if the latter has created a source of danger which has the potential to harm the pursuer. This principle is neatly illustrated in the Court of Appeal case of *Kimber v Gaslight and Coke Co*.[231] In that case, workmen, who were carrying out work in a private house, removed floorboards from part of a landing in the house. A visitor put her foot in the hole and was injured. It was held that the workmen, who had created the danger, were under a duty to warn the claimant of the existence of the hole. Such a duty arose quite independently from the occupation of premises.[232] Similarly, in the Court of Appeal case of *Fisher v Ruislip-Northwood Urban District Council*[233] the plaintiff was injured when his car collided with a surface air-raid shelter during the hours of darkness. It was held that the defendant local authority was under a duty to give the claimant adequate warning of the danger. Again, in the Inner House case of *Mooney v Lanark County Council*[234] the tenant of a new council house entered into occupation of the house before the entrance path to the premises had been completed. A metal toby protruded from the surface of the path. The pursuer, who was visiting the wife of the tenant, tripped over the toby and was injured. It was held that since the local authority had created the danger, it was under a duty to warn visitors to the premises about the danger.[235]

Again, in the Court of Appeal case of *Kane v New Forest District Council*[236] a planning authority required a developer to construct a footpath before allowing the development to commence. The footpath ended on the inside of a bend of a road. This had impaired visibility of pedestrians to road users. The claimant was struck by a car when he emerged from the footpath. In a striking out action, the court accepted the proposition that the defendant claimant had a 'positively powerful case'[237] to the effect that the planning authority owed him a duty of care, in terms of the law of negligence, on the grounds that the latter had created the danger in question. For May LJ the defendant owed the claimant a duty of care, since it had assumed a responsibility to those who might wish to use the footpath to ensure that it was not opened until the danger was removed.[238]

Whereas in the above cases there was a close nexus between the defenders/defendants and the creation of the dangerous situation, which was the subject matter of the action, in the Court of Appeal case of *Begum v Maran (UK) Ltd*[239] (which

---

231 [1918] 1 KB 439.

232 Ibid at 445 (per Bankes LJ).

233 [1945] KB 584.

234 1954 SC 245.

235 See also *Bell v Commissioner of Police of the Metropolis* [2024] EWHC 379. Police were held to have breached their duty of care to the claimant, by taking possession of B's son's passport from the son's mother, and then returning the passport to her without good reason (thereby allowing her to abduct the son) and without putting in place appropriate measures to prevent his abduction. The police had, in effect, created a source of danger and owed the claimant a duty of care to prevent the child's abduction.

236 [2002] 1 WLR 312.

237 Ibid at 318 (per Simon Brown LJ).

238 Ibid at 319.

239 [2022] EWCA Civ 326.

was a striking out action) the relationship between the defendant and the relevant dangerous situation was more tenuous, or remote. In that case, the deceased had been working in a shipyard in Bangladesh. He had fallen to his death while demolishing an oil tanker in the shipyard. Maran Tankers Management ('MTM') operated and managed the vessel which was owned by a related company ('CSME'). MTM agreed with the defendant ('M') to provide shipbroking services to M in respect of the vessel. M had agreed with CSME to act as their brokers, to arrange for the ship's sale and demolition. The proposed sale was not directly to the shipbreakers themselves, but to a demolition cash buyer. The vessel was sold (to 'H'). H took the ship to be demolished in Bangladesh. The vast majority of oil tankers are broken up in Bangladesh where working practices are dangerous. The court accepted the fact that M had known that the ship would be demolished there.

Coulson LJ was of the view that by virtue of M's playing an active role in sending the ship to be demolished in Bangladesh, knowingly exposing workers to significant dangers which working on a large vessel entailed, M had created a dangerous situation.[240] It was, therefore, arguable that the defendant owed the deceased a duty of care.[241]

We see in *Begum* that the court held that an individual who simply facilitated the creation of a dangerous situation was held liable for the harm sustained by the claimant. However, as we have noted above[242] the law sets its face against imposing an affirmative duty to protect another person from harm inflicted by a third party. Goudkamp and Nolan express reservations about allowing the 'creation of a danger' principle to erode, to an unacceptable extent, the fundamental rule that there is no liability for failing to control third parties, and result in a duty of care being placed on defendants, who were involved only in a peripheral, or historical, way in the chain of events that led to the injury of the claimant.[243] The authors argue that liability should, save in exceptional circumstances, be placed on immediate wrongdoers, as opposed to on defendants, whose actions merely enable or facilitate wrongdoing by others. The author would endorse this view, with a reservation to the effect that the person who facilitates wrongdoing may sometimes have considerably more financial means, and therefore be more capable of compensating a potential victim, than the immediate wrongdoer. To make the latter liable seems, in the author's view, to flout notions of fairness and justice, as well as being contrary to public policy.

OMISSIONS AND PUBLIC AUTHORITIES

In this section of the chapter we turn our attention to the potential liability of public authorities, in terms of the law of negligence, with special reference to omissions on the part of a public authority, the upshot of which is that the pursuer sustains

240 Ibid at [64].

241 Ibid at [71]. For a discussion of *Begum* see D Brodie 'Supply Chains and Worker Exploitation' (2021) *Jur Rev* 109.

242 See p.34 above.

243 *Winfield and Jolowicz Tort* n 129 at 5-039.

harm.[244] Liability on the part of public authorities for failing to act represents a grey and indeed, untidy area of the law of negligence. For the purposes of the section, the author had discussed delictual liability for omissions under separate functions, or public authorities, for example, 'The Police'. However, this is done simply for the sake of convenience. The separate categories or functions should not be regarded as either self-contained or water-tight categories.

THE POLICE

The most important function of the police is, of course, the prevention of crime. The author concentrates on the potential liability of the police for failing to apprehend criminals, who proceed to harm members of the public. However, we have already observed that subject to certain exceptions, the courts are unwilling to impose liability on the defender for acts of third parties. Therefore, to what extent, if any, does this approach by the courts extend to the police for failing to prevent a criminal from harming members of the public?[245]

The general rule is that the courts are unwilling to place an affirmative duty on the police to prevent third parties from inflicting harm on members of the public. This approach is well illustrated in the House of Lords case of *Hill v Chief Constable of West Yorkshire*.[246] In that case, the mother of one of the victims of the 'Yorkshire Ripper' (Peter Sutcliffe) sued the Chief Constable of West Yorkshire for the failure on the part of the police to apprehend Sutcliffe before he murdered the claimant's daughter. It was held that, whereas it was reasonably foreseeable that if Sutcliffe was not apprehended, he would harm individuals such as the deceased, he had posed no special distinctive risk to her.[247] She was simply a member of the general public who could be harmed by Sutcliffe. In short, there was no proximity between the parties. No duty of care was, therefore, owed by the police to the deceased. A further reason as to why the police did not owe the deceased a duty of care rested in public policy. Lord Keith stated:

> A great deal of time, trouble and expense might be expected to have to be put into the preparation of the defence to the action, and the attendance of witnesses at the trial. The result would be a significant diversion of police manpower and attention from their most important function, that of the suppression of crime.[248]

In *Calveley*, which has been briefly discussed above,[249] one of the grounds for the House of Lords deciding that the police authority did not owe the claimant police

---

[244] For a detailed discussion of the subject see C Booth and D Squires *The Negligence Liability of Public Authorities* (OUP, 2006). See also D Nolan 'The Liability of Public Authorities for Failing to Confer a Benefit' (2011) 127 LQR 260.

[245] For a useful discussion of the potential liability of the police to prevent crime, see S Tofaris and S Steel 'Negligence Liability for Omissions and the Police' [2016] CLJ 128. See also M Burton 'Failing to Protect: Victims' Rights and Police Liability' (2009) 72 MLR 283.

[246] [1989] AC 53.

[247] Ibid at 62 (per Lord Keith).

[248] Ibid at 63.

[249] See n 138 above.

officers a duty of care, for its alleged failure to conduct disciplinary proceedings properly or expeditiously, was that to make the police liable would be contrary to public policy, in that it would prejudice the fearless and efficient discharge by police officers of their vitally important public duty of investigating crime, by requiring them to act under the shadow of a potential action for damages for negligence by the suspect.[250]

Hill was followed in the House of Lords case of *Brooks v Commissioner of Police of the Metropolis*.[251] In that case (which was a striking out action) the claimant had been the victim of a serious racial attack, in which his friend L had been killed. The police had been severely criticised in an inquiry resulting from L's death. The claimant claimed that the police had failed to take reasonable steps to assess whether he was a victim of crime, and, if so, then to accord him *inter alia* adequate protection and support which was commonly afforded to key witnesses of a serious crime. However, the House, in following *Hill*, held that the police did not owe the claimant a duty of care, in terms of the law of negligence. Essentially, the House held that the police's function of protecting, assistance and support commonly afforded to key witnesses of crime fell to be equated with the function of the police in investigating crime.

Hill fell to be considered again by the House of Lords in *Van Colle v Chief Constable of Hertfordshire Police* and *Smith v Chief Constable of Sussex Police*[252] which were conjoined appeals.

In *Van Colle* an accused person ('B'), who was about to stand trial on charges for theft, approached witnesses and attempted to dissuade them from giving evidence. Over the same time, incidents of fire damage to the property of witnesses' property had occurred, and were investigated, but they were not attributed to B. Some of the incidents were reported to the police, including two telephone calls to the claimant's son, the second of which was aggressive but did not contain an explicit death threat. No steps were taken to protect the claimant's son. Shortly after the second phone call, and shortly before he was due to give evidence, he was shot dead by B. The claimant brought an action against the chief constable, claiming that the police had failed to protect the claimant's son from harm, of which the officer in charge of the case should have been aware.

The basic question which the court was required to answer was if the police were alerted to a threat that D may kill or inflict violence on V, and the police took no action to prevent that occurrence, and D did kill or inflict violence on V, may V or his relatives obtain civil redress against the police, and if so, how, and in what circumstances? The claimant founded solely on the deceased's rights in terms of Art 2 of the ECHR, which provides that 'Everyone's life shall be protected by law. No one shall be deprived of his life intentionally.' Lord Bingham stated that in the ECHR case of *Osman v UK*[253] it had been held that a state was required to take appropriate steps to safeguard those within its jurisdiction.[254] The scope of that positive obligation was the subject of the dispute in *Osman*, and also formed the basis of the instant case. In

[250] [1989] AC 1228 at 1238 (per Lord Bridge).
[251] [2005] 1 WLR 1495.
[252] [2009] 1 AC 225.
[253] (1998) 29 EHRR 245.
[254] [2009] 1 AC 225 at [28].

Osman the court had held that the liability of the state would lie in such circumstances only if it was established that the authorities either knew or ought to have known at the time of an immediate risk to life of an identified individual or individuals, from the criminal acts of a third party, and they had failed to take the necessary measures. However, Lord Bingham concluded that as far as the instant case was concerned, there were no grounds for the police to suspect that the deceased was at immediate risk of harm from B. The claimant's action against the defendant therefore failed.[255]

The facts in *Smith* were analogous to those in *Van Colle*. The claimant ('S') reported to the police that he had received threatening telephone, text and internet messages from his former partner, following a breakup of their relationship, including threats to kill him. S had provided the police with details of his former partner's history of violence, and his address and the content of the messages. The officers declined to look at the messages and neither took a statement from him nor completed a crime form. However, they did take steps to trace the calls. Shortly after, S was seriously assaulted by his partner and sustained serious injuries. S claimed that the police owed him a duty of care to prevent him from being harmed by his former partner. However, the House, in rejecting S's claim, was firmly of the view that the decision in *Hill* was not undermined by *Osman*. Indeed, the House was of the view that the right to life which was enshrined in the Convention had no influence on the development of the law of negligence in this area. In short, the common law should be allowed to stand on its own feet, along with the rights which were conferred by the Convention.[256] The *Osman* principle should not be mirrored by an introduction of a common law duty of care.[257]

The potential liability of the police for failing to protect the public from harm fell to be considered again by the Supreme Court in *Michael v Chief Constable of South Wales*.[258] In that case, the police had failed to respond timeously to an emergency phone call which had been made by the deceased, who was the daughter of the claimant. The daughter claimed that she was under immediate physical danger from her ex-partner. However, by the time the police arrived at the daughter's house she had been murdered. In deciding in favour of the defendant police authority, in endorsing the learning in *Hill* and *Van Colle*, the court held[259] that the defendant did not owe the deceased a duty of care. Lord Toulson stated that the duty of the police for the preservation of the Queens Peace was owed to the public at large and did not involve the close or special relationship ('proximity' or 'neighbourhood') necessary for the imposition of a private law duty of care.[260]

However, in the view of the author, the courts may be too willing to accept the view that the police should, to all intents and purposes, be immune from potential

[255] Ibid at [41]. The remainder of the House concurred.

[256] Ibid at [82] per Lord Hope.

[257] Ibid at [137] per Lord Brown. For a useful discussion of *Van Colle* see C McIvor, 'Getting Defensive about Police Negligence: The *Hill* Principle, the Human Rights Act 1998 and the House of Lords' [2010] CLJ 133.

[258] [2015] AC 1732.

[259] By a majority.

[260] Ibid at 1765.

liability in terms of the law of negligence, except in special circumstances, for failing to protect a victim from harm. The dissenting judgment of Lord Kerr is instructive and one the author, with respect, would endorse. His Lordship stated that whereas it would be difficult to predict, with confidence, the operational consequences of the police being held liable in negligence, such difficulty should not prompt a refusal to recognise liability, which by all conventional norms should be found to exist.[261] A large part of such difficulty stemmed from the lack of empirical evidence to support the feared outcomes (that is, 'defensive' policing, diversion of manpower) which were identified in *Hill*. His Lordship added that such a lack of evidence had prompted *Hill* to be distinguished by the Supreme Court of Canada. Lord Kerr concluded by stating that as far as the instant case was concerned, policy reasons to preclude liability on the part of the police had not been established.[262]

Whereas in the above cases the court was required to ascertain if the police owed a duty of care to members of the public to protect them from harm from a third party, in *Rathband v The Chief Constable of Northumbria Constabulary*[263] the question which fell to be answered by the court was whether the learning in *Hill* was applicable to a situation in which the defendant police authority had failed to take the necessary preventative action to protect a member of its own force from harm which had been inflicted by a member of the public.

The facts of the case were that, in the early hours of a summer's morning, PC Rathband was on duty in a police vehicle, which was parked. In the early hours of the previous day, one Raoul Moat, who had been released from prison, had shot and injured his former partner and had killed her current partner. Moat had been the subject of an extensive police inquiry. In the early hours of the same day, Moat had made a 999 call in which he outlined his supposed grievances against the police. Moat also threatened to kill or injure police officers. He concluded his call by saying that he was currently hunting for officers. Less than nine minutes later he shot PC Rathband in the head, at close range. Rathband sustained serious injuries, including loss of his eyesight, as a consequence.

The fundamental question which fell to be answered by the court was whether the defendant owed PC Rathband a duty of care. Males J stated that this question fell to be answered by applying the tripartite test in *Caparo*.[264] The judge stated that this approach had been affirmed by the Court of Appeal in *Robinson v Chief Constable of West Yorkshire Police*.[265] Mann J observed that whereas all three elements of the test were in dispute, the real issue between the parties was whether, in the circumstances of the case, the imposition of a duty of care on the defendant was fair, just and reasonable.[266] However, these concepts were closely connected with the principle of public policy.[267] The judge went on to state that the performance of the Chief

[261] Ibid at 1782.
[262] Ibid at 1783.
[263] [2016] EWHC 181.
[264] Ibid at [84].
[265] [2014] EWCA Civ 15 (overruled). See p.26 above.
[266] [2016] EWHC 181 at [86].
[267] Ibid at [91].

Constable's duty, as a quasi-employer of police officers, was outweighed by the public policy which was represented by the *Hill* principle, and that it would not be fair, just and reasonable for a duty of care to be owed by the defendant, in the instant case.[268]

The issue of whether the police were liable in terms of the law of negligence for failing to protect an individual from harm inflicted by a third party recently came before the Court of Appeal in the *Chief Constable of Northamptonshire Police v Woodcock*[269] where the court heard two conjoined appeals. The facts of the cases were relatively straightforward.

In the first appeal, the claimant ('W') was attacked and seriously injured by her former partner ('G'). W brought proceedings against the Chief Constable of Northamptonshire Police, alleging that the police owed her a duty of care to protect her from attack and were in breach of that duty. W's claim was dismissed at first instance.

In the second appeal, a man ('MP') was sentenced to a total of ten years imprisonment for a number of offences, including two offences of child rape. Five victims of his sexual offences brought actions against the police, alleging that the police owed them a duty to protect them against MP and were in breach of that duty. Their claims were dismissed at first instance. They appealed.

W's case

The court stated that firstly, the common law did not impose liability for omissions or for failure to act.[270] Secondly, the police did not owe a duty to individuals to protect them from harm which had been caused by the criminal actions of a third party. Thirdly, foreseeability of harm was not in itself sufficient to give rise either to such a duty or to the narrower duty to warn, for which W contended. The court held that W's case fell within the general rules. It was not a novel case which called for an assessment of whether it would be fair, just and reasonable to impose liability on the Chief Constable. The court then considered whether W's case fell within one or more exceptions to these general rules.

Firstly, the court addressed the question whether the police had assumed responsibility to W to protect her from attack. The court held that for the court to conclude that the police had assumed responsibility to the claimant, it would usually be necessary for the claimant to show something in the way of specific representation or promise by the police to take particular action.[271] It would also be necessary to show that the representation or promise was acted on, though that would not be required if, for example, the case concerned an assumption of responsibility to a vulnerable child. The court stated that in the instant case, the police had done nothing which could be regarded as an assumption of responsibility to warn W, or to prevent an attack on her by G.[272] The police had not promised W that they would warn W of any sightings

[268] Ibid at [114].
[269] [2025] EWCA Civ 13.
[270] Ibid at [120].
[271] Ibid at [121].
[272] Ibid at [122].

of G near her home, and had not promised to pass on to her any information which they had received, alerting them to a danger. Nor had the police promised to respond within any particular time to any information alerting them to a risk of attack. The call handler who had taken a phone call from a neighbour of W alerting the police to the danger G posed to W had said nothing which could be construed as an assurance that the police would pass on the neighbour's information to W, or would otherwise prevent any attack on her.

Secondly, W claimed that the call handler who had taken the neighbour's phone call had caused the neighbour to refrain from taking protective action which she otherwise would have taken.[273] However, in rejecting that claim, the court held that there was no evidence to the effect that the police could reasonably have foreseen that the call handler's words to her would cause the neighbour to refrain from taking action which she otherwise would have taken.[274]

Thirdly, W claimed that the police had control over G and therefore came under a duty to W.[275] However, the court rejected that argument.

The court concluded that W's case was a case in which nothing which the police did made matters worse.[276] In short, nothing which the police did had made matters worse than they would have been if the police had taken no action at all. The police did not owe W a duty of care.[277]

CJ's case

The court held that the serious failures of the police were omissions and failures to act.[278] They were not positive acts which had made matters worse. If the police had not taken any action at all, none of the claimants would have been in a better position. MP's sexual interest in the children would have remained undetected and the abuse of his victims would have occurred. The general rule that there is no liability for negligent omissions to act, therefore, applied.[279]

However, *Woodcock* should be contrasted with the earlier case of *Sheratt v Chief Constable of Greater Manchester Police*.[280] In that case, the claimant was the partner of the deceased, and also father to her children. The claim arose out of the death of the deceased, who was found dead in her home. She had taken her own life. The court was required to determine whether the defendant owed the claimant a duty of care. The facts of the case which gave rise to the claim were relatively simple. The defendant, Greater Manchester Police, received a phone call, early one evening, from the mother of the deceased. The mother had expressed concern about the welfare of her daughter. The mother was reassured by the call handler that there was no need for her to visit the daughter's house, since the police would arrange for the daugh-

[273] Ibid at [123].
[274] Ibid at [125].
[275] Ibid at [126].
[276] Ibid at [127].
[277] Ibid at [133].
[278] Ibid at [134].
[279] Ibid at [135].
[280] [2018] EWHC 1746. For a discussion of *Sheratt* see (2018) 145 *Rep Bul.* 5.

ter to be transferred to hospital. The phone call was graded as Grade 1 (emergency attendance). Shortly after, the call was downgraded to Grade 2 (priority attendance). That evening police officers attended the house where the deceased resided. They failed to gain access. On the morning of the following day, they obtained access to the house. The officers found the deceased. She had died from a drug overdose. The claimant claimed that on the basis that the defendant had received the phone call and, in turn, had created an incident log, informing the deceased's mother that they would deal with the incident, and agreeing that they would despatch officers, the defendant had accepted responsibility for the welfare of the deceased.

King J reviewed the relevant case law, including *Hill*.[281] That case law established the general principle to the effect that the police do not owe a private law duty of care in negligence to individual citizens for failure to comply with their public duty to investigate and prevent crime. However, the judge stated that there was an exception to this general rule.[282] That was where the police had assumed responsibility for the care of a particular individual. King J concluded that by virtue of the control room's response to the phone call which had been made by the mother of the deceased, the defendant had assumed responsibility for the welfare of the deceased.[283]Such an assumption of responsibility had established a relationship of proximity between the parties. The defendant, therefore, owed a duty of care to the deceased.

As far as the issue of reliance was concerned, King J stated that it was irrelevant that the assurances had been given to the mother of deceased, as opposed to the deceased herself.[284] His Lordship stated that what was of critical importance was the fact that the deceased was obviously a person who was in need of welfare assistance, which the defendant was offering to provide. The critical fact was that the defendant, through its call handler, knew that the mother was calling on behalf of her daughter, who was in no position to make the call for assistance directly for herself. For the judge, the defendant, in giving assurances to the mother, was focussed on a particular individual and a particular individual's welfare.[285] The police were not purporting to be performing their public duty of investigating or preventing crime. The police were performing the same function as the ambulance service, in coming to the aid of some person who was reported to be in need of welfare assistance. It was, therefore, irrelevant that the police (as opposed to another emergency service) had given the relevant assurances. The judge concluded by deciding that the defendant owed the deceased a duty of care.[286]

281 Ibid at [52]–[53].

282 Ibid at [57].

283 Ibid at [79].

284 Ibid at [80].

285 Ibid at [83].

286 Ibid at [84]. See also *Bell v Commissioner of Police of Metropolis* [2024] EWHC 379. The claimant's son was abducted by his partner, after his son's passport had been detained by police and then returned to her, without the claimant being aware of this. The claimant had been informed by police that the passport was in their possession. The claimant had relied on their assurances. It was held that the police owed the claimant a duty of care.

FIRE AUTHORITIES

In this section we discuss the potential liability of a fire authority for negligently failing to prevent fire from harming the pursuer.

In *Church of Jesus Christ of Latter-Day Saints (Great Britain) v Yorkshire Fire and Civil Defence Authority*[287] (which was a striking out action) a fire authority failed to extinguish a fire which had destroyed the claimant's premises because the authority had not ensured that certain fire hydrants were in working order. The court held that the defendant did not owe the claimant a duty of care, on the grounds that whereas the damage was foreseeable, and that there was sufficient proximity between the parties, it was neither fair nor reasonable to impose a duty of care on the fire authority. Permitting such claims risked posing a new burden, which would be detrimental to the service and a distraction from its proper task of fighting fires. Furthermore, the imposition of a duty of care would create the possibility of financial claims, amounting to an unreasonable burden on the taxpayer. It was for the individual to ensure his property against the risk of fire – it was not for the community to do so for the individual.

Reluctance on the part of the courts to impose an affirmative duty on a fire authority, for failing to protect the pursuer from harm by fire, is seen again in *John Monroe (Acrylics) Ltd v London Fire and Civil Defence Authority*.[288] In that case, certain individuals caused an explosion on a piece of land which adjoined the plaintiff's premises. The plaintiff's premises were showered with flaming debris. Emergency services were called to the scene. When the fire brigade arrived, they satisfied themselves that the fires had been extinguished on the waste ground. However, they did not inspect the plaintiff's premises. The fire crews then left. If they had inspected the premises they would have seen smouldering debris and combustible materials, which later resulted in the premises being seriously damaged by the fire.

Rougier J held that the fire authority did not owe the claimant a duty of care at common law. This was the case because there was neither sufficient proximity nor a special relationship between the fire authority and the owner of any property that was on fire to ground a common law duty of care on the former, for having failed to extinguish the fire.[289] Furthermore, it was contrary to public policy to impose a common law duty of care on a fire authority in such circumstances.[290] A number of factors combined to make it contrary to public policy to impose a duty of care. These factors were, in particular:

1. No extra standard of care would be achieved.
2. The imposition of a duty of care would lead to defensive fire-fighting.
3. If the efficiency of the emergency services was to be tested, it was not to be done by private litigation.
4. The fire brigade acted for the collective welfare of society.

[287] *The Times*, 9 May 1996; [1996] 2 WLUK 420.
[288] [1996] 4 All ER 318.
[289] Ibid at 329.
[290] Ibid at 331.

5. If one imposed a duty of care on fire authorities, that would 'open the floodgates', and encourage claims against fire authorities which (in relation to successful claims) would require to be subscribed by the general public.

The above cases illustrate the general principle that, notwithstanding the fact that the defender has acted negligently in attempting to perform a 'rescue', the defender has not made matters worse. The defender has simply failed to confer a benefit on the pursuer. However, if the cause of the fire is attributable to a positive act on the part of the defender, the courts are willing to impose liability on the part of the defender. For example, in *Capital and Counties plc v Hampshire County Council*[291] the claimants were tenants of a commercial building which consisted of three separate blocks. A fire in one block was attended by the defendant authorities fire brigade. The building was equipped with a sprinkler system in its roof space. In the course of fighting the fire, the station officer in charge of the operation ordered that the sprinkler system be shut down. The fire went out of control, as a result of this action. The building was destroyed. The plaintiffs sued the defendants in negligence. The court held that the defendants owed the plaintiff a duty of care in law on the grounds that the very act of shutting down the sprinkler system generated a relationship of proximity between the defendants and the plaintiffs.[292]

The leading Scottish case concerning the potential liability of a fire authority for failing to tackle a fire effectively is the Inner House case of *A J Allan (Blairnyle) v Strathclyde Fire Board*.[293] In that case, the owners of a farmhouse called the fire service to attend to a fire, which had broken out from a stove in the kitchen. The fire service attended and extinguished the fire. In the early hours of the following morning the fire reignited, and the farmhouse was completely burned down. The pursuers claimed that this had occurred as a result of smouldering rotten timber in the roof space. However, the Inner House held that the defender did not owe the pursuer a duty of care. According to Lady Paton, whereas a fire authority owed a duty of care to the general public, including the pursuers, such a duty was to take care not negligently to add to the damage which the pursuer would have suffered if the fire service had done nothing.[294] In other words, the defender was simply under a duty to refrain from inflicting fresh injury. Furthermore, the defender had not assumed any responsibility to the pursuers.

AMBULANCE AUTHORITIES AND COASTGUARD

The extent to which the ambulance service owes a duty of care to the public, in the manner in which it responds to '999' calls, was considered by the Court of Appeal in *Kent v Griffiths*.[295] The facts of the case were simple. The claimant had suffered an asthma attack. At 1625hrs her doctor telephoned '999' and asked for an ambulance to

291 [1996] 1 WLR 1553.

292 The *Capital and Counties*, *John Munroe* and *Church of Jesus Christ* decisions were upheld on consolidated appeals by the Court of Appeal: [1997] QB 1004.

293 2016 SC 304.

294 Ibid at 316.

295 [2001] QB 36.

take the claimant to hospital, immediately. The ambulance service promised to send an ambulance to convey her immediately to hospital. However, the ambulance did not arrive until 1705hrs. The delay was attributable to fault on behalf of the defendants. Shortly before the claimant arrived at the hospital at 1717hrs, she suffered a respiratory arrest which caused brain damage. If the ambulance had arrived in reasonable time, as it should have done, there was a high probability that the arrest which the claimant had suffered would have been averted. The court held that the ambulance service should be regarded as part of the health service, in relation to which the law already imposed a duty of care, in relation to the treatment of patients.[296] A distinction fell to be drawn between the ambulance service responding to an emergency call and the police or fire service responding to calls for assistance. In the last analysis, the defendants owed the claimant a duty of care.

Kent was followed in the Outer House case of *Aitken v Scottish Ambulance Service*.[297] In that case, the pursuer was the mother of a young woman who had suffered an epileptic fit. An ambulance was called by the pursuer's son. The ambulance service emergency medical dispatch centre, after eliciting information about the daughter's condition and medical history, and also advising how the daughter should be treated, informed the son that an ambulance had been dispatched, as well as a rapid response unit. However, the ambulance arrived late, despite the son having made a second phone call to the defendants, emphasising that the situation was urgent. The woman died as a result of her fit.

The issue to be determined by the court was whether the defenders owed the deceased a duty of care. Lord Mackay was of the opinion that it would be possible for the pursuer to establish at proof, that by the defender's eliciting information about the deceased's medical history from her brother, advising that an ambulance was on its way, giving advice as to how his sister should be treated until the ambulance arrived and also dispatching a rapid response unit, the defenders had established a relationship of proximity with the deceased.[298]

Finally, in the first instance case of *OLL Ltd v Secretary of State for Transport*[299] (which was a striking out action) eight children and their teacher were taken on a canoeing trip, with two instructors from the plaintiff's challenge centre. The party got into severe difficulties at sea. Four children died. A search and rescue operation was undertaken by the coastguard, who was later alleged to have failed to respond promptly and to have miscoordinated the rescue attempts of others. The court held that the coastguard did not owe the plaintiff a duty of care to respond to an emergency call. Nor did the coastguard owe the plaintiff a duty of care where the former had misdirected other rescuers outside its own service.

---

[296] Ibid at 52 (per Lord Wolff MR).

[297] 2011 SLT 822.

[298] Ibid at 837.

[299] [1997] 3 All ER 897.

ROADS AUTHORITIES

Roads can be potentially very dangerous. The poor design and layout of a public road, the lack of road markings and warning signs as well as the dangerous physical condition of the surface of the road can pose a risk to road users. Again, ungritted roads in winter can be particularly hazardous. Roads authorities in Scotland and highway authorities in England are creatures of statute and are placed under a series of statutory duties, and can exercise powers, the general object of which is largely to promote the security of road users. This section discusses the potential liability of roads and highway authorities for the negligent, or non-exercise, of their powers or duties, the upshot of which is that the pursuer sustains injury.

In the House of Lords case of *Stovin v Wise (Norfolk CC third party)*[300] the claimant was seriously injured when his motorcycle collided with a car, which was being driven by the defendant, who was turning out of a side road. The defendant's visibility had been limited because a bank on adjacent railway land had obstructed her view of the corner in question. The council, the highway authority, knew that the junction was dangerous and had accepted the recommendation of its surveyor that part of the bank be removed, provided the owner of the land agreed. The owner had made no response to the council's proposal before the plaintiff's accident. The defendant authority joined the highway authority as third party to the proceedings.

The trial judge held that the council was in breach of its common law duty of care and was 30 per cent to blame for the plaintiff's injuries. The Court of Appeal dismissed the council's appeal. However, the House of Lords, by a majority of 3 to 2, reversed the decision of the court.

The House rejected the proposition that, simply because the Highways Act conferred a variety of powers on the highway authority to make roads in its area convenient and safe, that this automatically resulted in the law imposing a common law duty of care to the claimant to remove the obstruction which had caused the accident. Lord Hoffmann[301] stated that the council possessed a large battery of powers under the Highways Act 1980 for making roads convenient and safe.[302] However, the judge added that to determine whether the defendant owed the claimant a common law duty of care was not simply a matter of construction of the statute.[303] The policy of the statute was a crucial factor in determining liability. Lord Hoffmann added that the fact that Parliament had conferred a discretion on the defendant local authority must be some indication that the policy of the Act was not to create a right to compensation. The judge added that the need to have regard to the policy of the statute, therefore, meant that exceptions would be rare. Furthermore, in order that a public authority owed a duty of care at common law, for failing to exercise a statutory power, it would require to be shown: firstly, that it would, in the circumstances, be irrational not to have exercised that power, so that there was, in effect, a public law duty to act, and secondly, that there were exceptional grounds for holding that the policy of the

[300] [1996] AC 923.
[301] With whom Lords Goff and Jauncey agreed.
[302] Ibid at 946.
[303] Ibid at 952.

statute required compensation to be paid to persons who suffered loss, because the power was not exercised.

Lord Hoffmann added that the question as to whether anything should be done about the embankment was firmly within the area of the council's discretion.[304] As the council were not under a public law duty to do the work, the first condition was not satisfied. Lord Hoffmann added that even if the first condition was satisfied, the second would not be, as there were no grounds upon which it could be said that the public law duty should give rise to an obligation to compensate persons who had suffered loss because it was not performed.

The House of Lords was required to consider the liability of a highway authority, in terms of the law of negligence, in *Gorringe v Calderdale MBC*.[305] In that case, the claimant was injured in a road traffic accident. Her vehicle was in collision with a bus, which had been hidden behind the sharp crest of a road until she reached the top of the crest which was followed by a curve. Seeing a bus approach she braked. The car skidded and hit the bus. The claimant was severely injured. The layout of the road may have given her the impression that the bus was on her side of the road. She brought an action against the highway authority, claiming that the highway authority caused the accident by failing *inter alia* to institute proper safety measures, including the provision of adequate road signs. However, the House held that the defendant highway authority did not owe her a duty of care. The House held that s39 of the Road Traffic Act 1988, which *inter alia* imposed a broad duty on highway authorities to prepare and carry out a programme designed to promote and improve road safety, did not create a common law duty of care, and thus a private right of action.

It is instructive to compare the judgments of their Lordships.

According to Lord Steyn, in order to ascertain whether a breach of statute confers a private right to sue, the basic question was whether the relevant statute excluded a private law remedy.[306] The judge went on to doubt the utility of applying the public law concept of irrationality as a condition precedent to the court imposing liability on a public authority, in terms of the law of negligence.[307]

In turn, Lord Hoffmann rejected the use of public law concepts to determine whether a duty of care was owed to the claimant.[308] The judge stated that he found it difficult to imagine a case in which a common law duty could be founded simply upon the failure (however irrational) to provide some benefit which a public authority had power (or a public law duty) to provide.

Lord Scott was of the opinion that if a statutory duty did not give rise to a private right to sue for breach, that duty could not create a duty that would not have been owed at common law, if the statute was not there.[309] The judge then expressed the opinion that he rejected the proposition that a common law duty of care could grow parasitically out of a statutory duty, not intended to be owed to individuals. That

304 Ibid at 957.
305 [2004] 1 WLR 1057.
306 Ibid at 1059.
307 Ibid at 1060.
308 Ibid at 1067.
309 Ibid at 1078.

would be the case, notwithstanding the fact that the defendant authority had acted outwith its discretionary powers.

Both Lords Rodger[310] and Brown[311] considered that it was against public policy that a road user should have the right to sue a highway authority for injury which had been caused by the road user's own negligence.

The above cases were reviewed by the Court of Appeal in *Sandhar v Department of Transport*.[312] The facts of the case were simple. The claimant's husband lost control of his vehicle on an icy road, which had not been gritted. He was killed. It was claimed that the authority owed the deceased a common law duty of care, on the basis that the highway authority had assumed responsibility to perform salting operations. However, the court held that, in order for an assumption of responsibility to create a duty of care, a particular relationship with either an individual or individuals was normally required.[313] An assumption of responsibility could not be based on a general expectation. Reliance was also required, on the part of the road user, for liability to lie. However, there was no evidence that the deceased had relied on an expectation that the road had been salted. The highway authority did not, therefore, owe the deceased a duty of care at common law.

The leading Scottish case on the potential delictual liability of a roads authority in relation to road users is now the Inner House case of *MacDonald v Aberdeenshire Council*.[314] In that case, the pursuer, the driver of a motor vehicle, raised an action against a roads authority, following an accident, whereby she had driven through a crossroads, into the path of another vehicle, the upshot of which was that the pursuer was injured, and both of her passengers were killed. The pursuer claimed that the accident had occurred as a result of the defender's failure to erect sufficient signage to alert drivers to the presence of the junction, and also to maintain road markings, which had been worn away over a period of time. The Lord Ordinary dismissed her action as fundamentally irrelevant, on the basis that the defender did not owe the pursuer a duty of care to maintain signage and road markings at the junction.[315] The pursuer reclaimed.

The most important issue which required to be addressed by the Inner House was, in effect, whether a common law duty of care, in terms of the law of negligence, could be 'carved out', as it were, of the general power which was conferred on a local roads authority under s1(1) of the Roads (Scotland) Act 1984, *inter alia*, to manage and maintain roads in its administrative area.

Lady Paton expressed the view that, if a roads authority became aware of a hazard on a road, Scots law would impose a duty of care on a roads authority to users of the road.[316] Such a consequence would be in keeping with Scots law, as it had developed, and would follow from the application of tests, such as the reasonable foreseeability

310 Ibid at 1085.
311 Ibid at 1086.
312 [2005] 1 WLR 1632.
313 Ibid at 1645 (per May LJ).
314 2014 SC 114.
315 2012 SLT 863.
316 2014 SC 114 at 125.

of harm, proximity of relationship and what would be fair, just and reasonable.[317] Lady Paton added that, even if the pursuer's averments were proved, she would not be entitled to a remedy, because it was not reasonably foreseeable that an accident had been likely to occur at the junction.[318] The judge concluded by stating that, on the facts of the particular case, and on the averments of the case, the common law did not impose a duty on the defender.[319]

Lord Drummond Young cautioned against uncritically adopting English decisions as representing the law of Scotland, and vice versa.[320] For the judge, a roads authority was liable in Scots law for failing to deal with a hazard which existed on roads under its control.[321] A hazard, for this purpose, was something which would present a considerable risk of an accident to a person proceeding along the road, with due skill and care. Such a view was supported by considerable authority in Scots law. The judge added that for a roads authority to be liable to a person who suffered injury, because of the state of a road under its charge, two features were required to exist. First, the injury was required to be caused by a hazard, the sort of danger that would create a significant risk of an accident to a careful road user. Second, the authority required to be at fault in failing to deal with the hazard. That would mean that the pursuer was required to establish that a roads authority of normal competence, and using reasonable care, would have identified the hazard and would have taken steps to correct it, whether by altering the road, or by placing signs, or in extreme cases, by closing the road.[322]

Importantly Lord Drummond Young went on to discuss the relevance of English case law in relation to the law of Scotland.[323] The judge stated that if the facts in *Stovin v Wise*[324] had occurred in Scotland, the result would have turned on whether the bank in question was a hazard. The judge added that Scottish liability had always been recognised as a private law delictual remedy, which did not derive from any statutory powers. Lord Drummond Young went on to discuss the relevance of *Gorringe v Calderdale MBC*[325] to the law of Scotland.[326] The judge added that much of what was said in *Gorringe* supported the general approach of the Scottish common law. Lord Drummond Young added that if similar facts had occurred in a case before the Scottish courts, it was possible that the result would have been the same as that reached by the House of Lords.

The judge concluded by stating that the reclaiming motion be refused on the basis that the pleadings lacked specification.[327]

---

317 Ibid at 126.
318 Ibid at 127.
319 Ibid at 128.
320 Ibid at 130.
321 Ibid at 135.
322 Ibid at 316.
323 Ibid at 142.
324 See pp.58–59 above.
325 See pp.59–60 above.
326 Ibid at 143, 144.
327 Ibid at 146.

MacDonald, in effect, establishes the principle that a roads authority is liable for harm which is caused to a road user by a hazard (which it fails to remove) on a road. Furthermore, the hazard may be created by a variety of circumstances. However, what constitutes a hazard will fall to be determined on a case-by-case basis.

In *Robinson v Scottish Borders Council*[328] the Outer House was required to determine whether the presence of metal strips on the road surface on a bridge constituted a hazard. The pursuer was injured when he was crossing the bridge on his bicycle. Lady Wolfe held that the presence of metal strips on the road constituted a hazard.[329] Furthermore, the hazard should have been apparent to a roads authority of ordinary competence using reasonable care. In conclusion, the defender roads authority had, therefore, breached its common law duties which they owed to the pursuer.

The Inner House had an opportunity to apply the learning in *MacDonald* in *Bowes v Highland Council*.[330] In that case, the pursuers were relatives of a man who was killed in a road accident. The deceased was driving his vehicle when the vehicle crossed to the other side of the road, mounted the kerb, collided with a bridge parapet and fell into the water. Twelve of the stanchions which formed part of the parapet had broken off, as a result of the impact, and had swung out from the bridge. The defenders were the roads authority, which was responsible for managing and maintaining the bridge and its parapets.

The Lord Ordinary held that the defenders had owed a duty of care to the deceased and, furthermore, that the requisite standard of care which the law demanded of the defender was whether a roads authority, using reasonable care, would have identified the hazard and taken steps to correct it. The defender appealed.

The Inner House held that, in the light of *MacDonald*, roads authorities owed a duty of care to road users, at common law.[331] Furthermore, what constituted a hazard depended on many factors. In the instant case, the hazard consisted of the fact that the parapet of the bridge over the sea was in such a weakened state that its containment factor was unknown and, therefore, presented a hazard to safe passage over the bridge.[332] Lady Dorrian added that the application of the test, as to what constituted a hazard, required to be sufficiently flexible to recognise that a particular hazard was likely to arise, as a result of the combined effect of a number of factors.[333] In other words, the defective parapet could not be viewed in isolation. The judge added that the significant risk of falling from the bridge into the sea, rather than merely colliding with the parapet, was a manifest danger, against which the defender was bound to take preventative measures.

The Inner House allowed the defender's appeal, in part, on the basis that the deceased had negligently contributed to the accident.[334]

[328] 2016 SLT 435.

[329] Ibid at 444.

[330] 2018 SC 499.

[331] Ibid at 515 (per Lady Dorrian).

[332] Ibid at 516.

[333] Ibid at 517.

[334] The deceased was held to have been 30 per cent contributorily negligent for the accident; Ibid at 522. See also *Fairley v Edinburgh Trams Ltd* 2019 SLT 819. See 2019 SLT 99 for a discussion of *Fairley*.

In conclusion, a roads authority can potentially be held liable for a wide variety of hazards on a road, ranging from the presence of large craters or sinkholes[335] to the layout of a road,[336] the provision of inadequate signage/road markings,[337]and the existence of uneven surfaces.[338]

LOCAL AUTHORITIES

Local authorities provide a variety of services to the general public, ranging from the provision of education and social work to environmental health, planning and building control. Such services are provided by local authorities under their statutory duties and powers. In this section, the author concentrates on the potential liability of a local authority for failing to exercise its powers and duties, the upshot of which is that someone is harmed by such failure. In short, the author discusses whether the relevant authority is liable for such omissions. The leading cases are now discussed.

The House of Lords was required to address the issue as to whether a local authority owed a duty of care to a member of the public for failing to carry out its duties in *X v Bedfordshire CC*[339] where, in a striking out action, the House was required to determine five conjoined appeals.

In the first action, 'the *Bedfordshire* case', the plaintiffs, who were born between 1982 and 1990, claimed damages for personal injury, which arose out of breach of statutory duty and negligence by the defendant council. The plaintiffs alleged that between 1987 and 1992 they had suffered parental abuse and neglect, and despite the defendant local authority having received serious reports of such treatment, it had failed to investigate the matter adequately, or protect the plaintiffs from further harm. In particular, the plaintiffs alleged that prior to 1991, the council had failed to exercise their statutory powers to institute care proceedings under the Children and Young Persons Act 1969 and the Child Care Act 1980, and thereafter, on the coming into force of the Children Act 1989, had failed to exercise their statutory duties to identify children in their area who were in need, and to take measures to protect them from harm. At first instance the plaintiff's claims were struck out.

In the other action, 'the *Newham* case', the plaintiff, M (who was born in 1983), and her mother claimed damages for personal injuries against the defendant local authority, the area health authority and a consultant psychiatrist, employed by the latter, arising out of breach of statutory duty and negligence. The plaintiffs alleged that in 1987, on the initiative of the local authority's social services department, the psychiatrist interviewed M, in the presence of a social worker employed by the local

335 *MacDonald* (above) at para. [36] per Lady Paton.

336 *Stovin* and *Gorringe* (above).

337 *MacDonald* (above).

338 *Robinson* and *Bowes* (above). See also *Laing v Paul and Williamsons* 1912 SC 196 where the defender local authority was held liable for an unstable pavement surface which resulted in a pedestrian being injured. See further, *Rush v Glasgow Corporation* 1947 SC 580. In that case, a local authority was held liable when the pursuer sustained personal injury on falling, after having placed her foot on a metal grating which had collapsed under her weight.

339 [1995] 2 AC 633.

authority, to ascertain whether, and if so, by whom, M had been sexually abused; that having diagnosed abuse, the psychiatrist and the social worker mistakenly identified the abuser as the mother's cohabitee and had concluded that the mother could not protect M from further abuse. The plaintiffs also claimed that in reliance on that assessment, the local authority had obtained court orders removing M from her mother, placing her in foster care and restricting the mother's access to her. The plaintiffs' claim was dismissed at first instance and also on appeal to the Court of Appeal.

In three further cases ('the education cases') the plaintiffs claimed damages *inter alia* for negligence, and in two of the cases, for breach of statutory duty, arising under the Education Act 1944 and the Education Act 1981.

In the first action, 'the *Dorset* case', the plaintiff, a child born in 1978 who had special learning difficulties, initially attended a local primary school which was maintained by the defendant county council. In 1992 he began proceedings against the county council, claiming damages for breach of statutory duty and negligence, alleging that between 1985 and 1992 he had special educational needs; that in 1985 the council had failed to diagnose that he suffered from a special learning disorder; that after his difficulties were acknowledged, the council had wrongly identified the school he then attended as appropriate for dealing with his needs, and that the council had failed to make provision for all his problems, including the failure to refer P to an experienced psychologist. The plaintiff further claimed that in breach of their common law duty, the council had failed to recognise, or inquire adequately, into his condition or make proper provision for it.

In the second action, 'the *Hampshire* case', the plaintiff, who was born in 1973, had attended a local primary school (which was maintained by the county council) where he exhibited learning difficulties, consistent with dyslexia and behavioural problems. The plaintiff claimed that the council owed him a duty of care to use reasonable skill and care in the assessment of his educational needs, and that the school's headmaster had failed to refer him either to the council for formal assessment or to an educational psychologist for diagnosis. The plaintiff further claimed, *inter alia*, that the teachers' advisory centre maintained by the council, to which he had been referred, had also failed to ascertain his difficulty. At first instance the plaintiff's case was struck out.

In the third action, 'the *Bromley* case', the plaintiff, who was born in 1971, began proceedings in 1993, claiming damages against the local authority, alleging, *inter alia*, that between 1977 and 1986 the authority, in breach of ss. 7 and 8 of the Education Act 1981, had failed to provide placements for him at any reasonably appropriate school, and had only provided places at special schools, and that, in breach of its duty at common law to take reasonable care in the exercise of its statutory duty, it had failed to make proper inquiries into or assessments of the plaintiff's educational capacity. The plaintiff's claim was struck out at first instance.

In each case, the Court of Appeal allowed the respective appeals in part, holding that the claims in negligence should not be struck out. The parties appealed against the decision.

Abuse cases

In the House of Lords, Lord Browne-Wilkinson addressed the issue as to whether a local authority could be liable for the manner in which it exercised a statutory discretion. He stated that where Parliament had conferred a statutory discretion on a public authority, it was for the authority, not for the courts, to exercise the discretion: nothing which the authority did within the ambit of the discretion could be actionable at common law.[340] If the decision complained of fell outside the statutory discretion, it could (but not necessarily would) give rise to common law liability. The judge went on to state that if the factors relevant to the exercise of the discretion included matters of policy, the court could not adjudicate on such matters and, therefore could not reach the conclusion that the decision was outside the ambit of the statutory discretion. Therefore, a common law duty of care in relation to the taking of decisions involving matters of policy could not exist.

Lord Browne-Wilkinson turned to the *Bedfordshire* case. In refusing to impose a duty of care the judge stated, first, that the imposition of a common law duty of care would cut across the whole system set up for the protection of children at risk.[341] The system was inter-disciplinary, involving the participation of the police, educational bodies, doctors and others. To impose a duty of care on all the participant bodies would lead to almost impossible problems of disentangling, as between the respective bodies, the liability, both primary and by way of contribution, of each for reaching a decision found to be negligent. Second, the judge held that the task of the local authority and its servants in dealing with children at risk was extraordinarily delicate.[342] Legislation required the local authority to have regard not only to the physical well-being of the child but also to the advantages of not disrupting the child's family environment, for example under s17 of the Children Act 1989.

Third, Lord Browne-Wilkinson held that if liability in damages were imposed, local authorities would adopt a more cautious and defensive approach to their duties. There would be substantial temptation to postpone making a decision, for example to remove a child, until further inquiries had been made in the hope of getting more concrete facts. The upshot of this would be that the child being abused would be prejudiced by such delay, the increased workload inherent in making such investigations would reduce the time available to deal with other cases and other children. The judge added that the decision of the social worker whether to remove a child from its parents was a fertile ground in which to breed ill feeling and litigation, the cost of which, both in terms of money and human resources, would be diverted from the performance of the social services for which they were provided.

Education cases

Each of the three cases was brought against the local education authority, alleging failures in their performance of their statutory duties under the Education Acts, in particular, in relation to children with special educational needs.

---

340 Ibid at 738.
341 Ibid at 749.
342 Ibid at 750.

In the *Dorset* case, the plaintiff's negligence claim consisted of the plaintiff claiming that the authority had *inter alia* failed to make proper provision for his special educational needs in terms of the Education Act 1981. The plaintiff further alleged that the authority had provided a psychology service which had negligently advised the plaintiff's parents who had relied on that advice. At first instance, the claim was struck out. However, on appeal, the Court of Appeal declined to strike out the plaintiff's claim.

In the House of Lords, Lord Browne-Wilkinson stated that the 'courts should hesitate long before imposing a common law duty of care in the exercise of discretionary powers or duties, conferred by Parliament for social welfare purposes'.[343] The judge added that the aim of the Education Act 1981 was to provide for the benefit of society, as a whole, an administrative machinery to help one advantaged section of society. If the scheme failed to provide the benefit intended, that was a matter which was more appropriately remedied by way of the Ombudsman looking into the administrative failure than by way of litigation. The judge concluded by deciding that an education authority owed no common law duty of care in the exercise of the powers and discretions, specifically conferred on it by the 1981 Act, relating to children with special educational needs.

As far as the plaintiff's claim, where it was alleged that the defendant authority owed him a direct duty of care, was concerned, Lord Browne-Wilkinson held that once the authority had taken the decision to offer the plaintiff psychological advice, it came under a duty of care to those using the service to exercise care in its conduct.[344]

In *Bromley* the plaintiff claimed damages against the local authority for negligence, *inter alia*, for failing to secure the availability of efficient primary or secondary education; placing the plaintiff in special schools when he did not have any serious disability and should have been educated in an ordinary school; and failing to make arrangements for provision to meet the plaintiff's educational needs. On appeal against the decision of the Court of Appeal to refuse to strike out the plaintiff's claim in negligence against the authority, the House of Lords upheld that decision. Lord Browne-Wilkinson reiterated the view which he had expressed in the *Dorset* case that a defendant education authority did not owe a duty of care in relation to the exercise of the statutory discretions which were conferred on it under the Education Acts.[345]

The extent, if any, to which a local authority was liable, in terms of the law of negligence, for failing to carry out its duties to promote and protect children in its care was required to be decided in the House of Lords case of *Barrett v Enfield LBC*.[346] In that case, the plaintiff had been placed in the care of the defendant local authority, under a care order, when he was ten months old. He remained there until the age of seventeen. He claimed *inter alia* that the authority had been under a duty to show to him the same standard of care which would be expected of a responsible parent, to protect him from *inter alia* physical and psychological injury, and further claimed that the authority was under a duty to provide him with a home, where his safety would

[343] Ibid at 762.
[344] Ibid at 763.
[345] Ibid at 770.
[346] [2001] 2 AC 550.

be secured and monitored. He also alleged that the authority had failed to arrange for his adoption, or to provide him with appropriate and properly monitored placements. Both the trial judge and the Court of Appeal struck off the plaintiff's claim, as disclosing no reasonable cause of action. The House of Lords allowed the plaintiff's appeal.

Lord Slynn stated that where a statutory power was given to a local authority and damage was caused by what was done, pursuant to that power, the ultimate question was whether the particular issue was justiciable, or whether the court should decide that it had no role to play.[347] The two tests (discretion and policy/operational) were guides in deciding that question. The judge added that the greater element of policy which was involved, the wider area of discretion was accorded, the more likely it was that the matter was not justiciable, so that no action in negligence could be brought.[348] He added that a claim in negligence in taking a decision was likely to be barred, unless it was wholly unreasonable, so as not to be a real exercise of the discretion, or if it involved the making of a policy decision, involving the balancing of different public interests. Importantly, Lord Slynn added that acts done pursuant to the lawful exercise of the discretion could be subject to a duty of care, even if some element of discretion was involved.[349] It did not necessarily follow that having taken the child into care, the authority could not be liable for what it or its employees did in relation to the child, without it being shown that the authority had acted in excess of power. Lord Slynn went on to call for caution when one was deciding whether particular issues were justiciable or whether, if a duty was owed, it had been broken. The mere fact that something had gone wrong, or that a mistake had been made, or that someone had been inefficient, did not mean that there was a duty to be careful or that such a duty had been broken. The court should not be too ready to find in these situations that there had been negligence by staff who were largely skilled and dedicated.

Shortly after *Barrett* was decided the House of Lords was again required to determine to what extent, if any, a local authority, by failing to provide adequate educational services to its pupils under its statutory powers and duties, owed a duty of care to the pupils at common law, in *Phelps v Hillingdon LBC*.[350] On the question whether the

---

[347] Ibid at 571.

[348] Booth and Squires argue that if one abandons the ultra vires and policy/operational tests, it is not clear how the courts are to determine whether a case is suitable for judicial determination: C Booth and D Squires *The Negligence Liability of Public Authorities* (OUP, 2006) at 2.51.

[349] That a common law duty of care can be superimposed on the exercise of a discretion by a public body is illustrated the Inner House case of *K2 Restaurants Ltd v Glasgow City Council* [2013] CSIH 49. In that case, the defender local authority served a demolition notice under s13(1) of the Building (Scotland) Act 1959 requiring the demolition of part of the upper floor of a building by the owners of the building which the authority had deemed to be dangerous. However, the owners failed to do so. Acting under s13(2)(4) of the Act which conferred powers on the authority to demolish the building, the defenders, therefore, appointed a contractor to carry out the demolition works on its behalf. The council supervised the works. After the demolition works was completed, a portion of the brickwork which remained on the upper floors, collapsed, due to high wind, and damaged the pursuers' premises. The court held that once the authority had made the decision to demolish the building, it came under a common law duty of care to ensure that the works were carried out without negligence: at [42]. The defender was in breach of that duty: at [45].

[350] [2001] 2 AC 619.

education authority owed a direct duty of care to its pupils, Lord Nicholls expressed the view that that was 'an exceedingly difficult question'.[351] However, he refused to rule out the possibility that an education authority owed no common law duty of care in the exercise of its powers and discretions relating to children with special educational needs, which were conferred on the authority by the Education Act 1981.

The extent to which a local authority would be potentially liable in negligence in the way it used its discretionary powers was required to be decided by the Supreme Court in *N v Poole Borough Council*.[352] In that case, the claimants with their mother were placed by the defendant local authority in a council house, in a housing estate in Poole. The house was situated adjacent to the house of another family who, to the knowledge of the local authority, had persistently behaved in anti-social behaviour. As a result of that behaviour, the mother had complained to the chief executive of the defendant authority. The police had attended the house and had issued a formal warning to the family. That resulted in the family targeting the mother and her family, for abuse. The abuse continued over a period of years. These incidents were reported to the local authority. Various measures were taken against the family, including eviction and periods of imprisonment. However, the harassment continued. The claimants alleged that that had caused them physical and psychological harm.

The claimants argued that the local authority owed them a duty of care, in relation to the exercise of its functions under the Children Act 1989, and had also failed to protect them from harm, by allowing them to continue to remain on the estate. Under s17 of the Act, a general duty is placed on a local authority, *inter alia*, to provide a wide range of services, which are appropriate to meet the needs of children in its area. The provision of services includes the provision of accommodation. Section 47(1) imposes a duty on a local authority,

> where there is reasonable cause to suspect that a child in its area is suffering, or is likely to suffer from significant harm, to make such inquiries, as it considers necessary, to enable it to decide whether it should take any action to safeguard or promote the child's welfare.

The main question which the court was required to answer was whether a local authority could be liable in negligence, in relation to the performance of its functions under the Act.

Lord Reed, with whom the remainder of the court agreed, categorised the facts of the case as one in which the defendant authority had failed to protect the claimants from harm.[353] Furthermore, there had been no assumption of responsibility on the part of the defendant to the claimants.[354] Lord Reed explained that this was so because, in contradistinction to situations where a public body provided a service to members of the public, such as the provision of medical care by a hospital authority (where the courts have held that the authority had assumed responsibility to the individual using that service) in the instant case, the defendant local authority's investigating and monitoring of the claimants' position did not involve the provision of a

351 Ibid at 668.
352 [2019] 2 WLR 1478.
353 Ibid at 1504.
354 Ibid at 1505.

service on which either the claimants, or their mother, could be expected to rely. Lord Reed also added that a further reason why there was no assumption of responsibility on the part of the defendant authority was that neither the mother nor the claimants had entrusted their safety to the defendant local authority; nor had the latter assumed responsibility to the claimants.[355] The authority, furthermore, had not taken the children into care and, thereby, assumed responsibility for their welfare.

The extent to which a local authority was under a legal duty to enlist its statutory powers to protect third parties from harm was required to be considered again by the Supreme Court in *HXA v Surrey CC*.[356] The case concerned claims by HXA and YXA respectively, in the tort of negligence against two local authorities, namely, Surrey County Council ('SCC') and Wolverhampton County Council ('WCC'). Both HXA and YXA were children when they suffered sexual abuse or physical abuse by a parent, or a parent's partner. The claimants alleged that the local authorities owed a duty of care to the claimants to protect them from harm.

Lord Burrows and Lord Stevens (who delivered the judgment of the court) stated that the liability of local authorities in the tort of negligence, for a failure to protect against harm, had been explored and clarified by the Supreme Court in the context of alleged failures by a local authority's social services department in *Poole*.[357] The decisions in the instant case turned on the application of the decision and reasoning in that leading case. The court was required to determine the defendant's application to strike out by reference to assumed facts.[358] There had been no factual finding in the proceedings. However, both HXA and YXA had been subjected to severe abuse, in the case of HXA, by HXA's mother and partner, and in the case of YXA, by YXA's parents.

Their Lordships outlined the alleged facts of the case.[359]

HXA

HXA was born in 1988. She had three younger siblings. Their childhood was characterised by sustained abuse and neglect, perpetrated by their mother, and at a later date, by her partner whom she had met in 1996 and had married a year later. From at least 1993 there were a series of referrals to SCC about the mother's physical chastisement, verbal abuse and lack of supervision of her children. Between September 1993 and July 1994 five investigations were conducted under s47 of the Children Act 1989. During this time the names of HXA and her siblings were placed on the child protection register. In November 1994 the local authority had resolved to undertake a full assessment with a view to initiating care proceedings. However, no assessment was carried out. The local authority continued to monitor the family but on at least some occasions, no decisions or actions were taken, despite ongoing concerns being reported.

[355] Ibid at 1506.
[356] [2024] 1 WLR 335.
[357] Ibid at [1].
[358] Ibid at [5].
[359] Ibid at [6].

In 1996 HXA's mother had formed a relationship with A. Four years earlier he had been convicted of an assault on his own infant son. Thereafter, concerns about A's behaviour to HXA and her siblings were raised with the local authority by several sources. In 1999 there were allegations of sexual abuse of HXA and her younger sister SXA, by both A and A's father. It was alleged that she had reported the abuse to staff at her school which was run by the local authority's education department. The local authority resolved not to take any action beyond keeping safe work with HXA and SXA. In the event no such work was undertaken. In 2004 HXA moved out of the family home. In 2007 after SXA had made further allegations, as a result of which she was removed from her mother's care, under an emergency protection order, the police carried out an investigation, during the course of which HXA was interviewed. As a result of this investigation A and the children's mother were prosecuted. A was convicted of seven counts of rape of HXA between the ages of nine and sixteen and sent to prison for fourteen years. Her mother was convicted of indecently assaulting her and sentenced to nine months' imprisonment.

YXA

At the time of the appeal YXA was nineteen. He suffered from epilepsy, learning difficulties and autism spectrum disorder. Initially he lived with his parents in London, where the family home came to the attention of the local authority social services department. In 2007 when he was six years old, he moved with his family to the West Midlands. A few weeks after their arrival, an assessment by the local authority for that area, WCC, identified concerns about his parents' ability to care for him. In March 2008 a paediatrician advised the local authority that YXA was being excessively medicated and that he should be taken into care. Thereafter, an agreement was reached between the local authority and the parents under s20 of the Children Act 1989 ('the 1989 Act'); a pattern of respite care was established whereby YXA spent roughly one night a fortnight and one weekend every two months in foster care. In the course of the next eighteen months further concerns arose about YXA's treatment in his parents' care. There were allegations that the parents drank and took cannabis to excess, that they physically assaulted YXA and continued to administer medication excessively. With their consent, YXA was accommodated full time under s20. Care proceedings were then started, and a final care order was made in March 2011, on the basis of a care plan, under which YXA remained in long-term foster care.

Legislative context

The legislative context involved consideration of various sections of Parts 3, 4 and 5 of the 1989 Act. For the purposes of the appeal, the court was concerned with the provisions which were in force between 1996 and 2004 in the case of HXA, and between 2007 and 2009, in the case of YXA.[360] The court stated that several duties were imposed on local authorities in Parts 3, 4 and 5 of the 1989 Act.[361] In addition

[360] Ibid at [19].
[361] Ibid at [20].

to the duties imposed under the 1989 Act, s11(2) of the Children Act imposed a duty on local authorities to make arrangements for ensuring that their functions were discharged, having regard to the need to safeguard and promote the welfare of children.

The parties agreed that in the light of the House of Lords case of *X v Bedfordshire CC* the provisions of the 1989 Act and the Children Act 2004, which imposed duties on local authorities, did not create a statutory cause of action in tort.[362] The claims of HXA and YXA were advanced on the basis that the defendants owed them a common law duty of care, based on an assumption of responsibilityby the defendants.

The court proceeded to outline the statutory background.

Part 3 of the 1989 Act is concerned with the support for children and families by local authorities.[363] Part 4 deals with the care and supervision of children. Part 5 deals with the protection of children and is concerned with compulsory powers of intervention in the lives of children and their families.

Section 17 (which was contained in Part 3) is concerned with the provision of services for children in need, their families and others.[364] Section 17(10) provides *inter alia* that a child is to be taken to be in need if (1) he is unlikely to achieve or maintain, or to have the opportunity of achieving or maintaining, a reasonable standard of health or development without the provision for him of services by a local authority under the Act; (2) his health or development is likely to be significantly impaired without the provision of such services; or (3) he is disabled.

Section 17(1) imposes a general duty on a local authority to provide a range and level of services appropriate to meet the needs of children in its area.[365] It does not impose a duty to meet the needs of a particular child. Section 17(2) provides that for the purpose principally of facilitating the discharge of that general duty, every local authority has specific duties, set out in Sch. 2 of the Act. Such duties include a duty to take reasonable steps to identify the extent to which there are children in need within their area, a duty to assess the needs of any child who appears to be in need and a duty to take reasonable steps, through the provision of services under Part 3 of the Act, to prevent children suffering ill treatment or neglect, and to reduce the need to bring proceedings for care or supervision orders.

Section 20 in Part 3 is concerned with the provision of accommodation for children.[366] This section was of relevance to YXA's claim since he relied for there being an assumption of responsibility by the defendant local authority on the provision of regular accommodation in foster care under s20 between April 2008 and December 2009. Section 20(1) places a local authority under a duty to provide accommodation for any child in need within its area, who appears to them to require accommodation, as a result, *inter alia*, of there being no person who has parental responsibility for him, or the person who has been caring for him being prevented (whether or not permanently and for whatever reason) for providing him with suitable accommodation or care. Section 24(4) provides that a local authority may provide accommodation for

[362] Ibid at [21].
[363] Ibid at [22].
[364] Ibid at [23].
[365] Ibid at [24].
[366] Ibid at [26].

any child within its area (even though a person who has parental responsibility for him is able to provide him with accommodation) if it considers that to do so would safeguard or promote the child's welfare.

Section 22, which is contained in Part 3, imposes further duties on local authorities.[367] Section 22(3) provides that it is the duty of a local authority looking after any child to safeguard and promote his welfare. Since YXA was provided with accommodation by the local authority under s20, the local authority owed him a statutory duty under s22(3) to safeguard and promote his welfare.

The court went on to state that there was a fundamental difference between the general duty under s17(1) of the 1989 Act and the specific duty under s22(3).[368] Whereas under s17(1) every local authority is under a general duty to safeguard and promote the welfare of children in need within their area, by providing a range of services appropriate to their needs, under s22(3) a local authority looking after a child is under a specific duty to safeguard and promote his welfare. Prior to 2011 further duties were placed on local authorities under s23.[369] Regulations made under the section provided that before the local authority placed a child, the local authority was required, so far as was reasonably practicable, to make immediate and long-term arrangements for that placement, and promote the welfare of the child who is to be placed.

Section 31 in Part 4 provides that an application can be made to the court for a care order or a supervision order.[370] However, s31(2) provides that such an order can be made by the court only if it is satisfied that the child concerned is suffering or is likely to suffer significant harm, and that the harm, or likelihood of the harm, is attributable to the care given to the child, or likely to be given to him if the care order were not made, not being what it would be reasonable to expect a parent to give him. Under s33(3) while a care order is in force the local authority has the power to determine the extent to which the parent should exercise responsibility. In contrast, if a supervision order is made under s35(1) duties are placed on the supervisor, including for instance, a duty to advise, assist and befriend the supervised child.

A further power to intervene in the lives of children is contained in s44.[371] Section 44(1) allows a court to make an emergency protection order only if it is satisfied, for instance, that there is reasonable cause to believe that the child is likely to suffer significant harm ... if he is not removed to accommodation provided by or on behalf of the applicant. If an emergency protection order is in force, s44(4) authorises the removal of the child at any time to accommodation provided by and on behalf of the applicant, and his being kept there. It also gives the applicant parental responsibility for the child.

The court stated that YXA, as a child accommodated under s20, was owed a specific statutory duty by the defendant to safeguard and promote his welfare.[372] There

[367] Ibid at [27].
[368] Ibid at [28].
[369] Ibid at [29].
[370] Ibid at [30].
[371] Ibid at [32].
[372] Ibid at [42].

would be potential failures to comply with the specific duty owed to YXA under s22(3) if the local authority did not think in the longer term, or if it did not consider whether or not it should seek to take parental responsibility for the child, by applying for a care order.

The court then outlined the facts in *N v Poole*. The court stated that the principal question in law which was required to be answered in *Poole* was whether a local authority, or its employees, may owe a common law duty of care to children affected by the manner in which it exercises or fails to exercise its social services functions, and if so, in what circumstances.[373] Lord Reed stated that the legal thinking about the liability of public authorities had developed in recent years (that is, from about 1995 to about the date of the judgment in *Poole*).[374] During that period the courts had sought to reestablish the traditional understanding that had been disrupted by the approach taken in *Anns v Merton LBC*. That understanding stressed the crucial distinction between acts and omissions, that is, between on the one hand, harming the claimant and, on the other hand, failing to confer a benefit on the claimant, typically in the context of public authorities, by failing to protect the claimant from harm. Lord Reed rejected the submission that a public authority could not assume responsibility by operating a statutory scheme, but made clear that the operation of such a statutory scheme could generate an assumption of responsibility, if the defendant's conduct pursuant to the scheme met the criteria set out in cases such as *Hedley Byrne v Heller* and *Spring v Guardian Assurance*.[375] Local authorities investigating and monitoring the claimants' position did not involve the provision of a service to them on which they or their mother could be expected to rely.[376] The relevant statutory functions relied on by the claimants did not in themselves entail that the council assumed or undertook a responsibility towards the claimants to perform their functions with reasonable care.

The court went on to state that in the instant case the claimant was required to satisfy the court that there was arguably an assumption of responsibility to use reasonable care to protect HXA and YXA from the abuse that the local authority was aware of, or ought to have known about.[377] However, the court held that there was no such assumption of responsibility.[378]

In relation to HXA's claim, the claimant alleged that there was a child protection investigation after the defendant had received a referral alleging that HXA's mother had assaulted HXA.[379] It was also alleged that the defendant had resolved to undertake a full assessment, but did not do so. However, the court held that the statutory function relied on did not of itself entail the local authority's assuming responsibility to HXA to perform the investigation with reasonable care. Furthermore, the local authority investigating HXA's position did not involve the provision of a service

373 Ibid at [45].
374 Ibid at [48].
375 Ibid at [53].
376 Ibid at [54].
377 Ibid at [91].
378 Ibid at [91].
379 Ibid at [93].

to HXA. Rather, the investigation was to enable the local authority to bring care proceedings. Again, the internal decisions to carry out keep safe work and assessment, designed to keep the children safe within the family, and to find out further information, fell significantly short of being an assumption of responsibility to take reasonable care to protect HXA from the abuse.[380] They were merely initial steps to prepare the ground for a possible later application for a care order. There was, therefore, no relevant assumption of responsibility to HXA in respect of any of the alleged facts.

In relation to YXA's claim, the court held that providing YXA with respite accommodation did not constitute an assumption of responsibility to use reasonable care to protect YXA from the abuse.[381] Furthermore, YXA had conceded that the failure to investigate under s47, and to commence care proceedings under s31 did not amount to a relevant assumption of responsibility on the part of the local authority.[382] The court stated that given that in *N v Poole* there was no assumption of responsibility to protect the children from their abusive neighbours, it was difficult to see how in the instant cases, there was an assumption of responsibility to protect the children from a parent or a parent's partner.[383] The court concluded that there was no arguable duty of care owed to the claimants.[384]

In conclusion, the court held that there was no assumption of responsibility by the defendant local authorities to use reasonable care to protect HXA or YXA from abuse by a parent or a parent's partner.[385] There was no arguable duty of care owed. Both claims had correctly been struck out at first instance.[386]

CONCLUSIONS

We can observe, by way of conclusion, that the courts are reticent about allowing a pursuer to 'carve', as it were, a private right of action (in terms of the law of negligence) against a public body, from the statutory powers which Parliament has conferred on the public body. In short, in determining whether a public authority owes the pursuer a duty of care, for failing to invoke its powers, the upshot of which is that the pursuer sustains harm, the courts have firmly founded on private law principles, such as assumption of responsibility and reliance. Such an approach protects public authorities from the threat of indeterminate liability to a limitless class.[387] That is to say, the fact that the relevant public body was possessed with statutory powers (which it could have invoked to prevent the pursuer sustaining harm, or could have used to confer a benefit) is of secondary import. Indeed, Deakin (referring to *Poole*) argues

380 Ibid at [95].
381 Ibid at [97].
382 Ibid at [98].
383 Ibid at [101].
384 Ibid at [105].
385 Ibid at [109].
386 Ibid at [364]. See also *Hamilton v Sutton LBC* [2025] EWHC 1675.
387 C Booth and D Squires *The Negligence Liability of Public Authorities* (OUP, 2006) at 3.108.

that public bodies are not treated in any fundamentally different way to private bodies or entities.[388]

However, in considering the potential liability of public authorities in negligence, one should bear in mind the observations which were expressed by Lord Reed in *Poole*, to the effect that the cases which were decided between the decisions in *Anns v Merton LBC*[389] and *Michael v Chief Constable of South Wales*[390] and *Robinson v Chief Constable of West Yorkshire*[391] had been superseded by later developments.[392]

Factual duty of care

Thus far, what has been discussed is what one can describe as the 'notional' duty of care. That is to say, one has been considering whether the law of negligence accepts the proposition that a defender owes a duty of care to the pursuer, in certain circumstances. For example, does a manufacturer of a defective product owe a duty of care to the ultimate consumer of the product? However, once a court does decide that a duty of care is owed in such circumstances, the court must then consider whether, on the facts of a particular case, the defender owes a duty of care to the pursuer. In the words of Lord Porter, 'there is no such thing as negligence in the abstract. There must be neglect towards a person towards whom the defendant owes the duty of observing care …'.[393] This point can be illustrated by two famous cases. The first is American.

In *Palsgraf v Long Island Rail Co*[394] Mrs Palsgraf was standing on a railway platform when two men ran to catch a train. The second man, 'X', was carrying a small and ostensibly innocuous package. The defendants' servants, in attempting to assist X in boarding the train, carelessly dislodged the package from his arms. The package fell and exploded, since the package had contained fireworks. A heavy weighing machine which was situated at the other end of the platform was dislodged by the explosion. The plaintiff was injured by the machine. However, the court held that the defendants were not liable for their servants' negligence, on the grounds that it could not have been foreseen that their careless acts would have harmed the plaintiff. Judge Cardozo, speaking for the majority of the court, held that there was no liability because there was no negligence between the parties. Negligence required to be founded upon the foreseeability of harm to the person who was actually injured, not to someone else.

The Scottish equivalent of *Palsgraf* is the House of Lords case of *Bourhill v Young*.[395] In that case, the pursuer, a pregnant fishwife, had alighted from a tram when she heard the sound of a road accident. The accident had been caused by the negligence of the defender, a motor cyclist, John Young, who had been overtaking

388 S Deakin 'Liability in Negligence in Providing a Public Good: Really Not So Different'? [2019] CLJ 513 at 515. See also *Airport Authority v Western Air Ltd* [2020] UKPC 29; *DFX v Coventry City Council* [2021] EWHC 1382. See also *Hamilton v Sutton LBC* [2024] EWHC 1675.

389 [1977] 2 All ER 492.

390 [2015] AC 1732 (see p.50 above).

391 [2018] UKSC 4 (see p.26 above).

392 [2019] 2 WLR 1478 at 1491.

393 *Bourhill v Young* 1942 SC (HL) 78 at 116.

394 248 NY 339 (1928).

395 1942 SC (HL) 78.

the tram in which the pursuer had been travelling. The defender had collided with a car which was turning right and into his direction of travel. The pursuer sustained nervous shock as a result. She sued the estate of the deceased. The House held that, whereas motor cyclists and cyclists who use the roads owed a duty of care to fellow road users and pedestrians, on the facts of the case, the defender did not owe the pursuer a duty of care, on the grounds that the defender could not reasonably foresee that someone who was standing where the pursuer was situated, at the time when the accident took place, would have suffered nervous shock. The pursuer was not within the relevant risk area, vis-à-vis the defender.

Chapter 2

Negligent Misstatements

In this chapter the author discusses the potential liability of the maker of a negligent misstatement, on which a third party relies and sustains loss as a consequence. Here, the courts have required to adopt a more nuanced approach to determine whether the former owes the latter a duty of care. The reason for this is, indeed, obvious. In sharp contrast to negligent conduct which results in physical harm, negligent misstatements can potentially reach the whole world, through the medium of newspapers and the internet. It is foreseeable, indeed, that the misstatement could be relied on by an infinite number of individuals, to their loss. In the oft-cited words of Lord Pearce, in the House of Lords case of *Hedley Byrne v Heller*:[1] 'Words are more volatile than deeds. They travel fast and far afield. They are used without being expended and take effect, in combination with innumerable facts, and other words. Yet they are dangerous and can cause vast financial damage.' However, the courts are unwilling to allow limitless claims for damages, for an indeterminate amount, for an indeterminate time, to an indeterminate class.[2]

Until the landmark decision of *Hedley Byrne* the courts were unwilling to allow claims for loss which the pursuer had sustained by relying on a negligent misstatement. Such an approach was based, in no small measure, on the disinclination of the courts to allow claims for pure financial loss, in general.[3] The person suffering financial loss, by relying on a negligent misstatement, was restricted to relying on the tort of deceit, or the fact that the statement was made in the context of a contractual or fiduciary relationship.[4]

In *Hedley Byrne v Heller*, Easy Power, a firm, asked the claimant, Hedley Byrne, to do some advertising work for it. In order to ascertain whether Easy Power could pay the claimant, Hedley Byrne asked its bank, National Provincial, to obtain financial information about Easy Power, from its banker, Heller. Heller gave favourable references but, at the same time, stipulated that the statements were given 'without responsibility'. In reliance on those statements, Hedley Byrne placed orders, which resulted in a loss of £17,000. It sued the defendant bank. The House of Lords held that, in the absence of the disclaimer, the defendant would have been liable for the

---

1 [1964] AC 465 at 534.

2 *Ultramares Corporation v Touche* (1931) 174 N.E. 441 at 444 (per Cardozo CJ).

3 C Whitting *Street on Torts* (16th edn) (OUP, 2021) at 90.

4 *Candler v Crane Christmas* at [1951] 2 KB 164 at 191 (per Asquith LJ).

loss which had been caused by the claimant having relied on the negligent misstatements. However, the judges differed in their approach as to when the maker of a negligent misstatement would be liable.

According to Lord Morris, a duty of care would arise if someone possessed of special skill undertook, quite irrespective of contact, to apply that skill for the assistance of another person, who relied upon that skill.[5]

In turn, Lord Devlin took a narrower approach. He stated that for the maker of a negligent misstatement to be liable, there required to be a relationship that was equivalent to contract.[6] That was to say, that where there was assumption of responsibility in circumstances in which, but for the absence of consideration, there would have been a contract.

However, the House took the general view, to the effect that there required to be an assumption of responsibility, on the part of the maker of the statement, and reliance on the accuracy of the statement, on the part of the recipient, for liability to lie.

Furthermore, it is the performance on the part of the defender to apply his skill for the assistance of a third party, which implies a voluntary undertaking to assume responsibility to the latter.[7] Whether any responsibility is assumed for the accuracy of the statement, and the extent of any such assumption, is to be judged objectively, in context and without the benefit of hindsight.[8]

In *John Kenway Ltd v Orcantic Ltd*[9] it was accepted that *Hedley Byrne* represented the law of Scotland.

Hedley Byrne revolutionised the law relating to liability for the making of negligent misstatements.[10] For liability to lie, the House held (by founding on the concepts of assumption of responsibility, on the part of the maker of the misstatement, and reliance on the statement, on the part of the pursuer) that close proximity required to exist between the parties. By adopting such an approach, the number of potential pursuers who had suffered harm, by relying on a negligent misstatement to their detriment, would be reduced, and would also readily satisfy the courts' disinclination to allow limitless claims. However, in the words of Lord Hoffman in the House of Lords case of *Customs and Excise Commissioners v Barclays Bank plc*,[11] the concept of 'assumption of responsibility' is simply a slogan for the court to conclude that a duty of care is owed by the defender. Lord Hoffman went on to state that questions of fairness and policy entered into the court's decision.[12] Again, in the House of Lords case of *Smith v Eric S Bush*[13] Lord Griffiths stated that the phrase 'assumption of

5 [1964] AC 465 at 502, 503. See also *Biffa Waste Services Ltd v Scottish Ministers* [2025] CSOII 9.

6 Ibid at 529.

7 *Spire Property Development LLP v Withers LLP* [2022] EWCA Civ 970 at [59] (per Carr LJ).

8 Ibid at [60]. See also *Customs and Excise Commissioners v Barclay's Bank* [2007] 1 AC 181 at 190 per Lord Bingham; *Precis (521) v William M Mercer Ltd* [2005] EWCA Civ 114 at [20], [22] (per Arden LJ). See also *Henderson v Merrett Syndicates Ltd* [1995] 2 AC 145 at 181 (per Lord Goff). See also *JP SPC 4 v RBS International Ltd* [2023] AC 461.

9 1979 SC 422 at 426 (per Lord Dunpark).

10 [2016] 1 WLR 3169 at 3174 (per Longmore LJ).

11 [2007] 1 AC 181 at para. [35].

12 Ibid at [36].

13 [1990] 1 AC 831 at 862.

responsibility' could only have any real meaning if it was understood as referring to the circumstances in which the law would deem the maker of the statement to have assumed responsibility to the person who acts on the advice. That is to say, the concept did not comprise a self-contained 'working' formula which could be applied to the facts of any case, at the outset, to yield a just solution. Indeed, Stevens states that it is unsurprising that some judges have dismissed assumption of responsibility as no more than conclusory.[14] In the present author's view, the concept simply expresses the view that the defender has, by his conduct, forged a sufficiently close relationship with the pursuer for the court to impose a duty of care.[15] There is no comprehensive list of guiding principles to help the courts determine when an assumption of responsibility can be said to arise in a given case.[16] The concept is elusive indeed, and is being developed by the courts.

REFORMULATION OF *HEDLEY BYRNE*

The decision in *Hedley Byrne* was reformulated by the House of Lords in *Caparo v Dickman*,[17] which has already been discussed in the context of the development of the duty of care. In *Caparo* the claimants were shareholders in a company. Relying on a negligently prepared audit and report, which had been made by the defendants, the claimants purchased further shares in the company, and made an unsuccessful takeover bid. They sustained financial loss. The claimants sued the auditors in negligence. However, the House held that no duty of care was owed by the defendants to the claimants. As far as liability on the part of the maker of a negligent misstatement was concerned, Lord Oliver was of the view that the relationship between the defendant and the claimant required to possess four features, before liability would fall on the former. These were:

1. The advice was required for a purpose, either specific or generally described, which was made known to the defender, at the time the advice was given.
2. The defender knew that the advice would be communicated to the advisee, either individually or as a member of an ascertained class, in order that it should be used by the advisee for that purpose.
3. The defender knew that the advice would be likely to be acted upon by the advisee for that purpose, without independent inquiry.
4. The advisee acted on the advice to his detriment.[18]

---

[14] R Stevens *Torts and Rights* (OUP, 2007) at 35.

[15] For a general discussion of the concept of assumption responsibility in the context of negligent misstatements, see A Robertson and J Wang 'The Assumption of Responsibility' in K Barker et al (eds) *The Law of Misstatements* (Bloomsbury, 2015) Ch. 3.

[16] *Precis (521) v Willam M Mercer Ltd* [2005] EWCA Civ 114 at [24] (per Arden LJ).

[17] [1990] 2 AC 605. See p.18 above.

[18] [1990] 2 AC 605 at 638.

Purpose of the advice

In *Caparo* the defendants were held not to have owed the claimants a duty of care, because the advice which had been tendered in the negligently compiled audit was to fulfil the statutory requirements of the Companies Act 1985. That is to say, that the audit was not prepared to assist the claimants in deciding whether to purchase further shares in the company.[19] However, *Caparo* should be contrasted with the Court of Appeal case of *Morgan Crucible Co. plc v Hill Samuel and Co.*[20]In the latter case, the plaintiffs, a limited company which had taken over another company, brought an action against the directors and accountants of that company. The plaintiffs had made an unsuccessful bid for the company. The plaintiffs alleged that they had sustained financial loss by increasing their bid for the company, as a consequence of relying on a negligent profit forecast and financial statements, which had been made after their original bid for the company had been rejected.

The court held that it was arguable that the directors of the defendant company owed the plaintiffs a duty of care. This was the case, since when making the relevant representations, the defendant directors were aware that the plaintiffs would rely on the statements, for the purpose of deciding whether to make an increased bid.[21] The plaintiffs, in turn, did rely on the representations.[22] It was plainly arguable that there was a relationship of proximity between the parties, which was sufficient to give rise to duty of care.

That the defender is required to be aware of the purpose for which the pursuer requires the relevant information is further illustrated in the Court of Appeal case of *Reeman v Department of Transport*.[23] In that case, the claimants purchased a commercial fishing vessel. The Department of Transport had issued a certificate which indicated that the vessel was seaworthy, in terms of the relevant statutory requirements. However, the surveyor who had issued the certificate had made an error in calculating the vessel's stability. A year after the purchase the error came to light, and the vessel's certificate was withdrawn. As a consequence, the plaintiffs were unable to use the vessel, and could not afford to pay for modifications to make the vessel seaworthy. The plaintiffs sued the Department of Transport for negligence, in respect of the economic loss which they had sustained. However, the Court of Appeal held that defendants did not owe a duty of care to the plaintiffs, on the grounds that the purpose of the certificate and the statutory scheme, under which it had been issued, was to promote safety at sea.[24]The protection of those whose commercial interests might be affected by unseaworthiness of vessels formed no part of the purpose for which Fishing Vessel Certificates were issued.[25]

For liability to lie, the requirement that the representor is required to be aware of the nature of the transaction for which the relevant information is required, and

[19] See also *Peach Publishing Ltd v Slater and Co.* [1998] PNLR 364.

[20] [1991] Ch 295.

[21] Ibid at 319 (per Slade LJ).

[22] Ibid at 320.

[23] [1997] PNLR 618.

[24] Ibid at 630 (per Phillips LJ).

[25] Ibid at 631. See also *James McNaughton Paper Group Ltd v Hicks Anderson and Co.* [1991] 2 QB 213.

also that the representation would be acted upon by the pursuer, is neatly illustrated in the Supreme Court case of *Playboy Club London Ltd v Banca Nazionale del Lavoro SpA*.[26] The first claimant, who operated a casino, wished to obtain a financial reference from the defendant bank, in respect of a customer. In order to preserve the customer's confidentiality, the request for the reference was made on the first claimant's behalf, by the second claimant. Without knowing the purpose for which the reference was required, the bank provided a reference which was addressed to the third claimant. The reference stated that the customer was financially healthy, and capable of meeting his business commitments. However, in reality, the customer was in the process of opening an account in the bank, in which, subsequently, there were never any funds. The reference was reviewed by the second claimant, which was the owner of the first and third claimants. A cheque cashing facility was approved by the first claimant for the customer. Subsequently, the first claimant made losses, as a result of accepting counterfeit cheques from the customer. The first claimant sought damages from the bank.

The Court of Appeal held that no duty was owed by the bank to the first claimant. The only duty which was owed by the bank was to the third claimant, to whom the reference had been addressed. The first claimant appealed.

In dismissing the appeal, the Supreme Court held *inter alia* that for liability to lie, it was fundamental that the bank had assumed responsibility to an identifiable person, or group of persons, but not to an indeterminate group, or to the world at large. Furthermore, for liability to lie, the defendant was required to be fully aware of the relevant transaction, in relation to which the information had been sought, and also aware of the fact that the statement would be acted upon by the claimant.

However, as far the defendant's awareness of the nature of the relevant transaction was concerned, Lord Mance was prepared to accept that for liability to lie, it sufficed that the defendant bank was aware that the relevant information was being relied on for an unspecific purpose, namely, in relation to the customer's trustworthiness.[27] There was no reason in principle, in his view, why a duty of care should not arise in relation to so unspecific a purpose, provided that the representation was requested and given, in terms showing that it was intended to be, and would be relied on.

Again, in the Court of Appeal case of *Seddon v Driver and Vehicle Licensing Agency*[28] a classic sports car was constructed, using a mixture of original and new parts, which were manufactured to a 1964 specification. Following inspection, the Driver and Vehicle Licensing Agency (DVLA), acting under its powers in terms of the Vehicles Excise and Registration Act 1994, and subordinate legislation made under the Act, issued a document which stated that the vehicle had been manufactured in 1964, had a 1964 registration number and was also in the taxation class of 'historic vehicle'. Some years later, the DVLA became aware that the vehicle was being offered for sale. The DVLA decided to investigate the vehicle after it had been sold. The claimant subsequently purchased the vehicle for £250,000. After the DVLA had concluded its investigation, it decided that the vehicle could no longer be classed as historic and

26 [2018] 1 WLR 4041.
27 Ibid at 4051.
28 [2019] 1 WLR 4593.

would therefore be registered with a 'Q' registration number, which was issued when the age or identity of a vehicle was not known. The claimant sold the vehicle at a loss of £150,000. He then brought a claim in negligence against the DVLA, contending that since it already had doubts about the age of the vehicle, before he purchased it, the DVLA owed him a duty of care when performing its statutory functions.

The Court of Appeal, in affirming the decision of the court at first instance, held that the DVLA did not owe the claimant a duty of care, in terms of the law of negligence. There was no assumption of responsibility on the part of the DVLA to the claimant.[29] This was the case, simply because the claimant had not relied on the registration document for the purpose for which it had been provided. The purpose of the registration document was not to provide information to the claimant for the purposes of a commercial transaction. Furthermore, the DVLA was unaware of the identity of the claimant at the relevant time. It followed, therefore, that the defendant could not have expected the claimant to rely on the contents of the relevant document, without obtaining independent advice. Furthermore, the class of potential purchasers of the vehicle was not ascertainable at the time the information was given.[30] There was no proximity between the parties.[31] It would not be fair, just and reasonable to impose a duty of care on the DVLA, as to do so would open the door to wide-ranging and extensive liabilities, which would have a detrimental effect on the performance of the DVLA's statutory functions.[32]

In certain situations, the courts are willing to impose a duty of care on the defender, if the pursuer acts to his detriment upon the relevant statement, for some secondary purpose of which the former was, or ought to have been aware. For example, in the House of Lords case of *Smith v Eric S Bush*[33] (which is discussed below) a valuer who had been instructed by a building society negligently prepared the valuation of a house. The report stated that no essential repairs were required on the property. His report was shown to the plaintiff, who bought the house on the strength of the report. She sustained financial loss as a consequence. The primary purpose of the valuation was, of course, to allow the mortgagee to ascertain whether the house could be used as a security for a mortgage. However, the House held that the valuer owed the plaintiff a duty of care, on the basis that the defendant knew that the report would likely be relied on by the plaintiff in deciding whether or not to purchase the house.

Knowledge advice will be communicated to pursuer either individually or as member of ascertained class

The maker of the negligent misstatement is required to be in a position to be aware of the existence of the pursuer, either individually or as a member of an ascertained class, at the time the relevant statement was made. For example, in *Reeman* (above) Phillips LJ stated that when the Fishing Vessel Certificate was issued, those who

29 Ibid at [56]–[59] incl. (per Hamblen LJ).
30 Ibid at [75], [76].
31 Ibid at [77].
32 Ibid at [81], [82].
33 [1990] 1 AC 831.

might in the future rely on the certificate, when deciding whether or not to purchase the vessel, did not form part of a class that was capable of definition and delimitation, by identifiable characteristics.[34]

A similar point was made in the Court of Appeal case of *Goodwill v British Pregnancy Advisory Service*[35] (which was a striking out action) in which the defendants had arranged for a vasectomy to be performed on X. Shortly afterwards, the defendants informed him that the operation had been performed successfully, and that he no longer required to use any other method of contraception. Several years later, X commenced a sexual relationship with the claimant, who had been advised by X that the vasectomy had been successful. However, the claimant became pregnant. She sued the defendants, alleging that they owed her a duty of care in law, in relation to the economic loss which she had sustained as a result of the cost of bringing up her child, and also the reduction of her working hours. However, the court held that the defendants were not liable for her loss, since they could not have known, at the time the advice was imparted to X, that the advice would be communicated to the claimant, and also relied on by her, without independent inquiry. At the time when X had been advised that his vasectomy had been successful, the defendants were not aware of the claimant's existence. The defendants had not voluntarily assumed responsibility to the claimant. She was simply a member of an indeterminately large class of females who might have sexual relations with X during his lifetime. In the last analysis, there was no proximity between the parties to give rise to a duty of care.

As explained, above, in *Seddon*, since the DVLA was not aware of the identity of the claimant or the class of potential purchasers of the vehicle, at the time the former issued the registration document, the DVLA did not owe the claimant a duty of care. Again, in *Playboy Club*, above, since the defendant bank was unaware of the existence of the claimant, at the time it made the negligent misrepresentation about its client's creditworthiness, the bank did not owe the claimant casino a duty of care.

However, the defender need not know the precise identity of the pursuer, for liability to lie, provided that the class of persons of which the pursuer forms part is capable of being ascertained.[36]

Foreseeability, in that the defender knows that his advice might be relied on by the pursuer, is insufficient to ground liability.[37] That is to say, that the defender requires to be aware that the pursuer will likely rely on that advice.[38] Whereas in *Caparo* the House of Lords did not make intention, on the part of the defendant,

[34] Ibid at 632.

[35] [1996] 1 WLR 1397.

[36] *Valley Brook Investments Ltd v Huam Ltd* [2020] EWHC 1715 at [43] per Judge Eyre.

[37] *Galoo Ltd v Bright Graham Murray* [1994] 1 WLR 1360 at 1382 (per Glidewell LJ).

[38] In the Court of Appeal case of *Schubert Murphy (A Firm) v The Law Society* [2017] EWCA Civ 1295S had been acting for the purchaser in a conveyancing transaction and had relied on the defendants' 'Find a solicitor' to check on the person named as the solicitor to the vendor. The search confirmed the existence of the solicitor and firm. S transferred the purchase price to the firm after accepting an undertaking that the solicitor would discharge the vendor's mortgage over the property. However, there was no such solicitor or firm. S had been the victim of a fraud. The fraudster absconded with the money without having discharged the mortgage. The court refused to strike out the claim to the effect the defendants did not owe S a duty of care.

that the plaintiff should rely on the former's representation, as a condition precedent to his liability, in *Possfund Custodian Trustee Ltd v Diamond*[39] it was held that it was necessary that the defendant intended the claimant to rely on the former's statement and that, in turn, the claimant relied on that representation.[40] Such an intention, on the part of the defender, that the claimant should rely on his statement, was to be assessed objectively by the court. As stated above, in *Playboy* Lord Mance was also of the view that intention on the part of the maker of the negligent misstatement was necessary for liability to lie.

However, in the Inner House case of *Royal Bank of Scotland v Bannerman Johnstone and Maclay*[41] the court was of the view that intention on the part of the maker of a negligent misstatement that the relevant information, which was proffered to the pursuer, should be acted upon by him, was not necessary for liability to lie. In that case, the pursuers had made loans to a company, on the strength of the business plan, monthly management accounts and audited accounts of the company, which had been prepared by the defenders. The pursuers alleged that they had subsequently discovered after having been appointed receivers of the company, and its subsidiary, that the accounts had overstated the company's assets and profits. The pursuers claimed damages for the loss. The Lord Justice Clerk rejected the defenders' contention that for liability to lie, it was necessary that they intended that the accounts and suchlike should be relied on by the pursuers in deciding to make the loans to the company.[42] That is to say, that it was sufficient that the defenders knew that the relevant information was likely to be relied on by the pursuers.

Reasonable reliance

For liability to lie, whereas it is necessary that the defender knew at the time he made the relevant representation, that it would be relied on by the pursuer, it is also necessary that such reliance is reasonable. This point was emphasised in the Supreme Court case of *Steel v NRAM*.[43]In that case, the defender ('S') was a solicitor who acted for a company ('H'). H had bought a business park, part of which had been purchased with a secured loan, which had been provided by a professional lender, namely, NRAM. The business park comprised four units. The whole site was registered with the Land Register of Scotland in two separate titles. In 2005 unit 3 was sold. S acted for H in that sale. S negotiated on H's behalf for the release of the unit which had been granted in N's favour, over the whole site. The security package which had been granted by H consisted of a standard security over the land, and a floating charge over the assets of H. N agreed to the release of the security which had been granted, in return for the partial redemption of the loan. The transaction proceeded on that basis. However, N was not represented by a solicitor in the transaction. Indeed, it was not N's practice to obtain representation in such matters. S forwarded the deeds of

[39] [1996] 1 WLR 1351 at 1364 (per Lightman J).
[40] *Possfund Custodian Trustee Ltd v Diamond* [1996] 1 WLR 1351 at 1364.
[41] 2005 1 SC 437.
[42] Ibid at 448.
[43] 2018 SC (UKSC) 141.

restriction for execution by N, by which its standard security was restricted to units 1, 2 and 4.

In 2007 unit 1 was sold. In relation to that sale, N had stipulated to H that it would release its standard security on the unit, in return for a payment of £495,000, after which the balance of the loan would remain secured against units 2 and 4. H accepted these terms. On the eve of the sale, S sent an email to N. In that email, S stated that the whole loan was being paid off. Attached to the email were deeds of discharge. It had never been suggested to S or to anyone else that the whole loan was to be repaid. S's email was not queried by N, which duly executed the deeds. The upshot of this was that N's security over units 2 and 4 was discharged. H then went into liquidation. As a result, N sustained a loss amounting to almost £370,000.

However, the court held that S was not liable to N in respect of the loss the latter had sustained by relying on S's negligent misstatement. This was so, simply because S had not assumed responsibility for the accuracy of her representation. For the court to hold that S had assumed responsibility to N, it was of fundamental importance that it had been reasonable for N to have relied on what S had said and, furthermore, that S should have reasonably foreseen that N would have done so.[44] N had acted unreasonably in acting on S's representation without independent inquiry.[45] Indeed, the misrepresentation related facts which were wholly within N's knowledge. In short, there was no assumption of responsibility on the part of S to N. Therefore, S was not liable to N, in terms of the law of negligence.

Steel should be contrasted with the Court of Appeal case of *So v HSBC Bank plc*.[46] In that case, B operated a fraudulent high yield scheme through companies he controlled, including F. Investors' money was paid into the accounts of F with HSBC ('H'). The agreements under which investors invested in the scheme provided for F to issue an irrevocable bank instruction. H's employee stamped and signed various letters of instruction put forward by F and B. After being required by the claimants to verify that the relevant account was a segregated joint account, and after a reference letter had been given by H, the claimants transferred money into the account of F. However, the account was not a joint account. Most of the claimants' money was withdrawn and subsequently lost. The court held that H owed the claimants a duty of care. The truth of the representations which H had made were uniquely within the knowledge of H.[47] Furthermore, they were not verifiable by an independent expert.[48]

[44] Ibid at [19] (per Lord Wilson).

[45] In the Court of Appeal case of *McClean v Thornhill* [2023] EWCA Civ 466 (at [89]) Simmler LJ stated that when one was assessing whether the representee had reasonably relied on the reliance, the question whether it was reasonable for him to act without obtaining independent advice was highly relevant, and in many cases likely to be determinative.

[46] [2009] EWCA Civ 296.

[47] Ibid at [51] (per Etherton LJ).

[48] The claimants' claim failed on the basis that the effective cause of their loss was not on their reliance on the representations which had been made by H, but rather on representations which had been made by B (Ibid at [71]).

Without independent inquiry

It is also critical that the defender knows that the pursuer will likely act on the advice, without independent inquiry. This principle is neatly illustrated in the House of Lords case of *Smith v Eric E Bush*.[49] In that case, a valuer, who was commissioned by a building society to value a house, negligently prepared his survey report, a copy of which was given to the mortgagor. The report had failed to mention that the chimneys in the house were not adequately supported. The report stated that it was not a structural survey, and she was advised to obtain independent professional advice. However, relying on the report, the latter purchased the house, without obtaining independent advice. She sustained financial loss after one of the chimneys collapsed. She sued the valuer. The House held that the valuer owed her a duty of care, on the basis that his report would probably be relied on by the mortgagor in considering whether she should purchase the house. In so deciding, the House laid store by the fact that the house in question was of a fairly modest value and that it was widely recognised by surveyors that purchasers of such property would rely on their care and skill.[50]

Again, in *Bank of Scotland v Fuller Peiser*[51] M wished to purchase a hotel. M instructed the defenders to provide a valuation of the hotel. M then approached the pursuers for a loan in order to assist her securing the purchase of the hotel. The pursuers informed M that it was not their usual practice to advance money without a valuation. After the pursuers had received a copy of the valuation, M's application for an overdraft to the pursuers was accompanied by a hard copy of the valuation certificate, and the full report. The report contained a disclaimer. M was then offered an overdraft by the pursuers on condition that they were offered a standard security over the hotel. After M had bought the hotel and a standard security had been granted, M began to trade. However, the hotel was not successful. The pursuers then called up the standard security and sold the hotel. They claimed that the sale of the hotel raised less than the value which had been placed on the hotel by the valuation. The pursuers alleged that the defenders had over-valued the hotel, as a result of which they had sustained loss. The court held that, given the fact that the relevant transaction was a commercial as opposed to a domestic transaction, and that the pursuers were a large commercial entity, and could easily have obtained independent advice from another surveyor, the test of reasonableness under the UCTA 1977 was satisfied.[52] However, Lord Eassie stated *obiter* that he found it difficult to accept the proposition that the pursuers were not likely to rely on the report for the purposes of making a loan to M.[53] That is to say, the judge was prepared to accept the proposition that notwithstanding the fact that the pursuers were a bank and had received the valuation report as part of a commercial transaction, the defenders owed the pursuers a duty of care.[54]

49 [1990] 1 AC 831.

50 Ibid at 859 (per Lord Griffiths) and 872 (per Lord Jauncey).

51 2002 SLT 574.

52 Ibid at [20], [21].

53 Ibid at [22].

54 However, in *James McNaughton Paper Group Ltd* (n 24 above) Neill LJ stated *obiter* (at 127) that in a business transaction conducted at arm's length, it may sometimes be difficult for an advisee to prove

As stated above, in *Steel* the Supreme Court held that the defender did not owe the pursuers a duty of care, on the grounds that the latter had acted unreasonably by acting on the defender's representation without independent inquiry.[55]

DEGREE OF RELIANCE ON MISSTATEMENT

What degree of reliance on the defender's negligent misstatement does the pursuer require to prove, in order to succeed? That is to say, is it necessary for the negligent misstatement to play the sole role in inducing the pursuer to act to his detriment, or does it suffice that the advice assumes a less dominant role, and only contributes to inducing the pursuer to act to his detriment? The leading case on this point is the Court of Appeal case of *JEB Fasteners Ltd v Marks Bloom*.[56] In that case, the claimants entered into negotiations to take over a manufacturing company, which had started to trade in the same products as the plaintiffs. During the negotiations, the defendants who were the company's accountants, and who knew that the plaintiffs were negotiating to take over the company, produced audited accounts for the company's first year. In turn, the accounts were made available to the claimants. However, the accounts were partially inaccurate. In short, the accounts presented a somewhat sanguine view of the company. Whereas the claimants knew that the accounts were inaccurate, they did not appreciate the full extent of the inaccuracy. Their primary motive was to acquire the services of two directors of the company. The takeover was unsuccessful. The claimants lost money. They brought an action against the defendants, claiming damages for breach of the defendants' duty of care to the claimants, as prospective buyers of the company.

However, the court held that since the claimants had not relied on the negligent advice to any material degree, in making the unsuccessful bid, they could not succeed in a claim in negligence against the defendants. According to Donaldson LJ if the relevant misrepresentation played a subsidiary role in the mind of the decision-maker, the advice was not relied on in terms of the rule in *Hedley Byrne*.[57] In turn, Stephenson LJ was of the view that if the relevant representation played a real and substantial, though not by itself a decisive part in inducing a claimant to act to his detriment, that was sufficient to ground liability.[58]

ADVICE GIVEN ON INFORMAL OCCASIONS

Negligent information given on a purely informal occasion does not attract liability, since the law tends to the view that there is no assumption of responsibility on the part of the maker of the statement.[59] However, there may be certain ostensibly 'social'

---

that he was entitled to act on a statement, without taking any independent advice, or to prove that the adviser knew, actually or inferentially, that he would act without taking such advice.

[55] 2018 1 SC 437 at [38] (per Lord Wilson).

[56] [1983] 1 All ER 583.

[57] Ibid at 588.

[58] Ibid at 589.

[59] *Hedley Byrne v Heller* [1964] AC 465 at 482–3 (per Lord Reid).

occasions in relation to which a duty of care will be held to arise. For example, in the Court of Appeal case of *Chaudhry v Prabhakar*[60] the claimant wished to buy a second-hand car. The first defendant was a close friend of the claimant. However, the former was not a mechanic. The claimant asked the defendant if he could try to find her a second-hand car which had not been involved in an accident. The defendant agreed to do so, without remuneration. He did find a car and took it to the claimant. He told her that it was in very good condition and that he highly recommended it. The claimant asked him if the car had been involved in an accident, to which the latter replied, it had not. Furthermore, the defendant assured her that the car did not require to be examined by a mechanic. However, it soon transpired that the car had, indeed, been involved in a serious road accident and was, as a consequence, unroadworthy. Indeed, the car had been bought as salvage.

It was claimed, on behalf of the defendant, that he was simply under a duty to be honest. However, the court, by a majority, held that the defendant was liable in negligence. Stuart-Smith LJ found the defendant liable, on the basis that the defendant, in purchasing the car, had acted as the agent of the claimant. Stoker LJ stated, *obiter*, that even if the defendant had not conceded that he owed the claimant a duty of care, he would have found the defendant liable in negligence.[61] In Stoker LJ's view, the defendant had gone beyond what was required of him as a friend. This very assumption of responsibility by the defendant was enough, by itself, to bring the *Hedley Byrne* principle into play.

NATURE OF RELATIONSHIP BETWEEN DEFENDER AND PURSUER

As stated above, it is not sufficient to ground liability in the foreseeability that the pursuer will rely on the statement which is made by the defender. Some form of special relationship between the defender and pursuer is required. One important question which requires to be answered here is to what extent, if any, does the defender require to be in the business of providing such advice?

In the Privy Council case of *Mutual Life and Citizens Assurance Co Ltd v Evatt*[62] the plaintiff was a policy holder in Mutual Life. The plaintiff claimed that Mutual Life had gratuitously given him negligent information on the financial state of an associated company, on the strength of which he invested in that company, and had lost money. It was held (by a majority of 3 to 2) that Mutual Life did not owe the plaintiff a duty of care, on the grounds that the former did not carry on the business of providing advice on investments. Furthermore, Mutual Life had not claimed that it possessed the necessary skill and competence to provide such advice.[63]

However, in the Court of Appeal case of *Esso Petroleum and Co Ltd v Mardon*[64] a large oil company, Esso, gave misleading information to the potential tenant of

[60] [1989] 1 WLR 29.
[61] Ibid at 37.
[62] [1971] AC 793.
[63] Ibid at 809 (per Lord Diplock).
[64] [1976] 1 QB 801.

a garage, as to the throughput of the garage. He entered into the tenancy on the strength of that information. He sustained substantial financial loss. The court held that Esso owed the tenant a duty of care in negligence. According to Lord Denning MR it was sufficient that Esso professed to have, and did have, special knowledge or skill in estimating the throughput of a filling station.[65] In other words, it was irrelevant that the defendant was not in the business of tendering the type of advice on which the claimant had relied, to his detriment.

There is a strong presumption that if the maker of the statement is in the business of dispensing advice (that is, the defender has 'general knowledge') which he applies to the subject matter of a given inquiry or request, on the part of the pursuer, that the former assumes responsibility to the latter. Furthermore, if the defender is privy to information which is not widely available (as was the case in *Esso*) which he imparts to the pursuer, in such circumstances that reliance must be placed on its accuracy, the latter would be presumed to have assumed responsibility for the accuracy of the statement. Again, if the defender has some financial interest in the matter on which the advice is given, there is authority to the effect that the defender owes the pursuer a duty of care.[66]

In the House of Lords case of *White v Jones*[67] Lord Browne-Wilkinson stated that the categories of cases in which a special relationship (on which liability for making a negligent misstatement can be prefaced) can be held to exist, are not closed. However, in his Lordship's view, only two categories had been identified, namely:

1. where there is a fiduciary relationship; and
2. where the defendant has voluntarily answered a question or tenders skilled advice or circumstances where he knows or ought to know that an identified plaintiff will rely on his answers or advice.

MANNER IN WHICH INFORMATION IS IMPARTED

In ascertaining whether the defender has assumed responsibility towards the pursuer, the court takes into account the manner in which the information has been imparted by the defender to the pursuer. For example, in the Court of Appeal case of *Howard Marine and Dredging Co Ltd v Ogden and Sons (Excavations) Ltd*[68] civil engineering contractors asked a barge owner the capacity of a barge which the former intended to use to convey clay. The barge owners gave incorrect advice. However, the advice was given orally. As far as the common law claim was concerned, the court held that the barge owners were simply under a duty to be honest.[69] In the last analysis, there was no assumption of responsibility on the part of the barge owners to the contractors.

[65] Ibid at 820.
[66] See for example *Anderson (WB) v Rhodes (Liverpool) Ltd* [1967] 2 All ER 850.
[67] [1995] 2 AC 274.
[68] [1978] QB 574.
[69] Ibid at 592 (per Lord Denning MR).

DEFENDER EXERCISING STATUTORY DUTIES

To what extent, if any, is the maker of a statement, or the relevant statutory body, liable for making a statement if the statement is made in the course of the defender discharging a public duty? The leading case is the Court of Appeal case of *Welton v North Cornwall DC*.[70] In that case, an environmental health officer required the owner of food premises to carry out works which were quite unnecessary, in order to secure compliance with the relevant food hygiene legislation. Acting on this advice, the owners of the premises incurred substantial expenditure. After discovering that the bulk of the work which they had been advised to carry out was unnecessary, the owners sued the local authority, claiming damages for the unnecessary expenditure. The court held that the owner could recover damages from the local authority at common law under the rule in *Hedley Byrne v Heller*. According to Rose LJ[71] in determining whether a local authority was liable for loss which had been caused by someone relying on the negligent advice of officials, in the performance of the enforcement duties of the authority, there were at least three categories of conduct which could potentially give rise to a duty of care:

1. If the negligent advice was given in the course of statutory enforcement, such as the institution of legal proceedings, the service of improvement notices and obtaining closing orders, such negligent advice would only give rise to a duty of care at common law, provided that the imposition of such a duty was not inconsistent with, or tended to discourage, the due performance of the statutory duty.
2. If the local authority was offering an advisory service, insofar as that service was part and parcel of the authority's system for discharging its statutory duties, liability would be excluded, so as not to impede the due performance of these duties. However, if the advice went beyond that, the advice was capable of attracting liability on the part of the authority, and the fact that the service was offered, by way of a statutory duty, was immaterial.
3. If the conduct in question was outwith the scope of the relevant legislation, that is to say that the officer imposed detailed requirements which were coupled with threats of closure and close supervision, liability would lie at common law.

As far as the second category is concerned, it may, in the author's view, be difficult in practice to determine whether the advice in question is part and parcel of a local authority's system for discharging its statutory duties. For example, in relation to advice tendered by an environmental health officer the dividing line between what is required by law and that which is desirable from a public health viewpoint, and therefore, falling within a local authority's advisory service, is often fine.

[70] [1997] 1 WLR 570.

[71] Ibid at 580, 581.

NEGLIGENT MISSTATEMENTS MADE TO SOMEONE OTHER THAN PURSUER BY REASON OF WHICH PURSUER SUSTAINS LOSS

Thus far, we have discussed the potential liability of the defender who makes a negligent misstatement to the pursuer, who acts on that statement to his detriment. Attention is now turned to a situation where the pursuer sustains loss indirectly, that is to say, that the pursuer sustains loss not because he, himself has relied on the representation in question, but rather because the representation has been made to a third party, who in turn has relied on the representation, to the pursuer's detriment. The leading case on this point is the Court of Appeal case of *Ministry of Housing and Local Government v Sharp*.[72] In that case, the Ministry had registered a planning charge in the local land register after the payment of compensation to N, who had been refused planning permission to develop his land. Any later developer of the land would have been required to pay money to the Ministry before development could take place. Two years later, planning permission was granted. A prospective purchaser of the land requested an official search in the register of local land charges. However, the certificate omitted to mention the Ministry's charge, because of the carelessness of a clerk who was employed by the relevant local authority. The claimants accepted the fact that the purchaser was not liable to repay the sum because the certificate (which showed no charge) was, by virtue of English land law, conclusively in his favour. The Court of Appeal held, *inter alia*, the clerk liable for his negligence at common law.

Lord Denning MR swept aside any suggestion that a duty of care only arose when there was a voluntary assumption of responsibility.[73] In his view, the duty arose not from any voluntary assumption of responsibility, but from the fact that the person making the statement knew, or ought to have known, that others, being his neighbours in that regard, would act on the statement being accurate. That was enough to bring the duty into being. In other words, if it was foreseeable that the statement would be relied on, a duty of care would lie. In essence, the Court of Appeal decided the case by invoking mainstream negligence principles. That is to say, the defendant owed the claimant a duty of care, since the latter was the former's neighbour, in the Atkinian sense. In this context it should be emphasised that when *Sharp* was decided, the foreseeability test was at its zenith in terms of the development of the concept of duty of care.[74]

72 [1970] 2 QB 223.

73 Ibid at 268.

74 See also *Sebry v Companies House* [2016] 1 WLR 2499. In that case the High Court made a winding up order against a company. Companies House erroneously registered the company against the name of an unrelated company with a similar name. This had the effect of describing the claimant company as being in liquidation when it was not. The error was quickly removed from the register several days later. The company's suppliers refused to allow the company credit before supplying goods and services. The company's bank refused to lend it more money. It then went into administration. It was held that the defendant owed a duty of care when entering a winding up order, to ensure that it was not entered against the wrong company. Companies House owed the claimant company a duty of care.

See also the Sheriff Court Appeal case of *Commodity Solutions Services Ltd v First Scottish Searching Services Ltd* [2019] SAC (Civ) 4. In that case, it was held that a private firm of searchers searching a

The law was taken further forward in the House of Lords case of *Spring v Guardian Assurance plc.*[75] In that case, a former employer gave a reference to a potential employer of the claimant. The reference was negligently prepared. As a consequence of the unfavourable nature of the reference, the claimant failed to secure employment. He suffered economic loss. He sued his former employer contending that the latter owed him a duty of care in the law of negligence. The majority of the House accepted that a duty of care was owed by invoking the concepts of mainstream negligence.[76] However, Lord Goff was willing to extend the rule in *Hedley Byrne* to cover a situation where the claimant suffered economic loss, by virtue of a third party relying on a statement (in the instant case, the preparation of a reference) which had been negligently prepared by the defendant, to the detriment of the claimant.[77]

NEGLIGENT MISSTATEMENTS AND PHYSICAL DAMAGE

Whilst the majority of cases in which *Hedley Byrne* has been invoked concern claims for economic loss, the courts have applied the rule in *Hedley Byrne* to cover physical harm which has been caused by the reliance on a negligent misstatement. For example, in the Court of Appeal case of *Clay v A.J. Crump and Sons Ltd*[78] the owner of a site on which there were old buildings appointed an architect to plan and supervise its redevelopment. Demolition contractors were instructed to clear the site in accordance with the architect's plan. There was a wall on the site, which according to the plan was to be demolished before any building work was commenced. However, at the building owner's request, the demolition contractors left the wall standing, after the architect had sanctioned that course of action in a telephone conversation, during which he told the demolition contractor's managing director that it should be left standing 'if it was safe to do so'. Relying on the opinion of a foreman, the latter replied that it was. Although he visited the site, the architect never inspected the wall. The wall was left standing in a manifestly dangerous condition. After building contractors had moved on to the site, the wall collapsed, and a labourer who was employed by the building contractors was injured. The court, in deciding that the rule in *Hedley Byrne* could be expanded to cover the facts of the case, held that the architect owed the claimant a duty of care.

public register, namely the Register of Inhibitions and Adjudications, owed a duty of care to a creditor who had registered an inhibition.

75 [1995] 2 AC 296.

76 In *Glasgow City Council v First Glasgow (No 1) Ltd* 2020 SLT 75 the deceased had been killed after being struck by a local authority bin lorry the driver of which had lost consciousness. The latter had previously lost consciousness while in the employment of the defenders. The pursuers claimed that the latter owed the deceased a duty of care to disclose that fact in the job reference which the defenders had given to the pursuers. By applying the principles of mainstream negligence it was held that the defenders did not owe the deceased a duty of care.

77 Ibid 316–20, incl.

78 [1964] 1 QB 533.

Chapter 3

Pure Economic Loss

In this chapter liability for pure economic loss is discussed. Put simply, pure economic loss is not prefaced or founded on any physical injury to the pursuer or his property. Rather, the injury which the pursuer sustains sounds in purely financial or monetary terms. The general rule is that the common law duty to take care to avoid causing harm is restricted to loss caused by physical harm to the pursuer's person or property. In other words, there is no liability for pure economic loss. The courts in the United Kingdom have sternly set their faces against allowing claims for pure economic loss. This approach by the courts is founded on policy.

POTENTIALLY LARGE NUMBER OF PURSUERS

The courts fear that if claims for pure economic loss were allowed, it would encourage a multiplicity of claims, or in the words of Chief Justice Cardozo: 'Recovery of economic loss, in the absence of physical damage or personal injury would expose defendants to liability for an indeterminant time to an indeterminant class.'[1]

This somewhat apocalyptic vision of the consequences of allowing claims for pure economic loss was graphically illustrated by Gibbs J in the High Court of Australia case of Caltex Oil Ltd v The Willenstaad.[2] The judge stated:

> If a person committing an act of negligence were liable for all economic loss foreseeably resulting therefrom, an act of careless inadvertence might expose the person guilty of it to claims, unlimited in number, and crippling in amount. For example, if through the momentary inattention of an officer, a ship collided with a bridge, and as a result, a large suburban area, which included shops and factories, was deprived of its main means of access to a city, great loss might be suffered by thousands of persons, but to require the wrongdoer to compensate all those who suffered pecuniary loss would impose on him a burden out of all proportion to his wrong.[3]

The fear on the part of the courts for allowing claims for pure economic loss is further illustrated in the oft-cited Court of Appeal case of *Spartan Steel and Alloys Ltd v Martin and Co (Contractors) Ltd*.[4] The claimants owned a factory where they

---

1 *Ultramares Corp v Touch* 255 NY 170 (1931) at 179.

2 (1976) 136 CLR 529 at 551.

3 See also *Seddon v DVLA* [2019] 1 WLR 4593 at [81] (per Hamblen LJ).

4 [1973] QB 27.

manufactured steel. They obtained their electricity directly from the electricity board's power station via a cable. The defendants' workmen were digging up a road by the use of power-driven tools. They negligently damaged the cable which was situated under the road. The defendants knew that the cable supplied electricity to the power station. The electricity supply to the factory was shut off. This caused damage to a 'melt' which was being prepared. During the time the electricity was shut off (that is, 14.5 hours) it was established that the claimants could have put more 'melts' through the furnace. The claimants brought an action against Martin to recover all the damages which they had incurred. The court held that the claimants were entitled to recover damages for the value of the metal in the furnace when the power had failed. The claimants were also entitled to recover for the lost profit on that metal. However, the court held that the claimants were not entitled to recover damages for the lost profits, in relation to the 'melts' that could have been put through the furnace had the power supply not been affected. Such loss fell to be regarded as pure economic loss. It was against public policy to allow claims for such loss.[5] Lord Denning MR stated:

> [I]f claims for pure economic loss were permitted for this particular hazard, there would be no end of claims. Some might be genuine, but others might be inflated or even false. A machine might be in use anyway, but it would be easy to put in down to the cut in supply. It would be well-nigh impossible to check the claims.[6]

The issue of potential liability on the part of the defender to numerous individuals was required to be addressed in the Australian High Court case of *Perre v Apand Pty Ltd*.[7] In that case, the plaintiffs were potato farmers, whose farm was situated in South Australia. Their farms exported potatoes to Western Australia, where the price of potatoes was particularly high. The defendant negligently sold diseased potatoes to another farmer, S. The potatoes which grew from the seeds were diseased. That disease was named bacterial wilt. Western Australian regulations prohibited the import into that state of potatoes grown on property within 20km of an outbreak of bacterial wilt. The plaintiffs were unable to export any potatoes to Western Australia for five years. The plaintiffs, therefore, sustained economic loss. The plaintiffs sued the defendant in negligence. The court allowed the claim, by holding that the defendant owed a duty of care to the plaintiffs not to sell S diseased potatoes. In doing so, the court set store by the plaintiffs' degree of vulnerability to having its business interfered with, if the defendant sold diseased seed to one of its neighbours. Gleeson J observed that the law relating to liability for economic loss was a comparatively new and developing area of the law of negligence.[8] It had not yet developed to a stage where there had been enunciated a general principle which was applicable in all cases. Perhaps it never would.

As far as the defendant's argument to the effect that the imposition of a duty on it would flout the well-ingrained principle in the law of negligence that the law set its face against imposing a duty of care, in circumstances where this would expose the defendant to limitless liability, McHugh J stated that the plaintiffs were members of a

[5] Ibid at 36.
[6] Ibid at 38.
[7] (1999) 198 CLR 180.
[8] Ibid at [25].

class whose members, whether numerous or not, were ascertainable by the defendant, when it had supplied the diseased seed.[9]

Similarly, in the High Court of Australia case of *Caltex Oil*[10] a dredger which was owned by the defendant, during the course of its operations, negligently fractured an oil pipeline which lay in the bed of Botany Bay and connected an oil refinery on the southern shore with an oil terminal on the northern shore. The refinery and the pipeline were owned by an oil refining company. The terminal was owned by another company, namely, the plaintiffs. There was an arrangement between the plaintiffs and the refiner, under which the former supplied crude oil to the refinery for processing, and the refined oil was delivered through the pipeline to the terminal. The refined oil was the property of the owner of the terminal, but the arrangement between the refinery and the plaintiffs provided that the risk of loss or damage rested with the refiner. The agreement also provided that the plaintiffs had no proprietary or possessory rights in the pipeline. The plaintiffs incurred expense in transporting the refined oil from the refinery to the terminal while the pipeline could not be used. The court held that the plaintiffs could recover from the defendant the cost of alternately transporting its products until the pipe was repaired. The loss in question ranked, of course, as pure economic loss. However, the court held that a duty of care was owed by the defendant since they knew of the risk to the plaintiffs as a specific individual (as opposed to being a member of an unascertained class) that they would sustain economic loss by virtue of the defendant's negligence.[11]

A similarly more generous approach to a claim for pure economic loss was again displayed in the Canadian Supreme Court case of *Canadian National Railway Co v Norsk Pacific Steamship Co*.[12] In that case, the defendants' vessel collided with and damaged a bridge which crossed the Fraser River. The bridge was closed for several weeks. The railway company whose trains used the bridge sued the owners of the ship for the loss sustained by the former not being able to use the bridge. By a majority, the Supreme Court held that the plaintiff could recover for the pure economic loss which it had sustained by the former not being able to use the bridge. In the view of the majority of the court, there was sufficient proximity between the negligent act and the loss to ground liability. While the court recognised that the law should be chary of awarding damages for pure economic loss, there was no doctrinal reason bar to admitting such claims, if one adopted an incremental approach to the development to the law: that is to say, if one judged each case on its own particular facts. In the instant case, a decision in favour of the plaintiff would not manifest the odious spectre of indeterminate liability to an unlimited class of claimants.[13]

9 Ibid at [50].

10 See n 2 above.

11 For a discussion of *Caltex Oil* see W Horton Rogers 'Economic Loss in the High Court of Australia' [1978] CLJ 27.

12 [1992] 1 SCR 1021.

13 For a discussion of Canadian case law on the subject of pure economic loss, see P Giliker, 'Revisiting Pure Economic Loss: Lesson to Be Learnt from the Supreme Court of Canada' (2005) 25 LS 49.

The decision in the above cases can be contrasted with the approach taken by the court in *Pride and Partners v Institute of Animal Health*.[14] In that case, the claimants were farmers who had sustained financial loss as a result of an outbreak of foot and mouth disease (FMD) and consequent government restrictions on the movement of farm animals. It was claimed that the FMD virus had escaped from the defendants' laboratory. Whereas the defendants conceded that they did owe the claimants a duty of care in respect of the physical loss which the claimants had sustained as a result of the former's negligence, that duty could not be extended to include liability for financial loss which had been sustained as a result of lost business. In deciding in favour of the defendants, *Perre* was distinguished by Tugendhat J, on the basis that whereas in that case, the duty of care was confined to farmers whose farms were based within 20km of the farm on which the bacterial wilt broke out, in the instant case, the restriction zone extended to every farm in Britain. The potential number of claimants was, therefore, greater than that in *Perre*.[15]

We see the willingness of the courts to impose a duty of care on the part of the defender where the number of potential pursuers is numerically limited being displayed in the Court of Appeal case of *Barclays Bank plc v Fairclough Building Ltd (No 2)*.[16] In that case, Barclays Bank ('B') engaged Fairclough Building Ltd ('F') to carry out maintenance work at two warehouse units. Part of the work consisted of the cleaning of corrugated asbestos roofs. F contracted the cleaning of the roofs to C, who in turn, subcontracted the work to T. T carried out the cleaning by using a high-pressure hose. This caused an asbestos-contaminated slurry to enter the building and dry out, leaving dangerous levels of asbestos dust and fibres. A prohibition notice was served on the work by an environmental health officer, and remedial works at an estimated £4,000,000 were required. B obtained judgment against F. C compromised the third-party proceedings against it by paying F £1,250,000. In C's action against T, the judge found for the latter, on the basis that although T had warranted that in cleaning the asbestos roofs, it had and would use the skill reasonably expected of a competent contractor, it did not hold itself out as having expertise in relation to health hazards potentially created by working with asbestos. C appealed.

The Court of Appeal held that T owed C a duty of care in tort, as well as contract, to avoid causing economic loss to the latter. To hold T liable did not expose it to the risk of an unrestricted number of claims.[17]

MANNER IN WHICH THE PURE ECONOMIC LOSS IS CAUSED

The pursuer can sustain pure economic loss which is caused by (1) the defender harming property which belongs to another person, (2) the defender harming another person and (3) the defender harming property which belongs to the pursuer himself.

[14] [2009] EWHC 685.

[15] Ibid at [126].

[16] [1995] PIQR P152.

[17] Ibid at 168.

Defender harming property which belongs to another person

An early example of the courts disallowing claims for pure economic loss which derived from harm caused to property of a third person is seen in *Cattle v Stockton Waterworks Co*.[18] In that case, the claimant was employed by the owner of land to construct a tunnel under a road. The defendant water company's water main, which was situated in the vicinity of the tunnel, leaked. Water escaped into the tunnel. Work on the tunnel was delayed as a consequence. The claimant sustained pecuniary loss, since the contract which he had with the owner became less profitable. However, it was held the claimant could not recover from the defendant.

Another example of pure economic loss deriving from damage which has been caused to property of another is *Spartan Steel*, which has been discussed above, where the claimants' loss derived from damage which had been caused by damage to the electricity cable which belonged to the electricity board.

A more recent case concerning economic loss derived from the defender causing damage to property belonging to a third party is *Weller v The Foot and Mouth Disease Research Institute*.[19] In that case, there was an escape of the FMD virus from the defendants' premises, where they carried out experimental work, in connection with FMD. Cattle in the vicinity of the premises became infected. As a result, the Ministry of Agriculture, Fisheries and Food made an order closing two markets in the area. Auctioneers lost money as a consequence of being unable to auction cattle at these markets. They sued the defendants. It was held that since the auctioneers had simply sustained economic loss, because they did not own the infected cattle, they could not recover damages from the defendants.

Again, in the Inner House case of *Dynamco Ltd v Holland*,[20] contractors negligently carried out building operations. An underground electricity cable which was carrying power to a factory was damaged. Whereas no property of the occupiers was damaged, production in the factory was interrupted for 15.5 hours, the upshot of which was that the pursuers sustained financial loss. Lord Migdale underlined the general principle to the effect that Scots law sets its face against allowing the pursuer to recover for loss which did not stem from direct damage to the pursuer's property.[21] The judge added that the electricity which had been cut off did not belong to the pursuers.[22] The damage was done outside their premises and before the cable reached their meter. Furthermore, the cable which was damaged did not belong to the pursuers, and no part of their property was damaged.[23]

Another case which illustrates the disinclination on the part of the courts to allow claims for pure economic loss is *London Waste Ltd v Amec Civil Engineering Ltd*.[24] In that case, the claimants generated electricity from the burning of waste. Electricity

[18] (1874–75) LR 10 QB 453.

[19] [1966] 1 QB 569.

[20] 1971 SC 257.

[21] Ibid at 265.

[22] Ibid at 267.

[23] See also *East Lothian Angling Association v Haddington Town Council* 1980 SLT 213 and *Wimpey Construction (UK) Ltd v Martin Black and Co (Wire Ropes) Ltd* 1982 SLT 239.

[24] (1996) 53 Const. LR 66.

was, in turn, fed into the grid. The defendant was a building contractor. One day, when carrying out road improvements, with part of the work involving sheet piling, a subcontractor of the defendant severed the cable carrying electricity to the grid. The cable which was severed belonged to Eastern Electricity. As a result, the claimants suffered financial loss by being unable to supply the grid. It was held that they could not recover for this loss since the loss ranked as pure economic loss.

Another example of the courts unwillingness to allow claims for pure economic loss is seen in the House of Lords case of *Leigh and Sillivan Ltd v Aliakmon Shipping Co Ltd (the Aliakmon)*.[25] In that case, the claimant contracted to buy a quantity of steel coils, which were to be shipped from Korea. The claimant had expected to re-sell the coils. Contrary to the expectations of the parties, the property in the coils did not pass to the claimant buyers under the contract. The coils were damaged during the voyage because the coils had been badly stowed by the shipowner defendant. The claimant sued the defendant, whose negligence had caused the damage. It was held that since the claimant did not have either legal ownership or a possessory title to the coils at the time the damage took place, the claimant failed to recover damages. In short, the loss in question ranked as pure economic loss.

The *Aliakmon* was approved and followed in the Inner House case of *Nacap Ltd v Moffat Plant Ltd*.[26] In that case, the pursuers were laying a pipeline on behalf of the British Gas Corporation. The pipeline was owned by the latter. While the pipeline was in the course of being laid by the pursuers, and during the time the pursuers were contractually liable to the corporation for any damage caused to the pipeline, the pipeline was damaged. The pursuers sued the plant hirers responsible for negligently causing the damage, to recover the costs of repairing the pipeline. However, the court held that a distinction was required to be made between one having ownership, or a possessory right, in relation to the property damaged, and one where the pursuer simply had contractual rights to have the use of services of the property concerned, for certain limited purposes. In the instant case, any rights which the pursuers possessed in relation to the pipeline arose under the terms of contract between themselves and the corporation. The pursuers could not be regarded as having a possessory right or title in relation to the pipeline. In short, the pursuers had no title to sue. Therefore, the pursuers failed to recover damages from the defenders.[27]

However, *Nacap Ltd* should be contrasted with *North Scottish Helicopters Ltd v United Technologies Corp Ltd*.[28] The pursuer leased (or hired) a helicopter from a finance company. The terms of the lease placed all responsibility for keeping the helicopter operational on the lessees. The pursuers had unrestricted use of the helicopter and were responsible for its maintenance. The helicopter caught fire and was damaged. The pursuers sued the designers and manufacturers of the helicopter, and the manufacturers of a component, for damages for negligence. The defenders argued that the pursuers did not have title and interest to sue. However, it was held that

[25] [1986] AC 785.
[26] 1987 SLT 221.
[27] See also *Candlewood Navigation Corporation Ltd v Mitsui OSK Lines Ltd* [1986] AC 1.
[28] 1988 SLT 77.

the pursuers had a possessory and not merely a contractual right to the helicopter.[29] The effect of the lease was to put the pursuers in the position of being owners of the helicopter in substance, if not in legal title.

Harm caused by defective products

The manufacturer of a defective product could be potentially liable in negligence for the physical harm which has been caused by the defective product. For example, if a defective washing machine catches fire and burns the pursuer's kitchen, the manufacturer could be held liable. However, if the washing machine catches fire because of a defect, but the fire is contained within the washing machine itself, which requires to be discarded, the loss in question would simply rank as pure economic loss and, therefore, irrecoverable in terms of the law of delict.

Sometimes the fact that a product is defective may result in the pursuer suffering economic loss, on account of the product not being able to be used. Such loss is irrecoverable. For example, in the Court of Appeal case of *Muirhead v Industrial Tank Specialities Ltd*[30] the claimant was a fish merchant who ran a lobster factory. The lobsters were fattened up in tanks which were fed oxygen by pumps manufactured by the defendant. Unfortunately, the pumps were not suited to the United Kingdom's range of voltages. One day the equipment failed. Denied oxygen, the lobsters died. The claimant sued the defendant, *inter alia*, for the price of the lobsters, as well as the loss resulting from the pumps not being used. The Court of Appeal held that the claimant could only recover in respect of the financial loss which accrued from the dead lobsters. The claim for damages which derived from the pumps not being able to be used ranked as pure economic loss. There had been no reliance by the claimant on the manufacturer. Furthermore, there was insufficient proximity between the parties.

UNWANTED PREGNANCIES

The cases which we have looked at thus far have involved claims concerning physical harm which has been inflicted on property, and has caused loss to the pursuer. However, in the House of Lords case of *McFarlane v Tayside Heath Board*[31] the House was required to determine whether financial loss arising from an unwanted birth was recoverable. In that case, a couple were negligently advised that a vasectomy had been performed satisfactorily. The couple relied on that advice and refrained from using contraceptives. Mrs McFarlane became pregnant. The couple sued the defender health board, *inter alia*, for the cost of bring up the child. However, the House held that such loss ranked as pure economic loss and was, therefore, irrecoverable. In short, whereas the doctor who performed the ineffective vasectomy thereby assumed a duty of care to his patient to prevent a pregnancy, that duty did not extend to avoiding

[29] Ibid at 81 (per Lord Davidson).
[30] [1986] QB 507.
[31] [2000] 2 AC 59.

the costs that were associated with bringing up a healthy child if one happened to be born.[32]

THE BUILDING CONSTRUCTION CASES AND ECONOMIC LOSS

We now turn our attention to cases concerning loss arising from buildings which have been negligently constructed, the upshot of which is that the pursuer has sustained loss.

The first case which we look at, the facts of which were novel when the case was decided by the Court of Appeal in 1972, is *Dutton v Bognor Regis UDC*.[33] In that case, a builder developing a housing estate applied to a local council for permission to build a house on a certain plot and approval under byelaws made under the Public Health Act 1936. The relevant plans were passed by the defendant local authority. The council notified approval on a note which stated that all foundations and drains were required to be examined by the council's surveyor before being covered up. The work proceeded. One of the council's building inspectors inspected the foundations and orally approved them. The foundations were then covered up. The house was completed and then bought by C who, in turn, sold the house to the claimant. Since the house was almost new, she did not have the house surveyed. Soon after she moved in, serious defects developed in the interior structure of the house. It was then discovered that the internal foundations of the house had been built on the site of an old landfill site. This would have been apparent if a careful inspection had been made of the site. The claimant sued the builder and the local authority. Her action against the builder was settled. At first instance, the claimant's claim against the local authority succeeded. The local authority appealed. The Court of Appeal dismissed the appeal and held that the council were liable in negligence.

Lord Denning MR was of the view that the damage, which was the subject of the action, ranked not solely as economic loss but rather as physical damage to the house.[34] He was prepared to equate the duty owed by the manufacturer of a defective chattel with the duty of care owed by a negligent builder. However, Lord Denning was also prepared to hold that the council owed the claimant a duty of care to protect her from the harm which she had sustained.[35] The imposition of liability in such circumstances was in accordance with the policy of the law.

Sachs LJ was prepared to regard the loss which the claimant had sustained as physical.[36] However, the judge regarded any distinction between the type of loss the claimant had sustained as immaterial.

Dutton was decided at a time when Lord Atkin's foreseeability test was at its zenith in the development of the duty of care.[37] In *Dutton*, the Court of Appeal was prepared to accept the proposition that the council was under a duty at common

[32] Ibid at 76 (per Lord Slynn). See also *Rees v Darlington Memorial Hospital NHS Trust* [2004] 1 AC 309.
[33] [1972] 1 QB 373.
[34] Ibid at 396.
[35] Ibid at 398.
[36] Ibid at 404.
[37] See p.13.

law to protect a houseowner from harm which had been caused by an incompetent builder. However, the interesting point for the purposes of the section is that the court was prepared to classify the claimant's loss as physical harm.

It will be recalled that in *Anns v Merton LBC*[38] the House of Lords held that the defendant local authority owed a duty of care to lessees of flats for negligently failing to carry out its statutory building control inspection duties, the upshot of which was that the flats became damaged, by virtue of the fact that the flats had been built on foundations which were too shallow. The important point, in the present context, is that the House was prepared to regard the damage to the flats as physical damage.[39] However, progressively, the courts departed from *Anns* on this point.

However, before that transition is addressed, the decision of the House of Lords in *Junior Books Ltd v Veitchi Co Ltd*[40] deserves brief mention. In that case, the defenders, who were specialist subcontractors, laid a floor in a factory which was being constructed for the pursuers. There was no contractual relationship between the pursuers and the defenders. It was alleged that the floor had been negligently laid and had required replacement, which had occasioned economic loss to the pursuers. The pursuers successfully sued the defenders, notwithstanding the fact that the harm in question ranked as pure economic loss. The House held that the proximity between the parties was extremely close, just falling short of a direct contractual relationship.[41] Furthermore, the harm which had been caused was a direct and foreseeable result of the defenders' negligence. The defenders had been nominated by the pursuers as specialist subcontractors. The former therefore must have relied upon their skill and knowledge.[42]

Junior Books was thought to have been a landmark in the development of the duty of care, in that the House of Lords allowed recovery for economic loss deriving from a defective building. However, *Junior Books* has subsequently been regarded as having been decided on its own special facts.[43] Later cases display the courts reasserting their traditional stance, by disallowing claims for pure economic loss. We now discuss the leading cases illustrative of that approach.

We see the courts having to address the question, firstly, as to whether harm which derived from the defective state of a building itself ranked as pure economic loss and, secondly, as to whether that loss was recoverable in the law of tort, in the House of Lords case of *D and F Estates Ltd v Church Commissioners*.[44] In that case, the first defendants (D1) had commissioned the third defendants (D3) to build a block of flats. D3 had engaged subcontractors to carry out plastering work. The work was done negligently. The claimants who had bought a lease from D1, who were the

[38] [1978] AC 728.

[39] Ibid at 759 (per Lord Wilberforce).

[40] [1983] 1 AC 520.

[41] Ibid at 533 (per Lord Fraser).

[42] See also *Parkhead Housing Association Ltd v Phoenix Preservation Ltd* 1990 SLT 812.

[43] See for example *Muirhead v Industrial Tank Specialities* [1986] QB 507 at 528 (per Robert Goff). See also *Scott Lithgow Ltd v GEC Electrical Projects Ltd* 1989 SC 412 at 419 (per Lord Clyde). In the Court of Appeal case of *Robinson v P.E. Jones (Contractors) Ltd* [2012] QB 44 at 64 Brunton LJ castigated the decision in *Junior Books* 'as aberrant, indeed as heretical'.

[44] [1989] AC 177.

owners of the flats, brought an action against the builders (D3) claiming the cost of repairing the plaster. The House held that the loss in question ranked as pure economic loss, since no property, other than the flats themselves (that is, the defective plaster) had been damaged by the subcontractors' negligence. The claimants therefore failed to recover damages.

Another case which illustrates the resoluteness on the part of the courts to deny claims for pure economic loss is the Court of Appeal case of *Simaan General Contracting v Pilkington Glass Ltd*.[45] In that case, a new building was being constructed in Abu Dhabi. The claimants were the main contractors. The main contract specified for the incorporation of green glass units in the building. The subcontractors were responsible for fitting the glass in the building. The defendants supplied the wrong type of glass to the subcontractors, who fitted the glass in the building. The glass was rejected by the architect of project. As a consequence, the claimants suffered financial loss in replacing the units. However, the Court of Appeal held that the defendants were not liable to the claimants in tort, since the loss which the latter had sustained was pure economic loss. Furthermore, the claimants had not relied on the defendants.[46] The court did concede that where a specialist subcontractor was vetted, selected and nominated by a building owner, it might be possible to conclude that the nominated subcontractor had assumed a direct responsibility to the building owner. However, in the instant case the defendant had not assumed such responsibility for the quality of the glass to the claimants. In the last analysis, the defendants did not owe the claimants a duty of care.

A further illustration of the reluctance on the part of the courts to allow recovery for pure economic loss is seen in the Court of Appeal case of *Greater Nottingham Co-Op Society v Cementation Piling and Foundations Ltd*.[47] There, the main contract between the claimants and the main contractors provided for an extension and alteration works to the claimants' premises. The claimants also entered into a collateral contract with the defendants. However, that contract did not make any provision as to the manner in which the subcontracted works were to be carried out. The defendants carried out the piling work negligently, the upshot of which was that adjoining premises were damaged. Work was required to be suspended. The claimants sued the defendants for the financial loss which the former had incurred, in having to revise their building schedule, as a consequence. The court held that the claimants could not recover for the economic loss which they had incurred. In reaching this conclusion, the court considered the fact that the claimants had the opportunity to provide for such loss, by way of an appropriate term in the collateral contract, but had failed to do so.[48] The defendants had, therefore, not assumed responsibility to the claimants for the economic loss the latter had sustained.[49]

The pendulum has therefore swung away from *Junior Books* which should be regarded, at best, as a case which was decided on its own special facts, or at worse,

[45] [1988] QB 758.

[46] Ibid at 781 (per Bingham LJ).

[47] [1989] QB 71.

[48] Ibid at 100 (per Purchas LJ).

[49] Ibid 106 (per Woolf LJ).

as a case which no longer represents good law. The move away from *Junior Books* which underlines the point which has just been made is the House of Lords case of *Murphy v Brentwood DC*.[50] In that case, a local authority approved plans for the construction of a housing estate, under s64 of the Public Health Act 1936. The plans indicated that two of the houses were to be built on filled ground, on a concrete raft foundation. The claimant purchased one of the houses and took up residence there. Subsequently, serious cracks began to appear in the internal walls of the house. Wet patches began to appear in the lawn. Investigations revealed that the concrete raft had subsided differentially, so causing distortion and cracking. The claimant was forced to sell his house at a reduced price. The claimant sued the local authority in negligence. However, the House rejected his claim, on the basis that since the relevant damage was confined to the house itself, the claim ranked as one for pure economic loss. Such loss was, therefore, irrecoverable. In coming to that decision, *Anns v Merton LBC*[51] was roundly rejected. The House also rejected the so-called 'complex structure theory' which had gained some academic support, to the effect that if one considered a building as consisting of different components (that is, the foundations, walls, roof and suchlike) and, for example, the foundations were negligently constructed, the upshot of which was that the walls began to crack (as in the instant case), one could construe such damage as physical damage, in that the damaged component was a separate entity from the component which had caused the harm.

Murphy is authority for the proposition that if a building is negligently constructed, for the purposes of the law of delict, one requires to regard the building as an integrated entity. Therefore, any latent defect in the building (for example, defective foundations) which results in damage to other parts of the building (for example, load-bearing walls), ranks as pure economic loss and is, therefore, irrecoverable in terms of the law of delict.[52]

However, *Murphy* should be contrasted with the Privy Council case of *Invercargill City Council v Hamlin*[53] which related to an appeal from the Court of Appeal in New Zealand. In that case, the plaintiff owners of a house sued a local authority for negligently carrying out its inspectorial duties, in relation to a house which was being built, by virtue of the local authority building inspectors failing to observe that the foundations of the house were inadequate. As a consequence, the walls of the house began to crack with the passage of time. Whereas the loss which the owner of the house had sustained ranked as pure economic loss, the Board held that community standards and expectations demanded the imposition of a duty of care on the local authority and the builder, to ensure compliance with the byelaws.[54]

Murphy was considered in the Outer House case of *Stevenson v A & J Stephen (Builders) Ltd*.[55] In that case, the owners of a house which was damaged in a fire

---

50 [1991] 1 AC 398.

51 See p.15.

52 See also *Robinson v P.E. Jones (Contractors) Ltd* [2012] QB 44 and *Ulster Garden Villages Ltd v Farrans (Construction) Ltd* [2024] NIKB 230.

53 [1996] AC 624.

54 Ibid at 642 (per Lord Lloyd).

55 1996 SLT 140.

sought damages from the builders, who were also feudal superiors of the owners, on the grounds that the builders had failed to construct a fire stop between the garage, which adjoined the house, and the house itself. The fire had started in the garage and had spread to the adjoining house which was damaged. The pursuers maintained that the builders had shown a fire stop in the plans (which had been lodged for building control purposes) and also that the fire stop had complied with the relevant regulations. The pursuers also claimed that the defenders had obtained a completion certificate after the work had been completed, on the strength that the work had been carried out in accordance with the plans, and that the owners had relied on the fact the completion certificate had been obtained.

Lord Osborne, in allowing proof before answer, was prepared to accept that even if one assumed that the loss in question ranked as pure economic loss – the judge was unsure whether the damage which had been caused by the fire was, indeed, pure economic loss[56] – it was, at least, arguable that the pursuers could recover in a delictual claim. In so deciding, the judge laid considerable store by the fact that the misrepresentation the defenders had made in applying for a completion certificate was of fundamental importance in establishing a special relationship between the defenders and the pursuers, which, in turn, could render the latter liable for economic loss.[57]

In the author's view, it would seem that the loss in *Stevenson* was pure economic loss, since, first, the house and garage were a physical entity, and second, the damage in question arose from a latent defect within the building itself, albeit that fire was allegedly caused by a third party. Furthermore, the manner in which the latent defect manifests itself and causes harm to the pursuer is quite irrelevant as to whether the harm that the defect causes ranks as physical harm or pure economic loss. Furthermore, even if one accepts the pursuers' claim that the relevant harm which they sustained derived from their relying on the completion certificate, that certificate was granted by the buildings authority. Under s9(2) of the Building (Scotland) Act 1959 (repealed) such a certificate could only be granted if the authority was satisfied that the building complied with the conditions on which the relevant building warrant was granted. In the last analysis, the building authority was negligent in granting the completion certificate. One could, therefore, argue that the negligent act, on the part of the authority, broke the chain of causation between the negligent act of the defender and the harm which the pursuers had sustained, on the grounds that the intervening act on the part of the authority was unreasonable and therefore ranked as a *novus actus interveniens*.[58] In short, the damage the pursuers had sustained was too remote to allow them to recover.

[56] Ibid at 144.

[57] Ibid at 145.

[58] *McKew v Holland, Hannen and Cubitts* 1970 SC (HL) 20. See p.174 below.

Chapter 4

Psychiatric Injury 'Nervous Shock'

In this chapter the author discusses liability for psychiatric injury, or nervous shock.[1] Here, it should be emphasised that psychiatric injury is a term of art, or technical term, in the law of negligence. In the House of Lords case of *Page v Smith*[2] Lord Keith stated that nervous shock meant:

> a reaction to an immediate and horrifying impact resulting in some recognisable psychiatric illness. There must be some serious mental disturbance, outside the range of normal human experience, not merely the ordinary emotions of anxiety, grief, or fear.[3]

---

1 Jyoti and Ahuja state that the expression 'nervous shock' originated in terminology used by surgeons to describe the emotional sequelae of railway collisions; J Ahuja 'Liability for Psychological and Psychiatric Harm: The Road to Recovery' (2015) 23 Med LR 27 at 29.

2 [1996] AC 155 at 167.

3 In the *Shorter v Surrey and Sussex Health Care NHS Trust* [2015] EWHC 614 the defendant health authority negligently failed to diagnose the medical condition of the claimant's sister. She collapsed as a result of her condition. The claimant was made aware of this. Her sister was admitted to hospital a week later and died, roughly within twenty-four hours. The claimant was with her sister from the time of her admission until the time of her death. The claimant sustained psychiatric harm as a result of her experience. Swift J held that that could not qualify either as a 'horrifying event' or 'assault upon the senses'. The claimant could not, therefore, recover as a secondary victim (see below) of nervous shock: [2015] EWHC 614 at [213]. See also *Liverpool Women's Hospital NHS Foundation Trust v Ronayne* [2015] PIQR P20. In that case, the claimant was the husband of a patient of the defendant. The patient had been negligently treated by the defendant when a hysterectomy had been performed. The claimant claimed that he suffered psychiatric harm on seeing his wife's state during two specific episodes. Held, *inter alia*, the appearance of the claimant's wife and its impact on the claimant did not constitute a 'horrifying event' to allow the claimant to recover. See also *Doosey v Leeds Teaching Hospital NHS Trust* (2017) (unreported) and *O'Connor v The Royal Bournemouth and Christchurch Hospitals NHS Foundation Trust* (2017) (unreported); and *King v Royal United Hospitals Bath NHS Foundation Trust* [2021] EWHC 1576. However, in *Re (A Child) v Calderdale and Huddersfield NHS Foundation Trust* [2017] EWHC 824 a mother had given birth to a baby which had become stuck in the birth canal. The defendant's medical staff had been negligent in the delivery which had been delayed. The mother's mother was also present at the birth. Both had sustained nervous shock at what they witnessed. The court held that by virtue of the fact that both the mother and claimant had witnessed a shocking and horrifying event, both could recover damages against the defendant, as secondary victims of nervous shock. See (2017) 139 *Rep B* 6.

In other words, the pursuer cannot recover in respect of grief or sorrow. The injury in question requires to be a recognisable psychiatric illness.[4] However, the range of illnesses in respect of which the pursuer can recover is wide, ranging from morbid depression[5] and post-traumatic stress disorder[6] to chronic fatigue syndrome.[7]

In the recent Supreme Court case *Paul v Wolverhampton NHS Trust*,[8] which is discussed below, the court was of the view that there was no requirement that the event witnessed by the pursuer required to be horrifying, or that the harm which the pursuer suffered was caused by a sudden shock to the nervous system.[9]

THE DEVELOPMENT OF THE LAW

During the nineteenth century the courts displayed a robust approach to claims for psychiatric injury and denied pursuers the right to recover damages. For example, in *Lynch v Knight*[10] Lord Wensleydale stated that mental pain and suffering was something which the law could not value, and could not pretend to redress. Again, in the Privy Council case of *Victorian Railway Commissioners v* Coultas,[11] the defendants' employee, who was in charge of a level crossing, negligently allowed the carriage in which the plaintiff was travelling on to the railway line, as a train was approaching. The plaintiff feared that she might be killed. She sustained nervous shock as a consequence. However, the Board held that she could not recover damages against the defendants for this type of harm. There were two main reasons for such judicial reticence. Firstly, and probably more importantly, the courts were wary of admitting false, or imaginary, claims.[12] Secondly (and linked to the first), psychiatric medicine was in a jejune state of development. Judges regarded this form of injury as esoteric, and an area, in effect, where they should not tread.[13] However, things began to change towards the end of the nineteenth century. For example, in *Wilkinson v Downton*[14] the claimant's husband had gone to the races for the day. The defendant visited the claimant in her house and told her, by way of a practical joke, that her husband was lying seriously injured, in a pub, some miles away. As a consequence, the claimant suffered psychiatric injury. At first instance, she successfully recovered from the defendant in

4 *Hinz v Berry* [1970] 2 QB 40 at 42 (per Lord Denning MR); *Alcock v Chief Constable of South Yorkshire* [1992] 1 AC 310 at 410 (per Lord Oliver) and *Rorrison v West Lothian Council* 2000 SCLR 245. See also *Pridie v Dick* (1857) 19 D 287. Mulheron argues that the law has reached such a stage whereby something lesser than a recognised psychiatric illness should be sufficient to trigger a compensable injury in law: R Mulheron, 'Recognised Psychiatric Injury in Negligence Claims' (2012) 32 OJLS 77.

5 *Hinz v Berry* (n 4).

6 *White v Chief Constable of South Yorkshire* [1999] 2 AC 455.

7 *Page v Smith* [1996] AC 155.

8 [2024] UKSC 1.

9 Ibid at [78].

10 (1861) 9 HL Cas. 577 at 598.

11 (1888) 13 App. Cas. 222.

12 *Victorian Railway Commissioners v Coultas* (1888) 13 App. 222 at 226 (per Sir Richard Couch).

13 For a discussion of the historical development of the law relating to nervous shock see I Goold and C Kelly 'Who's Afraid of Imaginary Claims? Common Misunderstandings of the Action for Pure Psychiatric Injury in Negligence' (2022) 138 LQR 58.

14 [1897] 2 QB 57.

tort, on the basis that the latter had wilfully committed an act which was calculated (that is, the natural consequence of which was) to cause physical harm to her, that is, infringe her right to physical safety.[15] Whereas the injury which the claimant sustained was inflicted intentionally by the defendant, *Wilkinson* is notable, in that it demonstrates a willingness on the part of the courts to recognise psychiatric harm as a form of injury to the person.

However, as far as liability for psychiatric injury, which was caused by the negligence of the defender, was concerned, the courts made a tentative start, by allowing the pursuer to recover, if he suffered psychiatric harm because of fear of physical injury to himself. For example, in *Dulieu v White and Sons*[16] the claimant, who was pregnant, was working behind the bar of a public house. An employee of the defendant negligently drove a horse and van into the bar. The claimant feared that she would be injured. She sustained psychiatric harm as a consequence. It was held that since the defendant owed the claimant a duty of care not to injure her, she was entitled to recover damages.[17]

As far as the law of Scotland is concerned, the courts were disinclined to allow claims for nervous shock which the pursuer sustained simply by witnessing a traumatic event. For example, in *Campbell v James Henderson Ltd*[18] the pursuer witnessed a road accident in which her brother was injured, when he was hit by a passing van which was being negligently driven by an employee of the defender. As a consequence, she sustained nervous shock. Lord Ormidale, endorsing the learning in *Dulieu*, expressed the opinion that since the pursuer had sustained nervous shock by witnessing the accident, the defenders did not owe the pursuer a duty of care.[19]

Whereas the claimant recovered in *Dulieu* because she feared for her own safety, the courts gradually began to allow claims for negligently inflicted psychiatric harm where the pursuer had witnessed a traumatic event, in which his own personal safety was not imperilled. An example of such a change is seen in the Court of Appeal case of *Hambrook v Stokes Bros.*[20] In that case, an employee of the defendants left a lorry at the top of a hill, with the brake off and the engine running. No proper steps had been taken in order to secure it. The lorry took off, on its own accord, ran down the hill, hurtled past the claimant and ultimately crashed into a building, where the lorry came to rest. The claimant had just left her children at the foot of the hill. They were out of sight when the collision took place. The claimant immediately feared for the safety of her children. She was then told by a passer-by that a child, whose description matched that of one of her children, had been injured. The claimant sustained psychiatric injury as a consequence. She subsequently died. The court held that the claimant was entitled to recover, notwithstanding the fact that she did not fear for her

[15] There is little Scottish authority as to whether the deliberate infliction of psychiatric harm alone is actionable. However, *Wilkinson* was cited with approval by Lord Porter in *Bourhill v Young* 1942 SC (HL) 78 at 100.

[16] [1901] 2 KB 669.

[17] *Dulieu* was followed in the Outer House case of *Wallace v Kennedy* (1908) 16 SLT 485 at 487 (per Lord Johnston).

[18] 1915 1 SLT 419.

[19] Ibid at 422.

[20] [1925] 1 KB 141.

own safety.[21] In other words, it sufficed that the claimant feared for the safety of others, namely, her children. Bankes LJ emphasised[22] that, for the victim of psychiatric harm to recover, it sufficed either for him to have seen the accident or to have become cognisant of its occurrence, through the victim's own, unaided senses. Therefore, it was insufficient to have been told of the accident afterwards.

The next important landmark in the progression of the law relating to nervous shock was the House of Lords case of *Bourhill v Young*.[23] In that case, a pregnant Edinburgh fishwife sustained psychiatric injury by witnessing the immediate aftermath of an accident, in which the defender, a motorcyclist, was killed. He had been driving negligently. The House held that the pursuer could not succeed, since it was not foreseeable that someone situated where the pursuer was, at the time when the accident occurred, would have sustained injury, by way of nervous shock. However, in terms of the subject matter currently being discussed, the House did approve the learning in both *Dulieu* and *Hambrook*,[24] and reaffirmed the courts' acceptance of the fact that psychiatric harm ranked as a form of personal injury, in respect of which the law would allow one to be compensated. However, opinions were reserved as to whether the court would award damages only when the pursuer had experienced psychiatric harm by virtue of apprehending injury to himself, as opposed to a third party.

CONCEPTUAL PROBLEMS

One of the problems which the courts have been required to confront in dealing with claims which are based on psychiatric harm is whether to address the facts of the case from a 'duty of care' or a 'remoteness of damage' perspective. For example, in the Court of Appeal case of *King v Phillips*[25] a taxi driver omitted to look where he was driving. He reversed over a child who was riding a tricycle at the time. The child sustained only minor injuries as a consequence. However, the claimant, the child's mother, who was looking out of her window at the time the accident took place, heard the child scream. She also saw his tricycle under the taxi. However, she could not see the little boy. She sustained psychiatric shock as a consequence. The scene of the accident was situated some 64–73 metres from the point where it was witnessed by the claimant. The court held that the claimant failed in her action. For Singleton LJ the facts of the case required to be analysed from a 'duty of care' perspective.[26] The judge held that the defendant did not owe the claimant a duty of care in the Atkinian sense, in that the claimant was not within the requisite area of risk. Interestingly, in

21 In the Inner House case of *Currie v Wardrop* 1927 SC 538 the pursuer and her friend were walking by the side of a road. An omnibus came up from behind and knocked both down. The pursuer sustained nervous shock as a result, firstly, of fearing for her own personal safety, and secondly, of fearing for the safety of her companion. By a majority, it was held that as far as the award of damages was concerned, the court could consider the shock which she had sustained by fearing for the safety of her companion.

22 Ibid at 152.

23 1942 SC (HL) 78.

24 Lord Russell stated *obiter*, 1942 SC (HL) 78 at 86 that he preferred the dissenting judgment of Sargant LJ in *Hambrook*.

25 [1953] 1 QB 429.

26 Ibid at 435–6, incl.

describing the nature of the risk in relation to which the law demanded the claimant should be exposed, before a duty of care arose, Singleton LJ stated that he found difficulty in drawing a distinction between a risk consisting of physical injury and one consisting of nervous shock.[27] However, for Denning LJ (as he then was) the defendant owed the claimant a duty of care in law.[28] However, the shock which the latter had sustained was too remote to allow her to succeed.[29] It should be mentioned that *King* was decided before *The Wagon Mound*[30] (which concerned remoteness of damage) which will be discussed later.[31]

THE CURRENT LAW

It is now customary to divide victims who have sustained nervous shock into two main categories, namely, (1) primary victims and (2) secondary victims.[32]

Category (1) governs a situation where the pursuer is actively participating in the very events which give rise to injury, whereas category (2) deals with a situation in which the pursuer has witnessed a traumatic event, the upshot of which is that he sustains psychiatric harm.

However, in certain circumstances, the pursuer may be able to found an action, in terms of being both a primary victim and also a secondary victim of psychiatric harm. In other words, the distinction between primary victims is not always clear cut. This point is illustrated in the House of Lords case of *W v Essex County Council*.[33] The basis of the claimants' claim was that the defendant local authority had negligently placed a known sex abuser in their care, the result being that he had abused their children. The claimants claimed that they had suffered psychiatric injury as a consequence. The House felt itself unable to reject the proposition that, if the facts which were alleged could be proved, the claimants could be regarded as both primary and also secondary victims of psychiatric injury.

PRIMARY VICTIMS OF NERVOUS SHOCK

The courts have traditionally been more willing to allow claims for psychiatric injury which has been caused to those who have been participating, in some way, in the traumatic event in question, as opposed to those having simply witnessed that event. Such an approach is hardly surprising, since there are fewer compelling policy reasons to exclude liability for this form of injury than for psychiatric injury which

[27] Ibid at 437.
[28] Ibid at 441.
[29] Ibid at 442.
[30] [1961] AC 388.
[31] See Ch. 7 below.
[32] In *White v Chief Constable of South Yorkshire Police* [1999] 2 AC 455 at 478, Lord Griffiths attributed the distinction between primary victims and secondary victims to the opinion of Lord Oliver in *Alcock v Chief Constable of South Yorkshire Police* [1992] 1 AC 310 at 407. The Scottish Law commission recommended the abolition of these two categories: Report on *Damages for Psychiatric Injury* (Scot. Law Com. No 196, 2004) at p.2.
[33] [2001] 2 AC 592.

has been caused to someone who simply witnesses a traumatic event. Certainly, to admit claims of primary victims of nervous shock would not open up the frightful vista of potential limitless liability, on the part of the defender, to a large number of potential pursuers. For the pursuer to rank as a primary victim, physical participation in the particular events giving rise to the psychiatric injury is the very touchstone of liability. This point is neatly illustrated in *Dooley v Cammell Laird and Co Ltd*.[34] In that case, a crane driver sustained nervous shock when the rope of a crane which he was operating snapped because it was faulty, causing the load which he was lifting to fall into the hold of a ship from which the load was being lifted. He feared that he had killed some men working in the hold. He successfully recovered damages from his employer. *Dooley* is also authority for the proposition that the pursuer need not fear for his own safety in order to recover.

The leading case on primary victims of nervous shock is now *Page v Smith*.[35] In that case, the claimant was involved in a collision between his car and the car which had been driven by the defendant. The claimant did not receive any physical injuries. However, he had been suffering from a condition known as myalgic encephalitis, or chronic fatigue syndrome. The claimant claimed that as a result of the accident, his medical condition had become permanent. By a majority, the House of Lords held the defendant liable, notwithstanding the fact that it was not reasonably foreseeable, on the facts of the case, that the claimant would sustain psychiatric injury. According to Lord Lloyd, once it was established that the defendant was under a duty to avoid causing personal injury to the claimant (whom he had described as a primary victim)[36] it did not matter whether the injury which was sustained by the claimant was physical, psychiatric or both.[37] It sufficed to ask whether the defendant should reasonably have foreseen that the claimant would suffer physical injury, as a result of the defendant's negligence, so as to bring the former within the range of the defendant's duty of care. It was unnecessary to ask, as a separate question, whether the

[34] [1951] 1 Lloyd's Rep 271.

[35] [1996] AC 155. See also the Court of Appeal case of *Young v Charles Church (Southern) Ltd* (1997) 39 BMLR 146. In that case, Cook was erecting a structure consisting of scaffolding poles. He was assisted by two labourers, one of whom was the claimant, Young. As Young turned away, in order to fetch another pole, Cook raised a long pole. It came into contact with an overhead power cable. Cook was electrocuted. Young was within about 2 metres of Cook when the accident took place. It was held that Young had participated in the traumatic events which had given rise to his injury. Therefore, he ranked as a primary victim of nervous shock, and he could succeed in his action against the defendant.

[36] [1996] AC 155 at 184.

[37] Ibid at 190. See also the sheriff appeal court case of *Weddle v Glasgow City Council* 2021 SLT (Sh Ct) 277 which concerned the notorious 'bin lorry' accident which occurred in central Glasgow in December 2014. The pursuer, who was present at the scene of the accident, raised an action against the defender, claiming that she was a primary victim of nervous shock. However, the pursuer failed in her action, since when the accident took place, she was not within the foreseeable range of physical injury. For a discussion of this case see E Russell 'The Bystander and the Bin Lorry: *Weddle v Glasgow City Council* Considered' (2019) SLT 137; E Russell 'Revisiting Pure Psychiatric Injury – *Weddle v Glasgow City Council* (2023) Jur Rev 75. See also *Schofield v Chief Constable v Chief Constable of West Yorkshire Police* [1999] ICR 193; *Donachie v The Chief Constable of Geater Manchester Police* [2004] EWCA Civ 405; and *A v Essex County Council* [2004] 1 WLR 1881, where the claimants had suffered psychiatric harm as a result of being placed in risk of physical danger by reason of the defendants' negligence.

defendant should reasonably have foreseen injury by shock, and it was also irrelevant that the claimant did not, in fact, suffer any external physical injury.[38]

Page, which was accepted as representing the law of Scotland in the House of Lords case of *Simmons v British Steel plc*,[39] was followed in *Salter v UB Frozen and Chilled Foods Ltd*.[40] In that case, the pursuer was employed in a factory as a forklift truck operator. One day, two fellow employees were stocktaking in a cold store at the factory. They were lifted in a cage by the truck. When the cage reached the highest level, the men were required to 'duck' in order to avoid contact with the roof beams. However, on one occasion, one of the stocktakers who were being lifted by the pursuer's truck failed to do so. As a consequence, his head collided with a beam, and he was fatally injured. The pursuer sustained psychiatric injury by witnessing the horrific injuries which his colleague had sustained. The pursuer was not at fault. The pursuer sought damages from his employer. In allowing proof before answer, it was held that the pursuer ranked as a primary victim of nervous shock, since he had actively participated in the traumatic events which had given rise to his injury.

Work-related psychiatric injury

In the above cases the pursuer has sustained psychiatric harm by participating in a traumatic event. However, it is possible that one can sustain psychiatric illness over a period of time. An example of such a situation would be of one suffering psychiatric illness because of stress at work. Since the mid-1990s there have been a number of cases in which employees have sued their employers for subjecting them to a work environment which has caused them to succumb to psychiatric illness. The first reported case featuring this form of injury was the first instance case of *Walker v Northumberland County Council*.[41]

In that case, the claimant was employed by a local authority as an officer, with managerial duties for social services in certain areas of Northumberland. The population in that part of the country grew with the passage of time. However, there was no commensurate increase in staffing levels. The stress levels among staff increased. From 1985 onwards, the claimant produced reports which were intended to draw his superior's attention to the work pressures to which he and his staff were subjected. In 1986, the claimant suffered a nervous breakdown. He remained off work until early 1987. During his absence, his workload had increased. There was also a backlog of paperwork to deal with. He subsequently had a second mental breakdown and was then dismissed by the authority on the grounds of permanent ill health. The

38 For a discussion of *Page* see F McManus 'Nervous Shock-Back to Square One?' (1996) Jur Rev 159; H Teff *Causing Psychiatric and Emotional Harm* (Hart Publishing, 2009) at 77–83 incl. F Trindade 'Nervous Shock and Negligent Conduct' (1996) 122 LQR 22; S Bailey and D Nolan 'The *Page v Smith* Saga: A Tale of Inauspicious Origins and Unintended Consequences' [2010] CLJ 495. See also *RE(a minor) v Calderdale and Huddersfield NHS Foundation Trust* [2017] EWHC 824. For a discussion of *RE(a minor)* see (2017) 139 Rep B 6. See also *Zeromska-Smith v United Lincolnshire Hospitals NHS Trust* [2019] EWHC 980; and *YAH v Medway NHS Foundation Trust* [2019] 1 WLR 1413.

39 2004 SC (HL) 94 at 110 (per Lord Rodger).

40 2004 SC 233.

41 [1995] ICR 702.

claimant then sued the local authority for breach of its duty in failing to take steps in order to avoid exposing him to a health-endangering workload. Colman J held that an employer owed a duty of care to an employee not to cause him psychiatric harm, by the volume and character of the work which he was required to perform. The defendant had breached that duty to the claimant in relation to his second nervous breakdown. The former had failed to take the preventative measures which were commensurate with the reasonably foreseeable risk that the claimant would sustain psychiatric harm.[42]

Again, in the Outer House case of *Fraser v State Hospitals Board for Scotland*[43] a former charge nurse at the defender's hospital sued the hospital board, alleging that he had developed a depressive disorder as a result of a punitive work regime. In deciding that the defenders owed a common law duty of care to their employers, to avoid exposing them to the unnecessary risk of injury, Lord Carloway refused to draw a distinction between physical and psychiatric injury.[44] The law imposed a duty of care on an employer in relation to each form of injury.[45] However, the pursuer failed in his action, since he could not prove that his psychiatric illness was reasonably foreseeable.[46]

SECONDARY VICTIMS OF NERVOUS SHOCK

As noted above, a secondary victim of nervous shock is someone who has sustained psychiatric injury by witnessing a traumatic event. Essentially, the pursuer suffers nervous shock by witnessing someone being injured, or, less frequently, an inanimate object being damaged, the upshot of which is that the pursuer sustains a sudden assault on his senses.[47] The leading case on the subject of psychiatric injury being sustained by secondary victims is the House of Lords case of *Alcock v Chief Constable of South Yorkshire*.[48] In that case, the defendant was responsible for policing a football match, which took place in the Hillsborough Stadium in Sheffield. There was overcrowding in part of the stadium, which had been caused by the negligence of the police. Ninety-six spectators died as a result of being crushed. Many more were seriously injured. Pictures of the harrowing event were broadcast live on television. The claimants were all either related to or friends of the spectators who were involved in the disaster. Some witnessed the traumatic events from parts of the stadium itself, while others saw the events on television. However, all alleged that they had suffered nervous shock. The House of Lords held that in order for a claimant to succeed, it was necessary for them to prove that the injury which had been sustained by the claimant

---

42 See also *Levy v Allied Dunbar Assurance plc* [2000] 12 WLUK 423.

43 2002 SLT 1051.

44 Ibid at [119].

45 Ibid at [122].

46 See also *Rorrison v West Lothian Council* 2020 SCLR 245; *K v Chief Constable of the Police Service of Scotland* 2020 SC 399; *Yapp v Foreign and Commonwealth Office* [2015] ICR D13; *T v W* [2024] CSOH 44.

47 The Scottish Law Commission recommended the abolition of this requirement: Report on Damages for Psychiatric Injury (Scot. Law Com. No. 196, 2004) at p.4.

48 [1991] 1 AC 310.

was reasonably foreseeable, and that the relationship between the claimant and the victim required to be one of love and affection. Such affection would be presumed to exist in certain situations, such as when a parent, child, husband, or wife was injured. In other cases, however, a bond of love and affection would require to be proved. This would be the case in respect of remoter relationships: for example, between cousins. The claimant had also to establish propinquity, in respect of sustaining nervous shock, in both time and space, to the accident and the immediate aftermath. Finally, claimants required to sustain nervous shock by witnessing the event in question with their own unaided senses.

According to Lord Keith, for liability to lie, it required to be established that psychiatric harm was reasonably foreseeable.[49] There also required to exist a requisite relationship of proximity between the claimant and the defendant. The judge stated that the class of persons to whom a duty was owed was not to be restricted to certain relationships, such as husband and wife or parent and child.[50] The closeness of the tie would require to be proved by the claimant, though no doubt capable of being presumed in certain cases. Psychiatric injury to the bystander would not ordinarily be within the range of reasonable foreseeability. However, such individuals could not be entirely excluded from it if the circumstances of the catastrophe occurring very close to the bystander were particularly horrific. Lord Keith then went on to endorse Lord Wilberforce's decision in *McLoughlin v O'Brien*[51] and stated that it was necessary for the claimant to suffer nervous shock by virtue of seeing or hearing either the traumatic event itself or its immediate aftermath. The viewing of such an event on television could not be equiparated with actually witnessing such an event with one's unaided senses.

For Lord Akner, in order to establish liability for harm which had been caused by nervous shock, whereas the test of reasonable foreseeability was a vital step towards establishing liability, it required to incorporate the notion of proximity which was embodied in Lord Atkin's duty of care in *Donoghue*.[52] Who, then, was one's neighbour, as far as liability for nervous shock was concerned? Lord Akner endorsed Lord Wilberforce's dictum in *McLoughlin v O'Brian*[53] and stated that since nervous shock, by its very nature, was capable of affecting such a wide range of persons, there was a real need for the law to place some limitation upon the extent of admissible claims. This limiting exercise required to be put into effect by considering the following three elements:

1. the class of persons whose claim should be recognised:
2. the proximity of the claimants to the scene of the accident; and
3. the means by which the shock is caused.

As far as 1 was concerned, Lord Akner stated that it was foreseeable that those in a close family relationship with the victim would suffer nervous shock, on the basis that

[49] Ibid at 396.
[50] Ibid at 397.
[51] [1983] 1 AC 410at 423.
[52] Ibid at 402.
[53] [1983] 1 AC 410 at 422.

the love and affection associated with such relationships, was such that the defendant ought reasonably to contemplate that they might be so closely and directly affected by his conduct.[54] Whether the degree of love and affection in any given relationship (be that of relative or friend) was such that the defendant, in the light of the plaintiff's proximity to the scene of the accident, in time and space and its nature, should reasonably have foreseen the shock-induced psychiatric illness, required to be decided on a case-by-case basis.[55]

As far as 2 was concerned, the claimant's proximity to the scene of the accident required to be close, both in time and space.[56] However, it was not necessary that the claimant should witness the accident with his own unaided senses. It sufficed that the claimant witnessed the immediate aftermath of the accident. In the instant case, one claimant had identified his brother in the mortuary, some eight hours after the accident. However, this did not, in Lord Akner's opinion, constitute the immediate aftermath of the accident.

Finally, as far as 3 was concerned, Lord Akner held that although television pictures certainly gave rise to feelings of the deepest anxiety and distress, in the instant case, the simultaneous television broadcasts of what occurred could not be equated with the sight or hearing of the event, or its immediate aftermath.[57] However, it was possible that in certain circumstances, the simultaneous broadcast of a disaster could not be ruled out as providing the equivalent of the actual sight or hearing of the event, or its immediate aftermath. Lord Akner gave the example (which Nolan LJ had given in the Court of Appeal) of a situation where it was reasonable to anticipate that television cameras while filming and transmitting pictures of a special event of children travelling in a balloon in which there was media interest, particularly among parents, showed the balloon suddenly bursting into flames.

For Lord Oliver, the touchstone of liability in relation to psychiatric harm suffered by secondary victims of nervous shock was the proximity or directness of the relationship between the claimant and the defendant.[58]The notion of proximity in such a context depended largely on the court's perception of what was the reasonable area for the imposition of liability, rather than upon any logical process of analytical deduction. The judge went on to warn against confining liability only in relation to close relatives.[59] Furthermore, in certain circumstances, where the traumatic event was of horrific proportions, a bystander who was unrelated to the victim could possibly recover.[60]

The learning in *Alcock* was applied in the Court of Appeal case of *McFarlane v EE Caledonia Ltd*.[61] In that case, the claimant was employed on an oil rig, which was owned and operated by the defendants. One night, when the claimant was off duty

54 [1991] 1 AC 310 at 403.
55 Ibid at 404.
56 Ibid at 404.
57 Ibid at 405.
58 Ibid at 411.
59 Ibid at 415.
60 Ibid at 416.
61 [1994] PIQR P154.

and on a support vessel, a series of massive explosions took place on the rig. The closest the claimant came to the fire was 100 metres, when the support vessel moved in towards the rig, in an attempt to fight the fire and also render assistance. The claimant brought an action against the defendants, on the grounds that he had suffered nervous shock as a result of witnessing the horrific events. The court held that he could not recover, since he ranked as a mere bystander. Furthermore, there was no bond of love and affection between the claimant and the victims of the disaster.

Again, in the Inner House case of *Robertson v Forth Road Bridge Joint Board (No 2)*[62] the pursuers, Robertson and Rough, were working on the Forth Road Bridge. Rough noticed a large piece of metal sheeting lying on the carriageway. He therefore enlisted the assistance of the pursuers and another colleague, Smith, to remove the sheet. The metal sheet was loaded on to the back of a pick-up van. However, because of its size, the sheet protruded over one side. Smith, therefore, sat on top of the sheet. Robertson drove the van. Rough followed behind in another vehicle. As the vehicles were travelling towards the end of the bridge, a gust of wind blew Smith and the metal sheet off the van and over the side of the bridge. Smith was killed. In an action against their employers, both Robertson and Rough claimed that they had suffered psychiatric injury, as a result of witnessing the accident. However, the Inner House rejected their claim. It did not suffice that the pursuers could prove that they had sustained nervous shock in the workplace. Indeed, there was no separate category of liability which governed liability for nervous shock in the workplace. Rather, the ordinary rules which governed liability for nervous shock applied. Since the pursuers had not been participating in the traumatic event in question, they simply ranked as mere bystanders in the eye of the law, and could, therefore, recover only if they had a close emotional relationship with the victim, which they did not.[63]

The Hillsborough disaster featured again in the House of Lords case of *White v Chief Constable of South Yorkshire*.[64] In that case, a large number of police officers brought claims for psychiatric injury which they had suffered, as a result of tending the victims of the tragedy. At first instance, it was held that given the fact that the claimants simply ranked as secondary victims of nervous shock, and furthermore, since they were not rescuers, they could not recover in damages against the defendant, notwithstanding the fact that the relationship which they enjoyed in relation to the defendant was analogous to that obtaining between employer and employee. The Court of Appeal reversed that decision, on the grounds that the defendant's duty to the claimants derived from the employer-employee relationship. The defendant was, therefore, under a duty to protect the claimants from psychiatric injury, irrespective of whether the latter ranked either as primary or as secondary victims. The defendant successfully appealed to the House of Lords. Essentially, the majority of the House were of the opinion that the police who were at the stadium at the time the accident

62 1995 SC 364. For a discussion of Robertson see F McManus 'Nervous Shock in the Workplace' (1995) JR 240. See also *Hunter v British Coal Corporation* [1999] QB 140.

63 See also *Monk v PC Harington Ltd* [2008] EWHC 1879.

64 [1999] 2 AC 455. For an interesting discussion of the law relating to primary and secondary victims of nervous shock, see P Handford 'Psychiatric Injury in Breach of a Relationship' (2007) 27 LS 26. See also P Handford 'Psychiatric Injury in the Workplace' (1999) Tort L Rev 126.

took place, and had witnessed the traumatic events, were to be regarded as secondary victims of nervous shock, and were to be treated no differently from other bystanders.

The pursuer's relationship with the traumatic event

It is not necessary for a secondary victim of psychiatric harm to actually witness the relevant traumatic event. It suffices that he should witness the immediate aftermath of the event. In the leading case of *McLoughlin v O'Brian*[65] the claimant's husband and children were seriously injured when their car came into collision with a vehicle, which was being negligently driven by the defendant. The claimant suffered psychiatric harm on seeing her family seriously injured in hospital, some two hours after the accident had taken place. However, the House of Lords held that the claimant could recover damages from the defendant. It sufficed that the claimant had sustained psychiatric harm by experiencing the immediate aftermath of the accident. Furthermore, to allow such a claim would not flout public policy.[66]

However, in order to successfully recover as a secondary victim of psychiatric harm, by virtue of witnessing the immediate aftermath of an accident, the pursuer must have been aware that the victim was involved the accident. This point was poignantly illustrated in the Inner House case of *Young v MacLean*.[67] In that case, the pursuer was the mother of a pedestrian who had been killed when a motor vehicle, driven by the defendant, mounted a pavement in a residential street and struck the pedestrian. The pursuer was on her way to meet her son when he was killed. The pursuer did not see her son being killed. However, she had walked past the scene of the accident shortly afterwards. She saw the badly damaged vehicle. The pursuer then proceeded to the place where she had arranged to meet her son. When he failed to turn up, she became distressed. She was then informed by the police that her son had been killed. The pursuer suffered post-traumatic stress disorder. She claimed, *inter alia*, that she was a secondary victim of nervous shock. She succeeded in the Outer House. However, the Inner House held that the pursuer did not rank as a secondary victim of nervous shock, on the basis that when she saw the scene of the aftermath

---

65 [1983] 1 AC 410.

66 See also *Galli-Atkinson v Seghal* [2003] Lloyds Rep Med 285; mother able to recover after seeing body of daughter in a mortuary, two hours after the relevant accident had taken place. See also *Ravenscroft v Rederiaktiebologet*, *The Times*, 6 April 1992; mother taken to hospital where her son had died within two hours of being injured in an accident at work, which had been caused by the defendant's negligence. She did not see her son's body. She was informed of his death by her husband. The Court of Appeal held that she could not recover, on the basis that she had not seen her son's body. Cf *Taylor v Somerset Health Authority* [1993] PIQR P262; plaintiff's husband suffers heart attack, taken to hospital and dies. The defendant had negligently failed to diagnose his serious heart condition. Plaintiff went to hospital within an hour and informed of his death. The plaintiff sees her husband's body in the hospital mortuary and suffers nervous shock. Held; the plaintiff did not come within the 'immediate aftermath extension' to the rule that claims for nervous shock could not be sustained where the plaintiff did not hear or see the injury to a near relative which was said to have brought on the nervous shock. Furthermore, the communication of the fact of his death by a doctor and the subsequent sight of the body of her husband (which bore no marks or signs of the circumstances of the fatal heart attack) did not fall within the categories entitling her to recover.

67 2016 SC 135.

of the accident, she was unaware of its having any connection with her son. In other words, in order to succeed, the pursuer was required to establish that when she saw the immediate aftermath of the accident, she could immediately juxtapose, or connect, the scene of the accident with her son. That, she was unable to do. She, therefore, failed in her action.[68]

Young v MacLean should be contrasted with the recent Court of Appeal case of *Young v Downey*.[69] In that case, the claimant ('Y') was 4½ years of age at the time of the notorious Hyde Park bombing. She saw her father (a lance corporal) leave Knightsbridge Barracks ('the barracks'), heard the explosion and saw other soldiers return to the barracks covered with blood and embedded with nails. Y told her mother that 'Daddy should be coming home now.' However, he never did. He died of his injuries the following day. The question which the court was required to answer was whether Y could demonstrate the necessary relationship of proximity between the parties to entitle her to recover damages for her psychiatric injury from the perpetrator of the bombing, namely, Downey.

At first instance, the judge rejected Y's claim, on the basis that there was never, at the relevant time, any recognition by Y of her father as the primary victim.[70] After reviewing the evidence, the judge concluded that it never occurred to Y's mind that her father had been injured, or killed, or involved at all, in what she had heard and seen.[71] However, the decision at first instance was overturned by the Court of Appeal, essentially on the grounds that the trial judge had wrongly rejected the evidence of a medical expert and substituted his own opinion. The court went on to state that the injury to the secondary victim must have arisen from witnessing the harm or danger

[68] *Young* should be contrasted with *Werb v Solent NHS Trust* (2017) (unreported) (which was a striking out action). In *Werb* the claimant's son was a psychiatric patient in the defendant's hospital. He had been allowed to go home on leave, despite expressing feelings of being suicidal to the defendant's staff. On the day of his release he had started being treated with a drug which increases the risk of suicidal behaviour. While at home, he had expressed feelings of suicide. On his return to hospital, unsuccessful attempts were made by the claimant to contact the son's consultant. Hospital staff noted that the son was 'very suicidal'. However, the consultant did not see or assess the son. The following weekend, during the son's release from hospital, he committed suicide by throwing himself off a railway bridge. The claimant witnessed the immediate aftermath of the suicide, by virtue of seeing a mangled corpse on the railway line. However, at that time, the claimant did not realise that the corpse was that of his son. Shortly after (twenty-five minutes) his return home, he received a frantic phone call from his ex-wife (the son's mother) to the effect that the claimant's son was 'gone'. The claimant immediately returned to the bridge. The corpse of his son was still on the railway line. The claimant suffered psychiatric harm. The court accepted that the psychiatric shock in question did not result from a retrospective process but, rather, from a sudden unexpected and exceptional shock, which all occurred within the period comprising the claimant first seeing the body parts on the railway line, receiving the phone call from his ex-wife, and returning to the railway bridge, where he saw the remains of the corpse, which he now knew was that of his son. It was artificial to consider the telephone call, informing the claimant that the son was missing, separately from the two visits to the railway bridge, as they formed part of one whole. The court, therefore, rejected the defendant's contention that the shock had been caused by the retrospective communication of the son's death. In conclusion, the court refused to strike out the claimant's claim.

[69] [2025] EWHC Civ 177.

[70] Ibid at [15].

[71] Ibid at [17].

to the primary victim, so if the secondary victim did not witness the harm or danger, in the sense that they had no understanding of what was going on, the duty could not arise.[72] The second critical factor of the proximity of the defendant to a secondary victim was the close tie of love and affection which they had to the primary victim.[73] That relationship must bring with it some sentience, in the sense that someone without an understanding of their relationship with a loved one was in no different position to an ordinary bystander. The court went on to add that proximity must depend on all the circumstances.[74] If the judge were correct in relation to the facts which he found, no sufficient proximity would be established, in that firstly, Y did not appreciate that her father was in danger; secondly, Y had not made the association with the noise and the bomb and the wounded returning soldiers on the one hand and fear for her father on the other hand; and thirdly, Y was in no different position to any other child in the nursery that day, who heard the explosion and saw the aftermath. If those facts were correctly found, Y's injury would not have arisen from witnessing harm or danger to Corporal Young.

In the vast majority of cases concerning harm which has been sustained by secondary victims of psychiatric harm, the pursuer has witnessed a traumatic event which either has taken place or has become manifest shortly after the defender's negligent act which caused the relevant accident. In other words, there was a close temporal nexus between the negligent act of the defendant and the event which had caused harm to the pursuer. *Alcock*, *Frost* and *Robertson* provide good examples of such circumstances. However, the Supreme Court was required to address the question as to whether the claimant could recover damages, as a secondary victim of nervous shock, not by witnessing an accident but, rather, the death of a close relative, who had died as a result of medical negligence, in the conjoined cases of *Paul v Royal Wolverhampton NHS Trust*.[75] The claimants in all three appeals before the court had sustained psychiatric harm, by witnessing the death of a relative who had died as a result of a medical condition which the defendant had failed to diagnose and treat. The Court of Appeal struck out all three claims, on the basis that the passage of time between the negligent act and the later horrific event meant that the necessary legal proximity between the defendant and secondary victim or victims did not exist. The parties appealed to the Supreme Court. The court, by a majority, rejected the appeal.

The majority judgment was delivered by Lord Leggatt and Lady Rose.

The court stated that the key issue which was raised in the appeals was whether the claimants could recover damages in respect of psychiatric injury which had been caused by witnessing the death or injury of a close relative, not in an accident, but from a medical condition which the defendant had failed to diagnose and treat.[76] Each of the cases had involved such a claim. In two of the cases the claimants were present when their father or young daughter had died in shocking circumstances. In the third case, the claimant had come across her daughter in such circumstances, a

[72] Ibid at [21].
[73] Ibid at [22].
[74] Ibid at [23].
[75] [2024] UKSC 1.
[76] Ibid at para. [5].

few minutes after her death. In each case the claimants claimed that the death had been caused by the negligence of the defendant doctor, or health authority, in failing to diagnose and treat a life-threatening condition from which the deceased had been suffering. The court stated that a critical question which fell to be answered was whether or not the rules which had been developed in relation to accidents applied where, as a result of the negligence of a doctor, a person had died or manifested an injury from an illness, which proper treatment would have prevented.[77] The key question which the court was required to decide was whether the rules, which determined whether the necessary proximity existed between the parties to give rise to a duty of care, owed to a secondary victim of an accident, applied in cases of medical negligence, where there was no accident.[78] The court concluded that persons whom doctors ought reasonably to have in contemplation when directing their mind to the care of a patient did not include members of a patient's close family who might be psychologically affected by witnessing the effects of a disease, which the doctor ought to have diagnosed and treated.[79] Hence, there did not exist the relationship of proximity between the parties, necessary to give rise to a duty of care.

The decision in *Paul* is in conformity with the current approach which is being taken by the courts to the duty of care, in the wake of the decision of the Supreme Court in *Robinson v Chief Constable of West Yorkshire*,[80] where the court decided that a duty of care should be recognised if the facts of the case are either analogous or identical to a case which has previously been decided. Furthermore, in developing the law, the courts should develop the law incrementally. However, in *Paul* for the majority of the court to expand the duty of care to allow individuals who had witnessed the death of relative caused by medical negligence, as opposed to an accident, was simply an increment too far.[81]

Rescuers

We have seen that as far as secondary victims of nervous shock are concerned, the courts deny the victim a remedy unless the victim has a close bond of love and affection with the primary victim. However, what is the case as far as rescuers are concerned? In the first instance case of *Chadwick v British Railways Board*,[82] there was a serious railway accident in London, in which ninety people lost their lives. The accident had been caused by the defendants' negligence. The claimant, who lived near the scene of the accident, assisted with the rescue activities. As a result of his experiences, he suffered psychiatric harm. He sued the defendants, claiming that the defendants had owed the claimant a duty of care. It was held that, since it was reasonably foreseeable that the claimant would sustain nervous shock, he could recover damages. It was irrelevant that the claimant did not fear for his own safety. Whereas *Chadwick*

77 Ibid at para. [24].
78 Ibid at para. [127].
79 Ibid at para. [142].
80 [2018] AC 736. See p.26 above.
81 For a discussion of *Paul* see 2024 SLT 213.
82 [1967] 1 WLR 912.

was approved by the House of Lords in *McLoughlin v O'Brian*,[83] in *White* Lord Goff, in his dissenting judgment, expressed the view that the circumstances of *Chadwick* were wholly exceptional, and that it would be very rare that a person bringing aid and comfort to victims would be held to have suffered foreseeable psychiatric injury as a result.[84]

In the first instance case of *Wigg v British Railways Board*[85] a train driver came across the body of a person soon after that person had been struck by a door of the train which he had been driving and which had pulled away from a railway station. A guard had negligently allowed the train to commence its journey. The claimant sustained nervous shock. Tucker J was prepared to treat the claimant as a rescuer, since he had attempted to comfort the victim, whom he mistakenly believed was alive. It was foreseeable that the claimant would suffer nervous shock. He recovered damages from the Board.[86]

Whether or not a person is to be regarded as a rescuer is a question of fact to be decided on the facts of the case.[87] However, trivial or peripheral assistance, on the part of the pursuer, is not sufficient to allow that person to rank as a rescuer.

Injury to inanimate objects

To what extent, if any, can the pursuer recover for psychiatric harm which has been occasioned by his witnessing damage, which has been caused by the negligence of the defender, to an inanimate object? This question required to be answered in the Court of Appeal case of *Owens v Liverpool Corporation*.[88] In that case, the claimants, who were relatives of the deceased, were following a hearse which was carrying his coffin. A tram which was being negligently driven by an employee of defendant collided with the hearse. The glass side of the hearse was broken. The coffin was overturned. The coffin was in danger of being thrown onto the road. The claimants suffered nervous shock on witnessing the accident, or its immediate aftermath. It was held that the claimants could recover. However, the authority of *Owens* was doubted by Lord Oliver in *Alcock*[89] and may not represent good law.

More recently, the Court of Appeal was required to consider whether one could recover for psychiatric harm occasioned by one witnessing damage caused to an inanimate object in *Attia v British Gas*.[90] In that case, the claimant suffered nervous shock by witnessing the destruction of her home by fire. The fire had been caused by the defendant having negligently installed central heating in the premises. The Court of Appeal, in deciding a preliminary issue, held that she could recover for such harm,

[83] [1983] 1 AC 410 at 438 per Lord Bridge.

[84] [1999] 2 AC 455 at 484.

[85] *The Times*, 4 February 1984.

[86] The Scottish Law Commission recommended that a rescuer who sustains mental harm from what he experiences during a rescue operation should not be barred from recovery merely because he was not at risk from physical harm. *Report on Damages for Psychiatric* Injury (Scot Law Com No 196 at 3.52).

[87] Per Lord Griffiths in *White* above, at 464/465.

[88] [1939] 1 KB 394.

[89] [1992] 1 AC 310 at 412.

[90] [1988] QB 304.

if she could prove at the trial that psychiatric harm was foreseeable. It is doubtful whether *Attia* represents good law. However, if *Attia* does represent good law, one would have the anomalous situation where the Atkinian 'foreseeability test' applies in relation to psychiatric harm caused by witnessing harm caused to an inanimate object, whereas, in contrast, a pursuer would require to establish the existence of a bond of love and affection with the victim of an accident which the pursuer witnesses. In short, it would be easier to recover damages in relation to harm being inflicted to an inanimate object than to humans.

NOVEL CATEGORIES

Whereas traditionally the courts have categorised victims of psychiatric injury as either primary or secondary victims, the House of Lords case of *W v Essex County Council*[91] illustrates that the categorisation of potential victims of psychiatric injury is not closed. In *W* the first and second claimants signed an agreement with the defendant local authority to become foster parents. After receiving assurances that no sexual abuser would be placed with them and following a false representation by the defendant's social worker that G was not a known sexual abuser, the claimants agreed to foster him. A month later, the first and second claimants discovered that G had sexually abused their children. The claimants alleged that as a result, they had suffered psychiatric illness. The House, in refusing to strike out their claim, held that it could not be said that the psychiatric harm which the claimants had suffered was outside the range of psychiatric harm which the law recognised. However, Lord Slynn stated[92] that whereas the parents did not rank as either primary or secondary victims, the categorising of those claiming to be included as primary or secondary victims was not finally closed and was a concept still to be developed in different factual situations.

SENSITIVE PURSUERS

It is trite law that the courts will not protect the oversensitive.[93] This general principle finds expression in the law relating to psychiatric injury by the rule that the courts will not countenance claims for such injury unless the traumatic events would not have affected those of reasonable fortitude.[94]

CONCLUSIONS

In the House of Lords case of *White v Chief Constable of South Yorkshire Police*[95] Lord Steyn stated that the law relating to psychiatric injury was as a patchwork quilt of

91 [2000] 2 AC 592.
92 Ibid at 601.
93 See for example, *Heath v Brighton Corporation* (1908) 24 TLR 414.
94 See for example *Wigg v British Railways Board*, *The Times*, 4 February 1986; *Brice v Brown* [1984] 1 All ER 997.
95 [1999] 2 AC 455 at 500.

distinctions which are difficulty to justify. This is particularly true in relation to secondary victims of nervous shock. Here, the courts may have been over-mindful of admitting false claims. It could be forcefully argued that the panoply of artificial rules which the courts have incorporated in the law relating to nervous shock sustained by secondary victims is unfair and unjust in relation to victims of nervous shock. The *Alcock*, *White* and *Robertson* decisions poignantly epitomise the law's somewhat harsh approach to secondary victims, such an approach being driven by public policy.

Chapter 5

Breach of Duty of Care

INTRODUCTION

In a negligence action, if it is proven that the defender owes the pursuer a duty of care, the latter must prove that the former has breached that duty. In so doing, the pursuer requires to prove that the defender has failed to attain the standard of care which the law demands of the defender. The requisite standard of care, which is demanded of the defender, is a question of law. However, whether the defender meets that standard is a question of fact, which requires to be determined in the light of the circumstances of the case.[1] In *Caswell v Powell Duffryn*[2] Lord Wright stated:

> What is all-important is to adapt the standard of what is negligence, to the facts, and to give due regard to the actual conditions under which men work in a factory or mine, to the long hours of fatigue, to the slackening of attention which naturally comes from constant repetition of the same operation, to the noise and confusion in which the man works, to his pre-occupation in what he is actually doing, at the cost perhaps of some inattention to his own safety.

THE CRITERION OF THE REASONABLE MAN

Whether the defender has acted negligently is judged objectively. That is to say, that no account is taken of individual disabilities[3] or idiosyncrasies, except in relation to children, who are judged in terms of the standard of children of the age of the defender.[4] Therefore, it does not matter whether I am clumsy and have a very poor sense of direction and speed, I fall to be judged by the standard set by the hypothetical normal adult. The court's employing an objective test to determine whether the defender has been negligent was established during the mid-nineteenth century, and is neatly illustrated in *Vaughan v Menlove*.[5] In that case, the defendant negligently

---

[1] *McCann v J.R. McKellar* 1969 SC (HL) 1. *Campbell v Ord and Maddison* (1873) 1 R 149 at 153; *MacIntosh v MacIntosh* (1864) 2 M 1357. See also *Das International Ltd v Manley* [2002] EWCA Civ 1638 and *Dunnage v Randall* [2016] QB 639 at [127] per Vos LJ and *Waugh v James K Allen* 1964 SC (HL) 102 at 110 per Lord Upjohn.

[2] [1940] 152 at 178.

[3] *Dunnage v Randall* [2016] QB 639.

[4] *Yachuk v Oliver Blais Co Ltd* [1949] AC 386.

[5] (1837) 3 Bing NC 468.

constructed a hayrick on the boundary of his property. The hayrick caught fire as a result of spontaneous combustion. The house of the defendant's neighbour burnt down. In deciding that the defendant was liable for the damage, C J Tindall stated:

> Instead ... of stating that the liability for negligence should be coextensive with the judgement of each individual, which would be as variable as the length of foot of each individual, we ought rather, to adhere to the rule which requires in all cases, a regard to caution such as a man of ordinary prudence would observe.[6]

In *Blyth v Birmingham Waterworks Co*[7] Alderson B stated: 'Negligence is the omission to do something which a reasonable man, guided upon those considerations which ordinarily regulate the conduct of human affairs, would do, or something which a prudent and reasonable man would not do.'

More recently, in the House of Lords case of *Glasgow Corporation v Muir*[8] Lord MacMillan stated:

> The standard of foresight of the reasonable man is, in one sense, an impersonal test. It eliminates the personal equation and is independent of the idiosyncrasies of the particular person whose conduct is in question. Some persons are by nature unduly timorous, and imagine every path beset with lions. Others of more robust temperament, fail to foresee or nonchalantly disregard even the most obvious of dangers. The reasonable man is presumed to be free both from over-apprehension and from over-confidence.

The reasonable man is not a clairvoyant.[9] Nor is he a paragon of circumspection.[10] However, he must possess the prevision to foresee that others may act negligently,[11] but the defender is only under a duty to foresee negligence on the part of others if such negligence falls within the bounds of human experience.[12]

The application of the objective test was graphically illustrated in the Court of Appeal case of *Nettleship v Weston*.[13] In that case, the defendant asked the claimant, a friend and not a professional driving instructor, if he would give her driving lessons in her husband's car. After satisfying himself that the car was insured against risk of injury to a passenger, the claimant agreed to do so. During the lesson, the defendant stopped at a junction and then proceeded to turn left slowly. However, she failed to allow the steering wheel to return to its original position, the upshot of which was that the car travelled in a perfect curve, mounted the nearside pavement, and struck a lamppost. The claimant suffered a fracture knee, as a consequence. He sued the

6 Ibid at 475.

7 [1856] 11 Ex 781.

8 1943 AC 448 at 457.

9 *Hawkins v Coulsdon and Purley UDC* [1954] 1 QB 319 at 341 (per Romer LJ).

10 *AC Billings and Sons Ltd v Riden* [1958] AC 240 at 255 (per Lord Reid).

11 *London Passenger Transport Board v Upson* [1949] AC 155 at 173 (per Lord Wright). See also *Thorogood v Van den Berghs* [1951] 1 All ER 682 where Asquith LJ stated (at 691): '[A]n employer who has created or permitted a dangerous condition to arise is reasonably expected to foresee and provide against the possibility of injury resulting therefrom even though it results from the intermediation of an act of inadvertence by the employee and even though that act of inadvertence be of a character which cannot be precisely forecast and remains, in the event "unexplained".'

12 *Lang v London Transport Executive* [1959] 1 WLR 1168 at 1178 (per Havers J).

13 [1971] 2 QB 691.

defendant, claiming that she had breached the duty of care which she had owed to him. The trial judge dismissed the action, on the basis that the defendant was simply under a duty to do her best, and that she had discharged that duty in the circumstances. However, the Court of Appeal allowed the claimant's appeal. In essence, the court was of the view that in determining whether the defendant had attained the standard of care, which was demanded of her, no account should be taken of the fact that she was a learner driver. Megaw LJ (who dissented on a different point) stated[14] that the certainty of a general standard was preferable to the vagaries of a fluctuating standard.

Nettleship should be contrasted with the Australian case of *Cook v Cook*.[15] In that case, the defendant, who did not hold a driving licence, was invited to gain experience by driving in a car in which the plaintiff was a passenger. The plaintiff supervised the defendant. The defendant collided with a concrete post. The plaintiff was injured. The High Court of Australia held that the requisite standard of care, which was applicable, fell to be determined objectively. However, that standard was required to be adjusted, in order to meet the special relationship under which it arose. The special relationship between the plaintiff and the defendant transformed the relationship between driver and passenger in such a way that it was unreal to regard the relevant relationship as simply one of driver and passenger. In effect, the apposite standard of care which fell to be applied was circumscribed by that relationship, and was therefore that which could reasonably be expected of an unqualified and inexperienced driver. In other words, the requisite standard of care demanded of defendant fell to be modified by the defendant's personal attributes.

However, *Cook* was over-ruled in *Imbree v McNeilly*[16] and no longer represents the law of Australia.

The learning in *Nettleship* was applied in the Court of Appeal case of *Wilsher v Essex Area Health Authority*.[17] In that case, the claimant was an infant. He was born prematurely and was suffering from oxygen deficiency. A junior doctor wrongly inserted a catheter in a vein, rather than an artery. The baby was given too much oxygen and suffered physical harm. In deciding that the defendant health authority was vicariously liable for the harm caused by the negligence of the medical staff, the court stated that the standard of care which the law demanded of medical staff did not depend on the experience or lack of experience of a member of staff, but rather on the post which the doctor occupied.[18]

The objective test which is used to establish whether the duty of care has been breached applies, is of wide application, and extends to those in control of premises.

---

14 Ibid at 707.

15 (1986) 162 CLR 376.

16 (2008) 236 CLR 510.

17 [1987] QB 730.

18 *Wilsher* was followed in the Outer House case of *Andrews v Greater Glasgow Health Board* 2019 SLT 727. In that case, the deceased had died as a result of the negligence of a junior doctor. It was held that in determining the standard of care which the law demanded of the doctor his lack of experience was irrelevant. The standard of care fell to be judged by the post which the doctor occupied when the negligent act took place: at [107] per Lord Pentland.

For example in *Al-Najar v Cumberland Hotel (London) Ltd*[19] the claimants were guests at the defendants' hotel. One evening a thief entered the rooms where they were staying. He violently attacked and seriously injured the claimants. The claimants sued the defendants, arguing that they had breached their duty of care to protect them from the criminal acts of third persons. However, it was held that the hotel had not breached its duty of care to them. The defendants had taken all reasonable precautions to protect guests.[20] The defendants had acted as any other reasonable 4-star London hotel proprietor would have acted.[21] In the last analysis, the defendants had not breached their duty of care. They had simply been under a duty to take reasonable care to prevent the attacks on guests by intruders. The defendants were not under an absolute duty to prevent an attack.

Again, in the Court of Appeal case of *Wells v Cooper*[22] the claimant who was leaving the defendant's house via the back door was required to pull the handle hard in order to close the door. However, the handle came off in his hands. He fell and was injured. It had not been adequately secured to the door by the defendant, who was not a professional carpenter, but rather, an amateur. The court held the defendant had not breached his duty of care to the claimant. The defendant had been entitled to undertake the fixing of the handle to the door himself.[23] Furthermore, the standard of care by means of which the defendant fell to be judged was that of reasonably competent carpenter undertaking that task, not that of a professional carpenter.

In the earlier case of *Phillips v William Whiteley Ltd*[24] the claimant visited a jeweller in order to have her ears pierced. The claimant contracted an infection in an ear, since the jeweller had failed to take adequate precautions to sterilise his equipment. However, it was held that the defendants had not breached their duty of care to the claimant. The jeweller was simply under a duty to adopt the standard of care demanded of a jeweller, in terms of the precautions which he had taken. He was not to be judged by the standards one would demand of a surgeon.

Again, in the Court of Appeal case of the *Lady Gwendolen*[25] the claimants' vessel, which was transporting stout from Ireland to England, negligently collided with and sank another vessel. The claimants' main business was that of brewers. However, the court held that, in their capacity as shipowners, the appropriate standard of care which they were required to attain was that of a reasonable shipowner in the management and control of a vessel or fleet of vessels.[26] In judging whether the claimants had been negligent an objective test fell to be applied.[27]

More recently, in the Supreme Court case of *Darnley v Croydon Health Services NHS Trust*[28] the claimant presented himself at the defendant hospital's accident and

---

19 [2019] 1 WLR 5953.
20 Ibid at [229].
21 Ibid at [196].
22 [1958] 2 QB 265.
23 Ibid at 271 (per Jenkins LJ).
24 [1938] 1 All ER 566.
25 [1965] P. 294.
26 Ibid at 333 (per Sellers LJ).
27 Ibid at 345 (per Wilmer LJ).
28 [2019] AC 831.

emergency department with a suspected head injury. The receptionist informed the claimant that he would have to wait between four and five hours before being seen by a member of the medical staff. However, she did not inform him that he would be seen by a triage nurse within thirty minutes. The claimant waited nineteen minutes and then went home, since he was feeling ill. His condition deteriorated. He was taken back to hospital where he was operated upon to remove a haematoma. The claimant suffered permanent brain damage. It was held that the defendant owed the claimant a duty of care, and had also breached its duty, in that the receptionist had acted negligently. The standard of care which she was required to attain was set by an averagely competent and well-informed person, performing the function of a receptionist, at a department providing emergency medical care.[29]

The rule that one adopts an objective approach, in ascertaining whether the standard of care has been attained by the defender, is inflexibly applied. For example, in *Roberts v Ramsbottom*[30] the defendant suffered a stroke while driving his car. His ability to drive was impaired. Twenty minutes later his car collided with a car which was being driven by the claimant, who was injured. It was held that the standard of care, which was demanded of the defendant, was to be judged objectively. An impairment of judgement was irrelevant in judging the standard of care which fell to be applied. The defendant had continued to drive after becoming aware of his disability.[31] The standard of care applicable to the reasonably competent driver was applicable to the situation. The defendant was, therefore, liable.

However, in the Court of Appeal case of *Mansfield v Weetabix Ltd*[32] a lorry driver had been suffering from an illness, which impaired his mental capacity. The driver was unaware of his condition. During the course of a journey, his vehicle was involved in two incidents, by virtue of his driving erratically. Subsequently, his vehicle was involved in a minor accident with another vehicle. His vehicle then crashed into the claimant's shop, causing extensive damage. The court held that the relevant standard which fell to be applied was that of a reasonably competent driver who was unaware of his inability to drive.[33] The driver, therefore, had not breached the standard of care which the law demanded of him.[34]

However, if the defender is suddenly incapacitated, through no fault of his own, and injures someone, the defender is not liable.[35] Goudkamp and Nolan argue that to excuse the defender of negligence, in such circumstances, departs from the notion that one should inflexibly apply an objective standard, in determining the requisite standard of care required of the defender.[36] However, in the view of the authors, in such circumstances, the defender simply is not acting at all, and that, in the absence of an act (or failure to act where there is a duty to act) no one can incur liability in tort.

---

29 Ibid at [25].

30 [1981] 1 All ER 7.

31 Ibid at 16.

32 [1998] 1 WLR 1263.

33 Ibid at 1268.

34 See also *C(A Child) v Burcombe* [2003] CLY 3030.

35 *Dunnage v Randall* [2016] QB 639 at [127] per Vos LJ. See also *Waugh v James K Allen Ltd* 1964 SC (HL) 102.

36 *Winfield and Jolowicz on Tort* (20th edn) at 6.011.

That line of reasoning is consistent with the fact that a breach of duty in negligence consists of conduct that falls below the standard of the reasonable person.

Foreseeability of harm

Life is fraught with a multitude of risks, from crossing a road, to travelling on a train, to playing a round of golf, and to spectating at a football match. However, the law, in taking a realistic and practical approach, demands that the defender is simply under a duty to refrain from exposing the pursuer to reasonably foreseeable harm, as opposed to any harm, the occurrence of which is remote.[37] In the House of Lords case of *Bolton v Stone*,[38] Lord Porter stated: 'The quantum of danger must always be a question of degree. It is not enough that there is a remote possibility that injury might occur: the question is, would a reasonable man anticipate it?' Again, in *Bourhill v Young* Lord Macmillan stated:

> The duty to take care is the duty to avoid doing, or omitting to do anything the doing or omitting to do which may have as its reasonable and probable consequence, injury to others, and the duty is owed to those to whom injury may reasonably and probably be anticipated, if the duty is not observed.[39]

The question whether the defender has failed to reasonably foresee harm falls to be judged by the knowledge which a reasonable person would have possessed, at the time the accident took place, as opposed to how a reasonable person would have acted, with the benefit of hindsight. This point is illustrated in *Roe v Ministry of Health*.[40] In that case, in 1947, the claimant went into hospital for a minor operation. He was given a spinal injection by the anaesthetist. The fluid used for the injection was kept in an ampoule – that is, a very small glass container – which in turn was kept in a phenol solution. However, the phenol seeped into the ampoule through invisible cracks in its wall. At that time, it was not known that this was possible. The claimant was paralysed from the waist down. He sued the Minister of Health who was responsible for the hospital concerned. However, the claimant did not succeed, since the hospital had acted in a way in which any other reasonable hospital would have acted in the situation. The state of medical knowledge at the time was not such that the law imposed a duty on the defendant to act in any other way than it had done. In the last analysis, the anaesthetist had not been negligent.

However, whereas it is now firmly established that the defender falls to be judged by the standard of the reasonable man, in terms of the standard of care the law imposes, precisely *what* prophylactic or preventative measures are required of the defender, on any given occasion, is fact-sensitive and falls to be determined on a case-by-case basis. For example, in the House of Lords case of *Bermingham v Sher Bros*[41] a fire broke out in the defenders' warehouse. The fire brigade was called. The firemen obtained access to the attic floor by means of an internal staircase. The fire spread

[37] *Michaels v Browne and Eagle* [1955] 2 Lloyd's Rep. 433.

[38] [1951] AC 850 at 860. See also *Christmas v General Cleaning Contractors* [1952] 1 KB 141.

[39] 1942 SC (HL) 78 at 88.

[40] [1954] 2 QB 66.

[41] 1980 SC (HL) 67.

into the ceiling of the first floor. The ceiling, which was made of untreated hardboard, erupted in flames. The flames reached the staircase. Six of the seven firemen on the attic floor died from the effects of heat and suffocation. The widow of one of the firemen claimed that the occupiers of the warehouse owed the firemen a duty to take reasonable care for their safety. In particular, as far as the exercise of that duty was concerned, the occupier should have erected a screen separating the staircase from the first floor of the warehouse, in order to make the staircase a safe means of escape. The House held that the defenders did not owe the deceased a duty of care in law, on the grounds that the occupiers could not foresee the tactics which would be employed by the firefighters.[42] That was completely outwith the control of the occupiers. It would have been quite unreasonable to expect the occupier to foresee the course of events, and in particular, the probability that a particular means of egress would be used.

However, the defender should reasonably foresee that the disabled could be injured by the conduct of the former's activities, in the absence of relevant prophylactic measures. For example, in the House of Lords case of *Haley v London Electricity Board*[43] the defendant electricity board had dug a trench along a pavement. In order to guard the trench and to prevent pedestrians walking along the pavement, the Board's employees had placed a punner-hammer across the pavement. The long handle of the hammer stretched across the pavement and rested some two feet above the ground on some railings. The claimant was blind. His walking stick missed the sloping hammer. He tripped and fell. He was seriously injured as a result. It was held that the Board owed the claimant a duty of care. Furthermore, that duty had been breached. The Board should have foreseen the presence of blind persons on the pavement and should have taken requisite measures to protect or warn them of the relevant danger.[44]

In the earlier House of Lords case *Taylor v Glasgow Corporation*[45] which was cited in *Haley*, Lord Sumner stated that:

> [A] measure of care appropriate to the inability or disability of those who are immature, or feeble in mind or body, is due from others who know of, or ought to anticipate, the presence of such persons within the scope and hazard of their own operations.

Another example of the vulnerability of the individual being considered by the court in determining the standard of care required of the defender is seen in the House of Lords case of *Barber v Somerset County Council*.[46] In that case, the claimant, who was a school teacher, was employed at a local authority school. He suffered a mental breakdown and was unable to return to work. His employers knew that he had been suffering from stress and depression prior to his breakdown. However, they did nothing to help him. Given the fact that the defendants had either known, or ought to have known, of the claimant's problems, it was held that they ought to have initiated enquiries about his problems and attempted to ease them. It was held that the authority's failure to do so constituted a breach of duty of care.

---

[42] Ibid at 73 (per Lord Fraser).
[43] [1965] AC 778.
[44] Ibid at 797 (per Lord Evershed).
[45] 1922 SC (HL) 1 at 15.
[46] [2004] 1 WLR 1089.

In certain circumstances, the defender is placed under a duty to foresee that the unruly conduct of others may injure the pursuer, in the absence of relevant measures. For example, in *Hosie v Arbroath Football Club*[47] the pursuer was seriously injured when knocked down, and trampled upon, by a crowd at a football ground. The crowd had made a deliberate and concerted attack on a defective security gate, which eventually gave way. The defenders, the occupiers of the ground, were held liable on the grounds that it was reasonably foreseeable by the occupiers that an attempt might be used by an unruly crowd to force the gate, and that the collapse of the gate might pose a risk to the safety of the crowd.

Reid argues that the objective criterion set by the reasonable man or by the average level of intelligence may be harder to achieve for some individuals than others and, indeed, may be seen as imposing a form of strict liability on those individuals who genuinely had limited capacity accurately to assess hazards.[48]

Defender possessing superior skill, knowledge and so on

Whereas the law sets the standard of care objectively, in certain circumstances the courts are prepared to vary that standard, to consider the nature of the relationship between the defender and the pursuer. For example, in *Stokes v Guest, Keen and Nettlefold (Bolts and Nuts) Ltd*[49] the claimant's husband (the deceased) was employed as a tool-setter by the defendants at their factory. The deceased's work involved him leaning over machines in such a way as to bring the lower part of his body into contact with a film of mineral oil, the upshot of which was that his clothing became saturated with the oil. In 1965 the deceased developed cancer of the scrotum. He died in 1966. It was proved that the cancer had been induced by his exposure to mineral oil in the course of his work as a tool setter, and that his work with the defendants had played a part in the development of his condition. The claimant argued that the defendants either knew, or ought to have known, that contact with mineral oil gave rise to a risk of cancer and were negligent in failing to warn the deceased of the dangers to which he was exposed. It was further claimed that the defendants had failed to instruct him of the precautions which were required to be taken to detect and report the effects of the oil, and also failing to provide six-monthly examinations.

It was held, *inter alia*, that an employer was required to display the standard of care which one would expect of the reasonable and prudent employer.[50] However, where the employer had greater than average knowledge of the risks, he might be required to take more than the average or standard precautions. In the instant case, the defendants' medical officer was particularly well-qualified to advise his employers of the risks to which their employees were exposed. However, he had rejected, out of hand, periodic medical examinations of employees, despite such practice being recommended in a Ministry of Labour pamphlet.[51] He had also expressed the view that

[47] 1978 SLT 122.

[48] E Reid *The Law of Delict in Scotland* (Edinburgh University Press, 2022) at 10.07.

[49] [1968] 1 WLR 1776.

[50] Ibid at 1783 (per Swanwick J).

[51] Ibid at 1793.

the remedy lay in greater attention being paid by the workers to personal hygiene. However, personal hygiene would have had little effect on the detection of a cancer which the worker was incubating, from many years of previous exposure. In the last analysis, the defendants were held liable.[52]

However, the extent to which the law demands greater skill of the defender, who is possessed of superior qualifications, knowledge or experience, compared to that of his counterparts, represents a grey area of law. An authoritative decision of the Supreme Court is, therefore, required.

Children

Children are delictually responsible for their conduct. In the Inner House case of *Campbell v Ord and Maddison*[53] it was stated *obiter* that a child of four years of age could be capable of negligence in law. However, the law sets the requisite standard of care demanded of the child by reference to the age of the child in question.[54] The authority on this point derives mainly, but not exclusively, from cases concerned with the defence of contributory negligence which will be discussed in more detail later.[55] In the Privy Council case of *Yachuk v Oiliver Blais Co Ltd*[56] an employee of the defendant sold petrol to a child (aged seven), who burned himself with it. It was held that the standard of care which the law demanded of the child was set by reference to his age.[57] On the facts of the case, contributory negligence could not be imputed to the child. However, in *DE v S Garages Ltd*[58] an employee of the defendants sold petrol to the claimant (aged 13), who proceeded to burn himself, by misusing the petrol. He claimed that the defendants owed him a duty of care by selling him the petrol. By way of a defence, the former raised, *inter alia*, the defence of contributory negligence. The court held that the defendants owed the claimant a duty of care. However, the damages which the court awarded to the claimant fell to be reduced by one-third for contributory negligence.

The learning in *Yachuk* was approved *obiter* by Lord Robertson in *Fraser v Glasgow Corporation*.[59] In that case, a car had been left parked in a street in Glasgow. Its condition gradually deteriorated, until it was a write-off. The car had become a playground for children. A child, aged eight, was badly burned after he had dropped a piece of lighted paper into the petrol tank of the car. His mother sued the local authority on his behalf, claiming that they should have taken reasonable care to remove the car, on the grounds that it was obviously abandoned and constituted a hazard to children playing in the street. She failed in her action. However, Lord Robertson stated that had he found the defenders had been negligent, he would have rejected the defence of contributory negligence.

---

52 See also *Baker v Quantum Clothing Group Ltd* [2011] UKSC 17.

53 (1873) 1 R 149 at 153 (per Lord Cowan).

54 *Orchard v Lee* [2009] EWCA Civ 295; *Mullin v Richards* [1998] 1 WLR 1304.

55 See p.183 below.

56 [1949] AC 386.

57 See also *Galbraith's Curator v Stewart (No2)* 1998 SLT 1305.

58 2000, unreported.

59 1972 SLT 177 at 181 (affirmed by Inner House). See also *Wylie v Lilley* 1961 SLT (Notes) 33.

Again, in the Court of Appeal case of *Gough v Thorne*[60] the claimant, aged 13½ years was seriously injured while crossing a busy road. She had been beckoned to cross by the driver of a lorry, which had stopped to allow her to cross the road. She failed to observe if there was any oncoming traffic on the road. She was hit and injured by a car which had been driven by the defendant. In rejecting the defence of contributory negligence, Lord Denning MR stated that a child could only be found guilty of contributory negligence if he or she was of such an age as to be expected to take precautions for his or her own safety.[61]

HOW IS THE STANDARD OF CARE DETERMINED?

What factors does the court require to take into account in determining whether the defender has breached the required standard of care which the law imposes?

State of current knowledge

Where relevant, the court considers the state of current knowledge which pertains to the activity or task the defender was undertaking when he harmed the pursuer. The leading case is *Roe v Minister of Health*[62] which was discussed above.

Magnitude of risk

The greater the risk of injury, the greater are the precautions which the defender is required to take. In *Blyth v Birmingham Waterworks Co*[63] the defendant water board laid water mains which were 18 inches in depth. One year later, there was an extremely severe frost which penetrated the ground as far as the water mains. The water mains burst, and the flood damaged the claimant's premises. It was held that the defendant had not been negligent in laying the pipes, because it had taken reasonable precautions in the circumstances.

The leading modern case which illustrates the same point is the House of Lords case of *Bolton v Stone*.[64] There, the claimant, while standing in a quiet suburban highway which was situated outside her house, was struck by a cricket ball. She was injured. The ball had been struck from a cricket ground which was situated nearby. The claimant was 100 yards from the batsman when she was struck. The ball had cleared a 7-foot fence, which owing to a slope was 17 feet above the level of the pitch. The fence was about 78 yards from the batsman. Similar hits had occurred only about

[60] [1966] 1 WLR 1387.

[61] Ibid at 1390.

[62] [1954] 2 QB 66.

[63] [1856] 11 Ex 781.

[64] [1951] AC 850. However, in the Court of Appeal case of *Miller v Jackson* [1977] QB 966 cricket balls were hit from the defendant's ground six to eight times during one season, which constituted a breach of duty on the defendants' part.

six times in the previous 28 years.[65] It was held that since the likelihood of the injury occurring was small, the defendant had not broken its duty of care.[66]

Risk of serious harm

In determining the standard of care the law requires of the defender, the court considers not simply the likelihood of an accident occurring, but also the risk of serious injury (that is, its gravity) should an accident occur. The leading case on this point is the House of Lords case of *Paris v Stepney LBC*.[67] In that case, the claimant had only one good eye. He was struck in his good eye by a chip from a bolt. He claimed that his employers should have provided and also required him to wear goggles while conducting work. It was held that notwithstanding the fact that the claimant was just as capable of carrying out his work as a person with normal vision (and, therefore, the risk of an accident occurring was no greater than that in respect of a fully sighted person) it was necessary for employers, when considering which preventative measures should be taken, to consider the consequences of any accident occurring to the defendant.[68]

Utility of the defender's activities

The social utility, or usefulness, of the relevant activity in which the defender is engaging at the time the accident takes place is considered by the court. The greater the utility, the more likely it is that the court will hold that the relevant standard of care has been attained. For example, in the Court of Appeal case of *Daborn v Bath Tramways Motor Co Ltd*[69] the plaintiff was driving an ambulance with a left-hand drive. The vehicle was completely shut in at the back, the upshot of which was that she was unable to see anything behind her. She was unable to see a bus which was travelling behind her, and also that the driver was attempting to overtake her. As she was turning into a lane she collided with the bus and sustained serious injuries. The plaintiff brought an action against the defendants, namely the driver of the bus and his employers. The defendants unsuccessfully pled contributory negligence on the part of the plaintiff. Asquith LJ stated:

> [During] the war ... it was necessary for many highly important operations to be carried out by means of motor vehicles with left hand drives, no other vehicles being available. So far as this was the case, it was impossible for the drivers of such cars to give the warning signals which could otherwise properly be demanded of them. Meanwhile it was essential that the ambulance service should be maintained. It seems to me in those circumstances it would be demanding too high and an unreasonable standard of care from the drivers of

---

[65] Ibid at 859 (per Lord Porter).

[66] See also *Hilder v Associated Portland Cement Manufacturers Ltd.* [1961] 1 WLR 1434; *Lewis v Wandsworth LBC* [2020] EWHC 3205; *Brisco v Secretary of State for Scotland* 1997 SC 14 and *Gillon v Chief Constable of Strathclyde Police* 1996 Rep LR 165; *Zucci v Waitrose Ltd.* 30 March 2000 (unreported); *Whippey v Jones* [2009] EWCA Civ 452; *Tysall Ltd v Snowdome* [2007] CLY 4196; *Walker v Northumberland County Council* [1995] ICR 702.

[67] [1951] AC 367.

[68] See also *Walker v Northumberland County Council* [1995] ICR 702.

[69] [1946] 2 All ER 333.

> such cars to say to them: "Either you must give signals which the structure of your vehicle renders impossible, or you must not drive at all."

Again, in *Watt v Hertfordshire County Council*,[70] the claimant was a fireman. The fire station at which he was working received an emergency call that a woman was trapped under a lorry. Two of the claimant's colleagues threw a heavy jack onto the lorry in which they were to travel to the scene of the accident. However, the lorry was not equipped to carry such a jack. Jacks were normally transported to accidents in a purpose-made lorry. No such lorry was available at the time the emergency call was made. During the rescue journey, the jack rolled away from its original position on the lorry and injured the claimant. The Court of Appeal held that the duty of care which the defendant owed to the claimant had not been breached. In reaching its decision, the social utility of the journey, namely the rescuing of an injured person, was considered.

However, simply because the defender was participating in an activity which had some social worth or utility does not automatically exempt the defender from the need to take care. For example, in *Ward v London CC*[71] the driver of a fire engine, responding to an emergency call, drove through a red traffic light and injured the claimant at a road junction. It was held that the defendant could not use the fact that he was involved in a journey of social worth as an excuse for his breach of a duty of care to the claimant.[72]

The relevance of social utility in terms of the law of negligence was discussed in the Supreme Court case of *Tomlinson v Congleton BC*.[73] In that case, a local authority owned and occupied a public park in which there was an artificial lake. Swimming in the lake was prohibited. Relevant warning signs were displayed. On a hot day the claimant jumped into the lake and sustained serious injury. He claimed damages against the defendant, arguing that the accident had been caused by the negligence of the defendant, by reason of its breach of the duty of care which it owed to him under s2(2) of the Occupiers Liability Act 1957. That section provides that the common duty of care is a duty to take such care as is reasonable in all the circumstances of the case, to see that the visitor will be reasonably safe in using the premises for the purposes for which he is invited or permitted by the occupier to be there. Lord Hoffman stated:

> [The] question as to what amounts to such care as in all the circumstances of the case is reasonable, depends on assessing, as in the case of common law negligence, not only the likelihood that someone will be injured and the seriousness of the injury which may occur, but also the social value of the activity which gives rise to the risk, and the cost of preventative measures. These factors have to be balanced against each other.[74]

---

[70] [1954] 1 WLR 835.

[71] [1938] 2 All ER 341.

[72] See also *Wardell-Yerburgh v Surrey CC* [1973] RTR 46; *Purdue v Devon Fire and Rescue Service* [2002] EWCA Civ 1538. For a discussion of the relevance of social utility in relation to the standard of care see A Beever 'Negligence and Utility' (2017) 17 OUCLJ 85.

[73] [2004] 1 AC 46.

[74] Ibid at [34].

The recreational value of beaches was a factor which one required to consider in deciding whether it was reasonable to expect the defendant to destroy the beaches.[75]

Practicality of precautions

The easier it is to take measures to counteract the risk, in the particular circumstances concerned, the more likely the courts will decide that the appropriate duty of care has been breached. In the House of Lords case of *Latimer v AEC Ltd*[76] the floor of the defendant's factory was flooded during an exceptionally heavy rainstorm. Oil which was kept in troughs was washed on to the factory floor. The defendant put sawdust on the floor. However, there was not enough sawdust to cover the entire floor. The claimant, a factory worker, slipped on the floor and was injured. He sued the factory occupier. However, it was held that the defendant was not liable, on the grounds that he had taken all appropriate precautions, short of closing the factory.[77]

One can criticise the decision on the grounds that commercial profitability was given too much prominence by the court over the personal safety of employees.

Availability of resources

To what extent, if any, can the court consider the level of resources which the defender has at his disposal, when determining whether the standard of care has been breached? This issue fell to be determined by the court in *Walker v Northumberland County Council*.[78] In that case, the plaintiff suffered a nervous breakdown which had been caused by the strain of performing his professional duties as a local authority social worker. He sued his employer. The authority was held liable, on the basis that it had breached its duty of care to the claimant. In so deciding, Coleman J stated that the defendant could not shelter behind a policy not to increase staff.[79]

However, in certain situations, the courts seem willing to consider the defender's lack of resources. For example, in *Goldman v Hargrave*,[80] which concerned an action in nuisance and also negligence, a tree which was situated on the defendant's land was set alight by lightning. The defendant failed to effectively extinguish the fire. The ambient air temperature rose. Wind blew the fire to the plaintiff's property which was damaged. The Privy Council held that in deciding whether the defendant had breached his duty of care to the plaintiff, it considered it legitimate (given the fact that the nuisance had been foist on the defendant through no fault of his own) to judge the defendant in the light of his individual circumstances, as opposed to those of a hypothetical landowner.

The learning in *Goldman* was approved by the Court of Appeal in *Leakey v National Trust for Places of Historic Interest or Natural Beauty*.[81]

[75] Ibid at [42].
[76] [1953] AC 643.
[77] See also *Walker v Northumberland County Council* [1995] ICR 702.
[78] [1995] ICR 702.
[79] Ibid at 721.
[80] [1967] 1 AC 645.
[81] [1978] QB 849.

CUSTOM AND PRACTICE

The extent to which the defender was conforming with common practice at the time the accident took place is a factor which the court considers in determining whether the defender has breached the standard of care which the law demands of him.[82] In *Baker v Quantum Clothing Group Ltd*[83] Lord Mance stated that an employer could rely on his conforming to a recognised and established practice, to exonerate himself from liability in negligence, for failing to take further steps, unless the practice was clearly bad or, where in the light of developing knowledge about the risks involved in some location or operation, a particular employer had acquired greater than average knowledge of the risks. However, the fact that the defender has complied with trade practice is not conclusive evidence that his conduct is not negligent.[84] That is to say, that the court is required to decide on all the evidence before it, whether the defender has been negligent.[85]

The Bolam principle

It has just been stated that the courts have held that the defender may be held to have acted negligently, notwithstanding the fact that he has conformed to the relevant general practice. However, the English courts have recognised an important exception to that rule, which is known as the *Bolam*[86] principle. The rule applies to 'professionals'. However, the term 'professional' is vague and indeed defies attempts at precise definition. The bulk of cases where the *Bolam* principle has been invoked concern negligence claims against medical practitioners. However, the application of the principle is not confined to medics.[87] When the principle applies the defender will not have breached the duty of care which the law demands of him, provided he acts in conformity with the practice supported by a reasonable body of opinion within that profession. The upshot of this is that if there are conflicting views as to how a professional should act in a particular situation, the defender has not breached the duty of care which the law demands of him, if he has acted in conformity with the practice of one body. The application of the *Bolam* principle therefore obviates the need for the court to choose between competing views. Goudkamp and Nolan argue that the *Bolam* principle is objectionable, in that it involves an abdication by the courts of their responsibility to determine the amount of care that the law requires people to exercise.[88]

Shortly before *Bolam* was decided the issue of negligence, in a medical context, came before the Inner House in *Hunter v Hanley*.[89] In that case, the pursuer had

[82] See for example *Brown v Rolls Royce Ltd* 1960 SC (HL) 22; *Gray v Stead* [1999] 2 Lloyds Rep. 559; *Morton v William Dixon* 1909 SC 807; *Powell v Phillips* [1972] 3 All ER 864.

[83] [2011] 1 WLR 1003 at para. [21].

[84] *Cavanagh v Ulster Weaving Co Ltd* [1960] AC 145; *Baker v Quantum Clothing Group Ltd* [2011] 1 WLR 1003.

[85] *Brown v Rolls Royce Ltd* 1960 SC (HL) 22 at 28, 29 (per Lord Denning).

[86] *Bolam v Friern Hospital Management Committee* [1957] 1 WLR 582.

[87] See for example *Natixes S.A. v Marex Financial* [2019] EWHC 2549.

[88] *Winfield and Jolowicz on Tort* (20th edn) (Sweet and Maxwell, 2020) at 6.027.

[89] 1955 SC 200.

sustained injury as a result of the breaking of a hypodermic needle, while she was receiving an injection. She claimed that this had been caused by the negligence of a doctor failing to exercise the standard of care and competence which it was his duty to display, in giving the injection. Lord Clyde stated that in order to establish liability by a doctor, where deviation from normal practice was alleged, three facts required to be established:[90]

> First, it must be proved that there is a usual and normal practice; secondly it must be proved that the defender has not adopted that practice; and thirdly (and this is of crucial importance) it must be established that the course the doctor adopted is one that no man of ordinary skill would have taken if he had been acting with ordinary care.

The question which falls to be answered is to what extent, if any, is there a substantive difference between the *Hunter* test and the *Bolam* test? Whereas *Hunter* refers to 'no man of ordinary skill' *Bolam* refers to a practice supported by a 'reasonable body of opinion'. However, the difference between the tests is nice at best, and at worse, simply one of semantics. In the last analysis, the courts have not been willing to distinguish between the tests.[91]

In the House of Lords case of *Bolitho v City and Hackney Health Authority*[92] we see the court reasserting its right to decide whether the defendant was negligent. In that case, a child experienced breathing difficulties while in hospital. A nurse contacted the doctor in charge by telephone. The doctor did not attend. The child apparently recovered without the doctor having attended. Later that day, the child collapsed owing to the failure of its respiratory system, which resulted in him suffering a cardiac arrest. By the time his respiratory and cardiac functions were restored, he suffered brain damage. The plaintiffs claimed that a competent doctor would have arranged for prophylactic intubation, in order to provide an airway, and that this treatment would have prevented a cardiac arrest and subsequent brain injury. The trial judge held that since the doctor had acted in accordance with a body of responsible medical opinion, the duty of care had not been breached. The Court of Appeal upheld that decision. On appeal to the House of Lords, Lord Browne-Wilkinson stated that before the court accepted the views of exponents of the body of opinion relied upon, the court was required to be satisfied that such an opinion had a logical basis.[93]

Another exception to the *Bolam* principle was recognised in the context of medical negligence in the Supreme Court case of *Montgomery v Lanarkshire Health Board*.[94] In that case, the pursuer gave birth to a child which was born with severe disabilities. She claimed, *inter alia*, that she should have been given advice about the potential harm to her child if she had a normal delivery, and also about the possibility of alternative delivery by elective caesarean section. The court held that a doctor had a duty to take reasonable care to ensure that a patient was aware of material risks of

[90] Ibid at 206.

[91] See for example *Montgomery v Lanarkshire Health Board* 2015 SC (UKSC) 63; *McCulloch v Forth Valley Health Board* 2023 SC (UKSC) 91.

[92] [1998] AC 232.

[93] Ibid at 242. See also *Honisz v Lothian Health Board* [2006] CSOH 24.

[94] [2015] UKSC 11.

injury that were inherent in the relevant treatment.[95] In that respect, a fundamental distinction fell to be drawn between the doctor's role when considering possible investigatory or treatment options and, on the other hand, his role in discussing with the patient any recommended treatment and possible alternatives, and the risk of injury which might be involved.[96]

Emergency situations (agony of the moment)

If the defender is placed in a sudden emergency situation, which is not of his own creation, his actions must be judged in the light of those circumstances. For example, in the Court of Appeal case of *Marshall v Osmond*,[97] the claimant (a suspect) was struck by a police car as the claimant left his vehicle to make an escape. It was held that the police officer who was driving the police vehicle had not breached his duty of care to the claimant.

Again, in the Privy Council case of *Ng Chun Pui v Lee Chuen Tat*[98] the driver of a coach (which was owned by the defendants) lost control of his vehicle when another vehicle cut across his path. The coach collided with a bus, which was carrying passengers, who brought proceedings against the defendants. It was held that, in determining whether the driver was negligent, one was required to take into account the emergency in which the driver had been placed.[99]

Res ipsa loquitur

Res ipsa loquitur is an evidential device which the pursuer can avail himself of in attempting to prove that the defender has been negligent. The phrase literally means 'let the facts speak for themselves'. Whereas *res ipsa loquitur* is sometimes referred to as a doctrine, this terminology was criticised in the Court of Appeal case of *Lloyde v West Midlands Gas Board*[100] by Megaw LJ who stated that *res ipsa loquitur* was 'no more than a common-sense approach, not limited by technical rules, to the assessment of the effect of evidence in certain circumstances'. The judge went on to state:

> [*Res ipsa loquitur*] means that a plaintiff establishes negligence where: (i) it is not possible for him to prove precisely what was the relevant act or omission which set in train the events leading to the accident; but (ii) on the evidence, as it stands at the relevant time, it is more likely than not that the effective cause of the accident was some act or omission of the defendant, or of someone for whom the defendant is responsible, which act or omission constitutes a failure to take proper care for the plaintiff's safety.

In short, the very occurrence of the event tells its own story, and is also indicative of fault on the part of the defender.[101] The exact cause of the accident must be

---

95 Ibid at [82].
96 See also *Duce v Worcester Acute Hospitals NHS Trust* [2018] EWCA Civ 1307.
97 [1983] QB 1034.
98 (1988) 132 Sol Jo 1244.
99 See also *Christian v South East London and Kent Bus Co* [2014] EWCA Civ 944.
100 [1971] 1 WLR 749 at 755.
101 See for example *Woodhouse v Lochs and Glens (Transport) Ltd* 2020 SLT 1203

unexplained for the maxim to operate. In *Roe v Minister of Health*[102] Morris LJ stated that *res ipsa loquitur* was generally a short way of saying:

> I submit that the facts and circumstances which I have proved, establish a *prima facie* case of negligence against the defendant.

In other words, the pursuer proves the result, not any particular act or omission producing the result.[103]

The circumstances in which the doctrine can operate are restricted. The leading case is *Scott v London and St Katherine Docks Co*.[104] In that case, Scott was a customs officer. While lawfully walking past a warehouse he was hit by six bags of sugar. The bags were being lowered from an upper floor of the warehouse to the ground, by means of a crane. The area where the officer was working had not been fenced off, and no warning had been given. Erle CJ stated:

> There must be reasonable evidence of negligence. But where the thing is shown to be under the management of the defendant or his servants, and the accident is such as in the ordinary course of things does not happen if those who have the management, use proper care, it affords reasonable evidence in the absence of explanation by the defendants, that the accident arose from the want of care.[105]

Res ipsa loquitur is, therefore, a rule of evidence to the effect that in the absence of explanation by the defendants, the relevant accident does not occur without negligence on the part of the defendants. In the Supreme Court case of *David T Morrison and Co Ltd v ICL Plastics Ltd*[106] Lord Hodge approved[107] the dictum of Toulson LJ in the Court of Appeal case of *Smith v Fordyce*[108] in which the latter stated:

> The doctrine expressed in the maxim *res ipsa loquitur* is a rule of evidence based on fairness and common sense. It should not be applied mechanistically, but in a way which reflects its underlying purpose. The maxim encapsulates the principle that in order for a claimant to show that an event was caused by the negligence of the defendant, he need not necessarily be able to show precisely how it happened. He may be able to point to a combination of facts which are sufficient, without more, to give rise to a proper inference that the defendant was negligent.

Therefore for the maxim of *res ipsa loquitur* to apply:

1. There must be an absence of explanation.
2. The thing which caused the damage must be under the control of the defender or his servants.
3. The accident must be of a type which does not normally occur in the absence of negligence.

---

102 [1954] 2 QB 66 at 87.
103 *Clerk and Lindsell on Torts* (24th edn) at 7-208.
104 (1865) 3 H & C 596.
105 Ibid at 601.
106 2014 SC (UKSC) 222.
107 Ibid at [98].
108 [2013] EWCA Civ 320 at [61].

The absence of reasonable explanation

In order that the doctrine can be brought into play, there must be no explanation as to how the accident occurred. In the Inner House case of *Milne v Townsend*[109] Lord Adam observed that 'the *res* can only speak as to throw the inference of fault upon the defender in some cases where the exact cause of the accident is unexplained'. Again, in the House of Lords case of *Devine v Colvilles Ltd*[110] the pursuer was employed by the defendants at their Ravenscraig steelworks. The pursuer had jumped from a platform and had injured himself, following a violent explosion. The explosion had occurred in a hose which carried oxygen. The defenders were able to demonstrate that the likely cause of the explosion was the presence of dust particles in the flow of oxygen. However, that explanation did not establish that the defenders were not negligent, in that they had failed to demonstrate that they had exercised due care to prevent such particles gaining access to their plant. Therefore, the *res ipsa* doctrine applied.[111]

However, *Devine* was distinguished in *McQueen v The Glasgow Garden Festival (1988) Ltd*.[112] In that case, a spectator was struck by part of a steel launching tube which fragmented when a firework exploded within it during a fireworks display. It was agreed between the parties that the explosion had been caused by a defect within the firework which had caused it to explode on the ground rather than while airborne. The pursuer raised an action against the organiser of the display. She claimed, firstly, that the company were occupiers of the fireworks display area and, as such, were responsible for the detonation of dangerous articles, such as fireworks, in that area. Secondly, she claimed that fault on the part of the company was established by the doctrine of *res ipsa loquitur* by virtue of the bursting of the launching tube or explosion of the firework under the management of the company, being the *res* demonstrating fault. However, it was held that it was established that the explosion had been caused by a latent defect in the firework, and was not indicative of fault or omission on the part of the defenders. Rather, it was indicative of fault on the part of the manufacturer of the firework. In short, the cause of the accident had been explained. Therefore, the *res ipsa* doctrine could not be invoked against the defender.

If the defender can demonstrate a way in which the accident may have occurred without fault on his part, the cogency of the fact of the accident by itself disappears and the pursuer is left as he began, namely in such a position that he has to show negligence.[113] Similarly, if the cause of the accident is proved the *res ipsa* doctrine is redundant.[114] Again, if the cause of the accident is known, the *res ipsa* doctrine is

109 (1892) 19 R 830 at 836.
110 1969 SC (HL) 67.
111 See also *George v Eagle Air Services Ltd* [2009] 1 WLR 2133.
112 1995 SLT 211.
113 *Ballard v North British Railway Co* 1923 SC (HL) 43 at 54 (per Lord Dunedin). The majority of the House dissented from Lord Dunedin on a different point. See also *O'Hara v Central SMT Co.* 1941 SC 363.
114 *Barkway v South Wales Transport Co Ltd* [1950] 1 All ER 392 at 399 (per Lord Normand).

redundant.[115] In such cases, the burden of proof remains on the pursuer to prove that the accident had been caused by the negligence of the defender.[116]

The thing which caused the damage must be under the exclusive control of the defender

In order that the *res ipsa* doctrine can apply, the defender or his employees[117] requires to be in exclusive control of the thing which caused the relevant damage.[118] For example, in the Court of Appeal case of *Easson v LNER*[119] a child fell through the door of a train belonging to the defendant railway company, while the train was in motion. There was no evidence as to how the door opened. However, it was held that since the doors of the train were not continuously under the sole control of the defendant during the course of the journey, given the fact that passengers walk up and down corridors, the *res ipsa* doctrine did not apply.[120] Again, in the Inner House case of *McDyer v The Celtic Football and Athletic Club Ltd*[121] the pursuer was injured when a piece of wood fell from a canopy while he was in the defenders' stadium while attending a sporting event. The pursuer made no averments as to the cause of the accident. However, he relied on the principle of *res ipsa loquitur*. The court held that the *res ipsa* doctrine could apply to the facts of the case, given the fact that the defenders had exclusive occupation and control of the canopy from which the piece of wood fell.[122]

The accident must be of a type which does not normally occur in the absence of negligence

Common experience suggests that bags of sugar do not fall from hoists;[123] cranes do not collapse;[124]aircraft do not normally crash;[125] foreign objects are not normally found in food;[126] vehicles do not normally veer off course on the road;[127]and swabs are not left in a patient's body after an operation.[128] In the Court of Appeal case of

115 *Black v C B Richard Ellis Management Services Ltd* 2006 Rep LR 36.

116 *Ng Chun Pui v Lee Chuen Tat* [1988] RTR 298 at 301 (per Lord Griffiths).

117 *Cassidy v Minister of Health* [1951] 2 KB 343.

118 *Wing v London General Omnibus Co* [1909] 2 KB 652 at 663 (per Fletcher Moulton LJ). See also *Murray v Edinburgh District Council* 1981 SLT 253.

119 [1944] KB 421.

120 However, in the earlier case of *Gee v Metropolitan Railway Co* (1873) LR 8 QB 161 the plaintiff fell out of the defendant's train after he had applied slight pressure to a door which flew open shortly after the train had left a station. It was held that this could be evidence of negligence on the part of the railway company.

121 2000 SC 379.

122 Ibid at 386 (per the Lord President).

123 *Scott v London and St Katherine Docks Co* (1865) 3 H & C 596.

124 *Swan v Salisbury Construction Co Ltd* [1966] 1 WLR 204.

125 *George v Eagle Air Services Ltd* [2009] 1 WLR 2133.

126 *Chaproniere v Mason* (1905) 21 TLR 633.

127 *Milliken v Glasgow Corporation* 1918 SC 857; *Richley v Faull* (Richley, Third Party) [1965] 1 WLR 1454.

128 *Mahon v Osborne* [1939] 2 KB 14.

Ward v Tesco Stores Ltd[129] the plaintiff was injured when she slipped on a floor in the defendants' supermarket, after yogurt had spilled on the floor. It was held that the doctrine of *res ipsa* applied. Lawton LJ stated:

> The accident was of a type which does not happen if floors are kept clean and spillages are dealt with as soon as they occur. If an accident does happen because the floors are covered with spillage, then … some explanation should be forthcoming from the defendants to show that the accident did not arise from want of care on their part.[130]

Again, in the Court of Appeal case of *Cassidy v Ministry of Health*[131] the claimant suffered from Dupuytren's contracture. He went into hospital for an operation to treat two stiff fingers. Shortly after the operation, after a splint was removed from his lower arm and hand, it was discovered that his hand was virtually useless. He raised an action against the health authority. In order to prove negligence on the part of the latter, he relied on the *res ipsa* doctrine. Denning LJ stated,[132] as regards the claimant:

> I went into the hospital to be cured of two stiff fingers. I have come out with four stiff fingers, and my hand is useless. That should not have happened if due care had been used. Explain it, if you can.[133]

However, the *res ipsa* doctrine is now rarely successfully invoked in medical cases. Where a person claims to have suffered injury as a result of medical negligence, it is seldom obvious that the loss was caused by negligence on the part of the defender, in contrast to the inherent risk of the therapy. In short, the facts do not 'speak for themselves'. In the Court of Appeal case of *Ratcliffe v Plymouth and Torbay Health Authority*[134] the plaintiff went to the defendant's hospital for an operation. He was given a general anaesthetic and also a spinal anaesthetic to ease the pain he would suffer after the operation. The operation was a success. However, he was left with a neurological deficit on the right side from the waist downwards. He claimed damages for personal injury against the defendant, alleging negligence on the part of anaesthetist. At first instance his claim failed. On appeal, the plaintiff contended that his condition raised an inference of negligence on the part of the defendant which placed an onus of rebuttal on the latter. The court held that, whereas the *res ipsa* doctrine could apply in simple forms in medical cases (for example, when a surgeon cuts off the wrong foot or a patient wakes up during an operation in relation to which he had received a general anaesthetic), in practice, in contested medical cases, the evidence of the plaintiff which establishes the *res* is likely to be buttressed with expert medical evidence, to the effect that the matter complained of does not ordinarily occur, in the absence of negligence.[135] In other words, the application of the *res ipsa* doctrine is redundant.

---

129 [1976] 1 WLR 810.
130 Ibid at 814.
131 [1951] 2 KB 343.
132 Ibid at 365.
133 See also *Saunders v Leeds Western HA* [1993] 4 Med LR 355.
134 [1998] PIQR P170.
135 Ibid at 184 (per Brooke LJ).

The limitation of the *res ipsa* doctrine in non-medical cases is seen in *Stafford v Conti Commodity Services Ltd.*[136] In that case, an investor in the London commodities future markets gave the defendants, who were brokers, a substantial sum of money to invest on the market, after he had had a discussion with them. The commodities market was an unpredictable and rapidly changing market. The investor suffered a loss. He brought an action based on alleged negligence, on the part of the defendants. He relied on the *res ipsa* doctrine. He failed in his action, partly on the grounds that losses made on such an unpredictable market as the commodities market could not of themselves provide evidence of negligence on the part of a broker.[137] The *res ipsa* doctrine did not, therefore, apply.

136 [1981] 1 All ER 691.
137 Ibid at 697 (per Mocatta J).

Chapter 6

Factual Causation

After the pursuer has established that the defender owes him a duty of care, and that that duty has been breached, the former requires to prove that the defender's negligent conduct has caused harm to the pursuer. The courts rely on two main tests to determine whether the defender's negligence has caused harm to the pursuer. The first is the 'but for' test. The second is the material contribution test.

THE 'BUT FOR' TEST

In applying the 'but for' test the court ascertains whether, if the defender's conduct had not taken place, the pursuer would still have suffered the harm in question. In short, the court attempts to ascertain whether the defender's conduct was of any factual relevance, in relation to the harm which the pursuer sustained. The leading case which neatly illustrates the 'but for' test is *Barnett v Chelsea and Kensington Hospital Management Committee*.[1] In that case, three night-watchmen, including the claimant's husband, had drunk tea which had made them vomit. They went to the casualty department of the local hospital. The casualty officer was informed by a nurse about the men. However, he decided not to see them. Instead, he told them to go home and consult their own doctors. A few hours later, the claimant's husband died of arsenical poisoning. It was held that while the hospital owed the deceased a duty of care, and that it had acted negligently, the defendants were not liable since he would have died in any case. In other words, there was no causal link between the negligent conduct of the defendant hospital board and the harm which the deceased had sustained.

Again, in the House of Lords case of *The Empire Jamaica*[2] a collision was caused by the negligence of the officer who was on watch on the defendants' vessel. While there was no doubt that the owners of the ship were vicariously liable for the officer's negligence, under the relevant merchant shipping legislation, they were entitled to limit their liability if the collision was caused without their actual fault, or privity. As far as the owners of the ship were concerned, the only fault attributable to them was that the officer in charge did not hold the necessary mate's certificate. However, it was established that if the owners had indeed applied for such certificate, it would have

1 [1969] 1 QB 428. See also *Davies v Frimley Health NHS Foundation Trust* [2021] PIQR P14.
2 [1957] AC 386.

been granted. In other words, the lack of the certificate had not caused the damage in question. The defendants were, therefore, able to limit their liability.

Again, in the House of Lords case of *McWilliams v Sir William Arrol and Co Ltd*[3] a workman who was employed by the defenders was killed when he fell from a steel lattice tower which was in the course of erection. It was claimed by his widow that the defenders[4] were negligent in failing to provide him with a safety belt. The defenders were found to have been in breach of their duties to provide a safety belt. However, the pursuer failed in her action because the defenders proved that her husband would not have worn the harness in any event. In other words, the defenders' negligent omission was not the cause of his fall.

An illustration of the application of the 'but for' test, in a medical context, is seen in the House of Lords case of *Kay's Tutor v Ayrshire and Arran Health Board*.[5] In that case, Kay's son had been admitted to hospital with meningitis. He was negligently given an overdose of penicillin. Subsequently, he was found to be suffering from deafness. However, the House held that deafness was a very common *sequela* of meningitis. There was also no evidence to the effect that the deafness had been caused by the overdose. In short, there was no causal relationship between the overdose and the child's deafness. In other words, it could not be argued that, but for the overdose, the child would not have suffered deafness.

Again, in *Andrews v Greater Glasgow Health Board*[6] the deceased presented herself at a hospital with various symptoms, including stomach pains, diarrhoea, and vomiting. She was misdiagnosed and discharged later that day. Her condition deteriorated. She was returned to hospital the following evening. However, she died a few hours later. The court accepted the pursuer's claim that if the deceased's condition had been correctly diagnosed, she would have been given appropriate treatment. In short, but for the negligence of the hospital the deceased would have been successfully treated.

In order to succeed, the pursuer is required to prove a causal link between the defender's negligent conduct and his injury, on a balance of probabilities.[7] The burden of proof remains on the pursuer throughout the trial.[8]

Before concluding the discussion of the application of the 'but for' test, in terms of factual causation, mention should be made of the House of Lords case of *Chester v Afshar*.[9] In that case, the defendant, a neurosurgeon, advised the claimant to undergo a surgical procedure on her spine. However, the surgeon failed to tell her that the procedure carried a risk, even if the operation was carried out without negligence that she could suffer neurological damage. The claimant reluctantly consented to the procedure. She did sustain injury. She brought an action in damages against the defendant, in negligence. The trial judge found that the defendant had failed to warn

---

3 1962 SC (HL) 70.

4 The deceased's employers and the occupiers of the shipyard where the deceased had died.

5 1987 SC (HL) 145.

6 2019 SLT 727.

7 *Wardlaw v Bonnington Castings Ltd* 1956 SC (HL) 26; *Gregg v Scott* [2005] 2 AC 176 and *AW v Greater Glasgow Health Board* [2017] CSIH 58.

8 *Wilsher v Essex Area Health Authority* [1988] 1 All ER 871.

9 [2005] 1 AC 134.

the claimant of the small and unavoidable risk (that is, 1–2 per cent) of her sustaining neurological damage. The judge also found that, had the claimant been aware of the risk of damage, she would have sought advice on alternatives to surgery, and also that the operation would not have taken place when it did. However, the defendant had not been negligent in performing the operation. If the operation had taken place at a later date, the risk to the claimant would have remained the same. It was therefore improbable that she would have sustained any neurological damage. The judge held that there was a sufficient causal link between the defendant's failure to warn and the damage sustained by the claimant. That link was not broken by the fact that the claimant might have consented to surgery in the future. He concluded that the defendant was liable in damages. The Court of Appeal dismissed the defendant's appeal. The defendant appealed to the House of Lords. The appeal was dismissed by a bare majority.

It is instructive to compare the judgments.

Lord Bingham (dissenting) stated that the central question in the appeal was whether the conventional approach to causation in negligence should be varied where the claim was based on the doctor's negligent failure to warn a patient of a small (1–2 per cent) but unavoidable risk of surgery, when following surgery, performed with due care, such risk eventuated.[10] However, it was not shown that, if duly warned, the patient would not have undergone surgery with the same small, but unavoidable risk of mishap. After stating that the 'but for' test was a necessary, if not a sufficient, condition of establishing causation, Lord Bingham stated that, in the instant case, the test was not satisfied, in that the claimant had not established that 'but for' failure to warn, she would not have undergone surgery.[11] Her injury would have occurred, whenever the surgery was performed, and whoever performed it. However, for the judge, the essential question was whether the claimant was entitled to recover, notwithstanding the fact that she could not show that the defendant's negligence was a cause of her loss. After stating that, whereas a patient's right to be appropriately warned was an important right, the claimant's right should not be reinforced by awarding potentially very large damages for a violation of that right, not shown to have worsened the physical condition of the claimant,[12] Lord Bingham concluded that the defendant's appeal should be allowed.

Lord Steyn, in deciding in favour of the claimant, stated that as a result of the surgeon's failure to warn the patient, she could not be said to have given informed consent to the surgery, in the full legal sense.[13] Her right of autonomy and dignity could, and ought, to be vindicated by a narrow and modest departure from traditional causation principles. The claimant was entitled to succeed. That result was in accord with one of the most basic aspirations of the law, namely, to right wrongs.

Lord Hoffman (dissenting) stated that the purpose of the duty to warn someone against the risk involved in what he proposes to do, or allow to be done to him, is

---

[10] Ibid at 139–40.
[11] Ibid at 141.
[12] Ibid at 142.
[13] Ibid at 146.

to give him the opportunity to avoid or reduce that risk.[14] If he would have been unable or unwilling to take that opportunity, and the risk eventuates, the failure to warn has not caused the damage. It would have happened anyway. In the instant case, the claimant was required to prove that she would not have had the operation. The question which the court was obliged to answer was whether the claimant would have taken the opportunity to avoid the risk, not whether one would have changed the scenario in some irrelevant detail. The trial judge had found that the risk would have been precisely the same, whether it was done then or later, or by that competent surgeon or by another. Lord Hoffman stated that it followed that the claimant had failed to prove that the defendant's breach of duty had caused her loss. The defendant was, therefore, not liable.

Lord Hope stated that the question of law which required to be answered was whether it was sufficient for the claimant to prove that, if properly warned, the claimant would not in fact have consented to the operation which was in fact performed, and which resulted in her injury, or whether it was necessary for her to prove also that she would never have had the operation.[15] Lord Hope stated that whereas it could be said that the claimant would not have suffered the injury, but for the defendant's failure to warn her of the risks (as the claimant would have declined to be operated on, by him on the date the operation took place), it was difficult to say that his failure was the effective cause of the injury.[16] Lord Hope stated later that the 'but for' test was easily satisfied.[17] However, the risk of which she should have been warned was not created by the failure to warn. It already existed as an inevitable risk of the operative procedure itself, however skilfully and carefully it was carried out. The risk was not increased, nor were the chances of avoiding it lessened by what the defendant had failed to say about it. The judge stated that to expose someone to a risk to which that person is exposed anyhow is not to cause anything. The defendant's breach of duty did not cause the claimant's injury.[18]

Lord Hope then addressed the question whether in the unusual circumstances of the case, justice required the normal rules of causation to be modified. He stated that the function of the law was to enable rights to be vindicated and to provide remedies when duties had been breached. Therefore, on policy grounds, the test of causation had been satisfied in the instant case.[19] The injury was intimately involved with the duty to warn. The duty had been owed by the doctor who performed the surgery which the claimant had consented to. It was the product of the very risk she should have been warned about when she gave her consent. It can be regarded as having been caused, in the legal sense, by the breach of that duty. Justice required that the claimant be afforded a remedy. The injury which she suffered at the hands of the defendant was within the scope of the very risk which she should have been warned about, when he

14 Ibid at 147.
15 Ibid at 148.
16 Ibid 154–5.
17 Ibid at 161.
18 Ibid at 162.
19 Ibid at 163.

was obtaining her consent to the operation which resulted in that injury. The claimant was therefore entitled to succeed.

Lord Walker, in deciding in favour of the claimant, was of the view that the 'but for' test of legal causation was satisfied, since the claimant had sustained injury as a result of the operation she had on a particular day.[20] She had that operation on that occasion, simply because she had not been warned of the risks inherent in the operation.

For the majority, the 'but for' test of causation was satisfied, since the claimant would not have sustained harm on the particular day the operation took place if she had been warned of the risks inherent in the operation, notwithstanding the fact that the risks would have remained the same if the operation had been carried out in the future. However, for the majority, the claimant's right to be suitably informed was, in effect, a 'freestanding right' which the defendant had a duty to protect. Indeed, Stevens argues that the physical harm the claimant sustained was coincidental[21] to such a right.[22] By way of conclusion, the author would suggest that *Chester* was decided on its own special facts.[23] The decision requires to be reviewed by the Supreme Court.

THE MATERIAL CONTRIBUTION TEST

The pursuer may not be able to prove that he would not have suffered harm but for the negligent conduct of the defender. However, he may be able to satisfy a less exacting test, namely, the material contribution test, which is only applicable if the 'but for' test does not apply.[24] That is to say, that the pursuer may succeed if he can prove that the negligent conduct of the defender has materially contributed to the harm which he has sustained. For example, suppose A, B and C were neighbours. A negligently starts a fire on his premises, as does B on his premises. Both fires merge and destroy C's garden hut, although neither fire, of itself, has the capacity to cause such damage. However, either A or B, or both, would be liable, in terms of the law of negligence, if their respective negligent acts had materially contributed to the harm in question. In such circumstances, both A and B would be said to be jointly and severally liable for the harm which was caused. In the Court of Appeal case of *Bailey v Ministry of*

[20] Ibid at 166.

[21] In *Chester* Lord Walker stated (at 164) that the harm which the claimant had sustained was not coincidental, in that the harm which the claimant had sustained was the very misfortune which was the focus of the surgeon's duty to warn.

[22] R Stevens *Torts and Rights* (OUP, 2007) at 165. In the Court of Appeal case of *Duce v Worcester Acute Hospitals NHS Trust* [2018] PIQR P 18 at [88] Leggatt LJ categorised the right in respect of which the claimant in *Chester* was awarded damages for was the patient's right of autonomy and dignity. The judge goes on to argue that the invasion of such a right should be protected by an award of damages and not for the physical injury resulting from the operation. For a useful discussion of *Chester* see T Clark and D Nolan 'A Critique of *Chester v Afshar*' (2014) 34 OJLS at 659.

[23] In *White v Paul Davidson and Taylor* [2005] PNLR 15 the Court of Appeal declined to apply *Chester* in relation to a solicitor's negligent advice. Similarly, *in Beary v Pall Mall Investments* [2005] PNLR 35 the Court of Appeal declined to apply *Chester* in relation to negligent financial advice.

[24] *Zgonec v Pereira* [2025] EWCA Civ 171.

Defence[25] it was held that in order to materially contribute to the harm in question, the contribution must be more than negligible.[26]

The application of the test is well illustrated in the House of Lords case of *Wardlaw v Bonnington Castings Ltd.*[27] In that case, the pursuer's illness pneumoconiosis, which is a divisible disease (that is, the severity of the disease varies with the amount of dust which the pursuer had inhaled), was caused by an accumulation of disease in his lungs. The dust in question came from two sources. The defenders (Wardlaw's employers) were not responsible for one source. However, they could have prevented and were therefore negligent in relation to the other source (in other words, the 'illegal' source). The dust from the illegal source was not sufficient, in itself, to cause the disease. However, the pursuer succeeded in his action for damages, because the illegal source had made a material contribution to his illness. Lord Reid stated that whether or not the illegal source materially contributed to his disease was a question of degree.[28]

The learning in *Wardlaw* was taken further forward in the House of Lords case of *McGee v National Coal Board.*[29] In that case, the pursuer contacted dermatitis from the presence of brick dust on his skin. It was proved that some exposure to brick dust was the inevitable consequence of working with brick (that is, the 'legal source'). However, the employers had failed to provide washing facilities, in contravention of the relevant legislation (that is, the 'illegal source'). The pursuer was, therefore, forced to cycle each day with dust on his skin. However, whereas the pursuer could prove that the dermatitis was caused by the accumulation of brick dust on his skin, as a result of the two causes, he could not prove, on the basis of medical evidence, that the illegal source had contributed to his disease. The House held that the pursuer could succeed if he could prove that the state of affairs which had been brought about by the failure to provide the washing facilities, had materially increased the *risk* that the dermatitis might set in.

The Court of Appeal case of *Vernon v Bosley*[30] illustrates the application of the material contribution test. In that case, the defendant was carrying the claimant's daughters, as passengers, in a car which she was driving. The defendant drove the car negligently. The car crashed and fell into a fast-flowing river. The defendant managed to escape, but the children were trapped. The claimant, and his wife, were called to the scene of the accident, where they watched the rescue services make an abortive attempt to rescue the children. The children perished. The claimant claimed that he suffered nervous shock and psychological trauma, by reason of witnessing the immediate aftermath of the accident. The claimant further claimed that he had developed a post-traumatic stress disorder, which was complicated by a severe grief reaction which had been caused by the defendant's negligence. However, the defendant contended,

---

25 [2009] 1 WLR 1052.

26 Ibid at 1069 (per Waller LJ). See also *Tuffin v University Hospitals Coventry and Warwickshire NHS Trust* [2024] EWHC 3318 and *Kerr v Midlothian Council* 2025 SLT 268.

27 1956 SC (HL) 26.

28 Ibid at 621.

29 1973 SC (HL) 37.

30 [1997] 1 All ER 577.

inter alia, that the damage which the claimant had suffered had come about either wholly or partly as a result of his reaction to grief. The Court of Appeal held, following *Bonnington*, that where the claimant's injury was attributable to two possible causes, it was sufficient that the 'illegal' cause (here the nervous shock which stemmed from the claimant's witnessing the immediate aftermath of the accident) materially contributed to the injury in question.

The learning in *McGee* was taken further forward in *Fairchild v Glenhaven Funeral Services Ltd*.[31] In that case, Fairchild had been employed at different times, and for different periods, by more than one employer: E1 and E2. Both E1 and E2 had been under a duty to take reasonable care to prevent F from inhaling asbestos dust. However, both had failed to do so, as a consequence of which F contracted mesothelioma and died. The fundamental question which the House of Lords was required to answer was whether F could recover against E1 or E2, or both. On current limits of scientific knowledge F was unable to prove, on a balance of probabilities, that his mesothelioma was caused by his inhaling asbestos dust during his employment either by EI or E2, or both. Mesothelioma is an indivisible disease.[32] That is to say, that the severity of the disease is not proportionate to the extent of an individual's exposure to asbestos dust. The House held that in certain special circumstances, the court could depart from the usual 'but for' test of legal causation, and treat a lesser degree of causation as sufficient, namely that the defendant's breach of duty had materially contributed to causing the disease by materially increasing the risk that the disease would be contracted. *McGee* was, therefore, followed. Any injustice that might be involved in imposing liability in these circumstances was heavily outweighed by the injustice of denying redress to the victim. Lord Bingham stated:

> It can properly be said to be unjust to impose liability on a party who has not been shown, even on a balance of probabilities, to have caused the damage complained of. On the other hand, there is a strong policy argument in favour of compensating those who have suffered grave harm, at the expense of their employers, who owed them a duty to protect them against that very harm, and failed to do so, when the harm can only have been caused by breach of that duty, and when science does not permit the victim to accurately attribute, as between several employers, the precise responsibility for the harm suffered.[33]

The law was taken further forward in the House of Lords case of *Barker v Corus (UK) Ltd*.[34] In that case, it was held that on facts which were similar to those in *Fairchild* it was appropriate to apportion liability between the defendants, in accordance with the degree of risk to which they had exposed the claimant, by virtue of their negligence.

As far as liability in respect of mesothelioma is concerned, the Compensation Act 2006[35] reverses *Barker* and makes the person who is at fault jointly and severally liable (that is, *in solidum*) with any other person.

[31] [2003] 1 AC 32.

[32] For a discussion of an indivisible injury see *BAE Systems (Operations) Ltd v Konczak* [2018] ICR 1.

[33] Ibid at 67. C Whitting argues that the juristic basis for *Fairchild* is uncertain: *Street on Torts (*16th edn) (OUP, 2021) at 176.

[34] [2006] 2 AC 572.

[35] Section 3.

In both *Fairchild* and *Barker* the claimant employee was exposed to contamination from an illegal source, or sources, in a workplace. Indeed, the key requirement for potential liability on the part of the defendants was that all of the exposures were related to the claimant's employment, were due to breaches of duty by the claimant's successive employers, and also that it was impossible to prove which exposure, if any, had caused the disease. However, in *Sienkiewicz v Greif*[36] the question which fell to be answered by the House of Lords was whether the learning in *Fairchild* and *Barker* was applicable to a situation where only one source to which the claimant had been exposed was work-related, and the other was not.

In *Sienkiewicz* the claimant's mother had been exposed to asbestos dust between 1966 and 1984, during the period of her employment with the defendant. However, due to the location of her home, the deceased had also been exposed to low levels of asbestos in the general environment. Of the two sources, the latter was the more significant. Indeed, the tortious exposure had increased the risk of her contracting mesothelioma, by only 18 per cent. The House held that the learning in *McGhee*, *Fairchild* and *Barker* applied to the facts of the case. Therefore, the defendant was liable, in full, for the harm which the claimant's mother had sustained. According to Lord Phillips[37] the underlying premise, in the decisions in both *Fairchild* and *Barker*, was that it was not possible to determine causation, unless medical science allowed one to do so with certainty. The judge added that the law of causation did not deal in certainties. It dealt in probabilities. Lord Phillips went on to state[38] that both *Fairchild* and *Barker* developed the common law by equating 'materially increasing the risk' with 'contributing to the cause', in specified and limited circumstances, which included ignorance, and how causation of fact occurred. The law was capable of further development.

The Court of Appeal was required to decide whether the so-called '*Fairchild*' exception to the rules of causation applied to lung cancer, as opposed to mesothelioma, in *Henaghan v Manchester Dry Docks Ltd*.[39] In that case, the deceased, who had died of lung cancer, had been exposed to asbestos, *inter alia*, while he was employed successively by six employers (the defendants). However, biological evidence could not establish which (if any) of the exposures had triggered the cell changes in his body which had led to his contracting cancer. Lung cancer is an indivisible disease. However, statistical evidence could establish by how much the exposure, by each defendant, had increased the risk the deceased would contract the disease. The question which the court was required to answer was how the law should deal with the issue of causation between the claimant and each defendant, in these circumstances. At first instance, the trial judge applied the so-called '*Fairchild* exception', and had awarded damages against each defendant, in proportion to the increase of risk for which it was responsible. The claimant appealed. He argued that the trial judge should have held that since each defendant had materially contributed to the cancer, each defendant was liable for damages in full.

36 [2011] 2 WLR 523.
37 Ibid at 544.
38 Ibid at 548.
39 [2016] 1 WLR 2036.

It was agreed between the parties that the claimant's risk of developing lung cancer was increased by smoking, and also by asbestos exposure, and that on the balance of probabilities, he would not have developed the lung cancer if he had not been exposed to asbestos. It was also agreed that the risk that lung cancer would develop increased with the amount smoked and with the dose of asbestos received. Furthermore, it was agreed that if lung cancer did develop, the duration and severity of symptoms and the eventual outcome were not affected by the amounts of smoking or asbestos exposure, which had led to that increase in risk.

Lord Dyson MR stated that epidemiological evidence could establish that the deceased's exposure to asbestos had caused his cancer.[40] That was the case because such evidence established that the relative risk of cancer having been caused by exposure to asbestos was greater than 2:1. That is to say, that such risk was doubled. The court then addressed the question, in a multi-contributor case, of which contributor's asbestos had caused the cancer.[41] Lord Dyson stated that it could not be proved that the exposure, which was attributable to any individual defendant, had doubled the risk that the claimant would develop lung cancer. The judge stated that lung cancer was similar to mesothelioma in that lung cancer was an indivisible disease, whose severity did not depend on the extent of the exposure to asbestos. The judge went on to state[42] that in a case where scientific evidence did not permit a finding that the exposure, which was attributable to a particular defendant, contributed to the injury, one should apply the *Fairchild* exception. The factors which were identified in *Fairchild* existed in the instant case. That is to say, firstly, all defendants had conceded their breach of duty. Secondly, all parties had increased the risk that the deceased would contract lung cancer. Thirdly, all defendants had exposed the deceased to the same agency, which was implicated in the causation, namely asbestos fibres. Fourthly, medical science was unable to establish to which, if any, of the defendants there should be attributed the exposure, which actually caused the cell changes which initiated the genetic changes, culminating in the cancer.

Lord Dyson MR concluded that there was no reason not to apply the *Fairchild* exception to the facts of the instant case. There was no objection, in principle, in extending *Fairchild* to situations which were not materially different from *Fairchild*'s case. Indeed, principle required that in a situation which was truly analogous to that considered in that case, the *Fairchild* exception should be applied. Otherwise, the law in that area would be inconsistent and incoherent.

Thus far, what has been discussed is a situation where several factors (one or more of which may be attributable to the fault of the defender) operate concurrently, the upshot of which is that the pursuer either sustains harm or is exposed to an increased risk of harm. However, to what extent, if any, does the material contribution test apply to events which occur successively?

---

[40] Ibid at 2040.

[41] Ibid at 2041.

[42] Ibid at 2051.

The Privy Council was required to answer this question in *Williams v Bermuda Hospitals Board*.[43] In that case, the claimant ('W') had gone into the defendant's ('B') hospital, suffering from acute appendicitis. A decision was taken to scan his abdomen. There was a delay of over four hours between the doctor ordering the scan and the scan being performed. W had an appendectomy the same day. However, there were complications, causing injury to his heart and lungs, as a result of which sepsis developed incrementally, over a period of about six hours, prior to the operation. The plaintiff sought damages from the defendant hospital board, on the grounds that the complications were the result of the negligent delay in his treatment. The trial judge had found that there had been a culpable delay of at least 140 minutes prior to the operation. However, he held that the plaintiff had not proved that the delay had caused the complications. He, therefore, only awarded damages for the plaintiff's extra suffering during the period of culpable delay, prior to the operation.

The Court of Appeal for Bermuda allowed the plaintiff's appeal, holding that the breach of duty by the defendant had materially contributed to the plaintiff's injury. The defendant's appeal to the Privy Council was dismissed. The Board (speaking through Lord Tolson) held that where, on the balance of probabilities, an injury had been caused by two or more factors operating cumulatively, one or more of which was a breach of duty, it was immaterial whether the cumulative factors operated concurrently or successively. Successive events were capable of each making a material contribution to the subsequent outcome.[44] The trial judge had found that the injury to the plaintiff's heart and lungs had been caused by a single known agent, namely sepsis, and that its development and effect on the heart and lungs had been a single continuous process which had continued for a minimum period of 140 minutes longer than it should have done.[45] It was right, therefore, to infer on a balance of probabilities that the defendant's negligence had materially contributed to the process. In the last analysis, the Board held that the defendant's negligence had materially contributed to the injury to the plaintiff's heart and lungs.[46]

In reaching its conclusion, in favour of the plaintiff, the Board made brief reference[47] to the 'doubling the risk' test, which had sometimes been used or advocated as a tool in deciding questions of causation. However, the Board cautioned against the use of this test.[48]

The learning in *Williams* was applied in *John v Central Manchester and Manchester Children's Hospitals NHS Foundation Trust*.[49] In that case, the claimant had suffered a head injury. He was taken to a hospital which was managed by the defendant. A CT scan was performed six hours after his admission. He was subsequently transferred to another hospital, where he underwent surgery. The claimant claimed, *inter alia*,

[43] [2016] 2 WLR 774. For a discussion of *Williams* see S H Bailey, 'Material Contribution after *Williams v The Bermuda Hospitals Board*' (2018) 38 LS 411.
[44] Ibid at [39].
[45] Ibid at [42].
[46] See also *Andrews v Greater Glasgow Health Board* 2019 SLT 727.
[47] Ibid at [48].
[48] For a commentary on *Williams*, see J Stapleton and S Steel 'Causes and Contributions' (2016) 132 LQR 363.
[49] [2016] 4 WLR 54.

that the delay by the defendant in performing the brain scan had resulted in a period of raised intra-cranial pressure which had caused, or had materially contributed to, the brain damage which he had suffered. The defendant contended that only if the claimant could establish that damaging raised intra-cranial pressure, caused by the defendant's negligence, had caused his brain injury (by applying the classic 'but for' test of causation) could he recover against the defendant. In other words, it was insufficient to establish that the negligent act of the defendant had materially contributed to his injury.

However, Pickin J rejected that argument. In other words, the material contribution test was the appropriate test to apply.[50] The judge drew a distinction between first, what was an appropriate test in a case such as *John*, which concerned material contribution to injury, or damage, and second, a case which had as its focus risk rather than injury or damage. As far as the second was concerned, there required to be a single agent. As far as the first was concerned, the material contribution approach applied to both single agency and multiple factor cases. Therefore, the claimant was entitled to recover for the entirety of his injuries, without apportionment or deduction.[51]

The application of the material contribution test fell to be applied in *Thorley v Sandwell and West Birmingham Hospitals*.[52] In February 2002, the claimant ('T') was diagnosed with atrial fibrillation, which is a condition which causes an increased risk of blood clots and other medical conditions, including a stroke. T was prescribed warfarin, which is an anticoagulant. In March 2005, T suffered chest pain. On 27 April T was given a coronary angiogram, immediately after which he was discharged, on the grounds that the angiogram was uneventful. Shortly before being given the angiogram, T was advised to stop taking warfarin, between 23 and 28 April, because of the bleeding risk in that procedure. He restarted taking the warfarin at a reduced dose, on 29 April. However, on 30 April T suffered a severe stroke, which resulted in permanent and severe physical and cognitive disability.

T alleged that the defendant NHS Trust, ('S') had been negligent, in that the cessation of the warfarin should have been limited to the three-day period, namely, 24–26 April (incl) and then restarted at the full dose, no later than the day after the angiogram (that is, 28 April). T alleged that S had been negligent, on this basis. T further claimed that S's negligence had caused or materially contributed to his stroke. S admitted that the full warfarin dose should have been restarted after the angiogram. However, S claimed that T would have suffered a stroke, in any event. The trial judge, Soole J, held that S had not been negligent, beyond the extent which the trust admitted.[53] In the last analysis, it had not breached its duty of care to T.

However, the judge went on to address the issue of causation, in relation to T's stroke. The judge held that even if the omission of the warfarin for a period of more than three days did constitute a breach of duty, since T would have suffered a stroke in any event, he could not successfully rely on the 'but for' test of causation.[54] The

[50] Ibid at [97].
[51] Ibid at [105].
[52] [2021] EWHC 2604.
[53] Ibid at [80].
[54] Ibid at [137].

judge went on to conclude that the material contribution test had no application where there was a single tortfeasor and an indivisible injury.[55]

However, *Thorley* must be reconsidered in light of the recent Court of Appeal case of *Holmes v Poeton Holdings Ltd*.[56] In that case, the claimant had worked for the defendant 'Poeton' between 1982 and 2020. In 2014 he was diagnosed with Parkinson's disease. The claimant claimed damages, on the grounds that the defendant had breached its common law and statutory duty between 1982 and 1997 by exposing him to unsafe levels of trichloroethyline (TCE) in the course of his employment. At first instance, the trial judge found that the defendant was liable to the claimant for all the consequences of his having contracted the disease. In short, the claimant was awarded 100 per cent damages. The defendant appealed, on the grounds that the judge had applied the wrong test of causation for establishing causation in respect of an indivisible disease.

The defendant claimed, *inter alia*, that the evidence could only establish that the TCE may have caused an elevation of the risk of the claimant developing the disease. Furthermore, the defendant submitted that the doctrine of material contribution did not apply in cases of indivisible conditions. In short, the claimant required to establish the basis 'but for' test of causation but was unable to do so. The judge then rejected the defendant's submission that the material contribution test had no application in relation to an indivisible disease. He held that the claimant had been exposed to levels of TCE in his employment with the defendant which had amounted to a breach of duty and that such exposure had made a material contribution to the development of the claimant's Parkinson's disease. The defendant appealed.

The defendant argued, *inter alia*, that the trial judge had applied the wrong test for proving causation, namely that it was sufficient, in an invisible injury case, to demonstrate material contribution to the injury, regardless of whether but for the tort, the injury would have occurred in any event.[57]

Stuart Smith LJ stated that the appeal raised complex and difficult questions of law in an area which had been bedevilled by apparent inconsistency and imprecision at the highest levels on multiple occasions.[58] The judge went on to reject the defendant's submission that the learning in *Bonnington* was only applicable to cases involving divisible injury.[59] In short, such learning applied to cases involving indivisible injury.[60]

What requires to be discussed now is whether the rules governing factual causation, which were applied in the above cases, are applicable in a non-medical context

[55] Ibid at [151]. See also *Ministry of Defence v AB* [2010] EWCA Civ. 1317 at [150] per Lady Justice Smith. See also *Davies v Frimley Health NHS Foundation Trust* [2021] PIQR P 14.

[56] [2023] EWCA Civ 1377.

[57] Ibid at [28].

[58] Ibid at [30]. Steel argues that there is a risk of persistent confusion in this area of law unless the concepts of 'divisible' and 'indivisible' injury are properly defined: S Steel 'Material Contribution to Damage, Again' (2022) 138 LQR 540 at 545.

[59] Ibid at [71].

[60] The appeal by the defendant was, however, allowed on the grounds that on the evidence presented to the court, the claimant could not prove that the tortious exposure to the TCE had caused or materially contributed to the claimant's disease: Ibid at [119].

(that is, disease and clinical negligence cases). This question fell to be answered in *Chetwynd v Tunmore*.[61] In that case, the claimants claimed that the defendants had excavated lakes on their land, which had adversely affected the land owned by the claimants and, in particular, the water levels in fishing lakes (where they operated a commercial fishery) which were situated there. The claimants based their claim, *inter alia*, on negligence and nuisance. The claimants claimed that in order to recover damages from the defendants, it was sufficient if the claimants could prove that the defendants' excavations had materially contributed to the reduction of water levels in the claimants' lakes. There were other factors which could have caused a reduction in the water levels in the claimants' lakes. In deciding in favour of the defendants, Judge Reddihough observed that a common feature in cases such as *Bonnington Castings*, *McGhee* and *Fairchild* (where the 'but for' test had not been applied) there was one agent or condition which had been brought about by cumulative or consecutive causes, one of which involved fault on the part of the defendant, which resulted in the relevant disease or injury.[62] However, in the opinion of the judge, such learning could not be applied in the instant case, where the relevant facts were quite different.[63] The judge held that the 'but for' test of causation fell to be applied, in preference to the material contribution test. That is to say, that the claimants were required to prove, on a balance of probabilities, that but for the excavation of the defendants' lakes, their loss and damage would not have occurred. Since the claimants had failed to prove causation on the application of the former test, they failed in their action.[64]

SUPERVENING EVENTS

It may sometimes happen that an event (either as a result of the operation of nature or otherwise) which is unrelated to and occurs after the defender's negligent act (but before the relevant proof or trial) eclipses or negates the harm which has been caused by the defender's original act. To what extent, if any, can the defender, in such circumstances, argue that he is liable to compensate the pursuer only for any harm which existed up to the time the supervening act took place? The House of Lords was required to answer this question in *Baker v Willoughby*.[65] In that case, the claimant sustained an injury to his leg, on account of the defendant's negligence. Later, but before the trial, the claimant was shot in the leg during an armed robbery. His leg required to be amputated. The House held that the claimant could still recover damages against the defendant without any reduction.

However, in the Court of Appeal case of *Cutler v Vauxhall Motors*[66] the claimant grazed his ankle in an accident at work, for which his employers were liable in negligence. The graze caused ulceration of the leg, for which the claimant required an immediate operation to remove various veins. The court held since the claimant

[61] [2016] EWHC 156.

[62] Ibid at [31].

[63] Ibid at [33].

[64] Ibid at [150]. See also *Bell v Northumbrian Water Ltd* [2016] EWHC 133.

[65] [1970] AC 467.

[66] [1971] 1 QB 418.

would have needed the operation within five years, anyway, this fact could be considered when it awarded damages to the claimant. In short, no damages fell to be awarded for the financial loss the claimant had sustained as a result of the operation.

Again, in the House of Lords case of *Jobling v Associated Dairies Ltd*[67] the claimant was injured, by virtue of the defendant's negligence, in January 1973. He suffered backpain that was somewhat disabling. However, before the date of the trial, he suffered serious illness which was completely unconnected with the accident. That illness would have proved totally disabling from about the middle, or end, of 1976. The House held that the effect of the illness should be taken into account when one was assessing the amount of damages which should be awarded to the claimant. The House, in reaching that conclusion, cast doubts on the decision in *Baker*.

LOSS OF CHANCE

The question to be answered here is whether one can recover damages in respect of the loss of a chance, which has been caused by the negligence of the defender. For example, if the defender, a medical practitioner, wrongly diagnoses that the pursuer has a benign tumour, as a result of which the latter does nothing to have it removed, but it subsequently transpires that the tumour is, indeed, malignant, by which time nothing can be done to remedy the situation, it can be said that the defender denied the pursuer the chance, or opportunity, to take appropriate remedial action. We say that the defender has denied the pursuer a *chance* of recovery, simply because one does not really know whether it would have made any difference to the pursuer if the correct advice had been given timeously. For example, such a diagnosis might have revealed that nothing could have been done to cure the pursuer anyway, or if something could have been done, there is the possibility that the pursuer would have rejected any treatment. We now consider how the courts have dealt with the loss of chance, in terms of the law of negligence.

In *Kenyon v Bell*[68] a young child's eye was injured in a domestic accident. The injury was treated in a hospital casualty ward. The pursuer was sent home. However, the condition of the eye worsened. The eye had to be surgically removed. The pursuer claimed that the doctor who had treated the girl had been negligent, as a result of which the pursuer had lost her eye, or such negligence had denied the pursuer a material chance of saving the eye. However, Lord Guthrie refused to accept the proposition that the loss of the chance of saving the eye, of itself, was a legally recognised harm, in relation to which damages were payable.[69]

The right to recover in relation to a lost chance was again considered in *Yeoman v Ferries*.[70] In that case, the pursuer instructed a solicitor to raise an action against his employer, in respect of an industrial injury which he had sustained. The solicitor failed to act timeously. The claim against the employer became statute barred. The employee then raised an action, which was based on professional negligence, against

67 [1982] AC 794.
68 1953 SC 125.
69 Ibid at 128.
70 1967 SC 255.

the solicitor. In the Outer House it was held that the defender had deprived the pursuer of the right to sue his employer for damages.[71] The pursuer was therefore entitled to succeed in an action for damages against the solicitor.

The right to recover for a lost chance was considered by the House of Lords in *Hotson v East Berkshire Area Health Authority*.[72] In that case, a boy fell while he was climbing a tree. He injured his hip. He was taken to a hospital where he was misdiagnosed. His condition was in fact serious. He developed avascular necrosis. He brought an action for damages against, *inter alia*, the defendant health authority who admitted negligence in failing to diagnose and treat his injury promptly. However, it was proved that even if a correct diagnosis had been made, and the plaintiff had been treated promptly, there was a 75 per cent chance that avascular necrosis would have developed. At first instance, on this basis, it was held he was entitled to damages for the loss of the 25 per cent chance that he would have made a full recovery. The Court of Appeal dismissed an appeal by the health authority. However, the House of Lords held that since in 75 per cent of such cases, avascular necrosis develops, the plaintiff had failed to prove, on a balance of probabilities, that the negligence of the defendant had materially contributed to his condition. The claimant, therefore, failed in his action. However, the House did not reject the proposition that one could not sue in respect of a lost chance, in the law of tort.[73]

The right to recover damages for loss of chance was again explicitly recognised in *Kyle v P and J Stormonth Darling WS*.[74] In that case, the pursuer had been the defender in a sheriff court case, which he had lost. That decision had been unsuccessfully appealed to the sheriff principal, and thereafter an appeal was marked (that is, scheduled) to the Inner House of the Court of Session. However, the defender failed to lodge and deliver relevant papers before the court. The pursuer then raised an action for damages, alleging professional negligence and breach of contract against the solicitors. Lord Prosser, allowing proof before answer, held that since the pursuer had a reasonable prospect of success in the litigation in which he was involved, the loss of the right to appeal to the court had deprived him of a legal right, in respect of which he could seek redress, in the law of delict. The Inner House, on appeal, held that the loss of right to pursue a claim (that is, the chance) in the courts could form the basis of an action in delict. In so deciding, the court expressly approved the decision in *Yeoman*.[75]

The issue of lost chance was discussed again in the Court of Appeal case of *Allied Maples Group Ltd v Simmons and Simmons*.[76] There, the claimants, a retailing company, instructed the defendant solicitors to act for them in the takeover of assets of a company, among which were four department stores, leased by a subsidiary. The defendants negligently advised the claimants about the agreement. Certain contingent claims were made against the claimants by the lessors of the property. The claimants

71 Ibid at 264 per Lord Avonside.
72 [1987] AC 750.
73 Ibid at 786 per Lord MacKay; at 792 per Lord Akner.
74 1993 SC 57.
75 Ibid at 67 per Lord McCluskey.
76 [1995] 1 WLR 1602.

became aware of the claims only a year later. The claimants then brought an action against the defendants, contending that, on the balance of probabilities, there was a real chance the claimants would have successfully renegotiated the contract with the vendor. The claimants succeeded at first instance. The defendants appealed. The Court of Appeal, in dismissing the appeal held:

1. that the establishment of a causal link between the defendant's negligence and the claimant's loss, where the negligence consisted of some positive act, was a question of historical fact, to be determined on the balance of probabilities, in which case, once established, the fact was taken to be true, and the claimant was entitled to recover damages in full;
2. that where the quantification of the claimant's loss depended upon future uncertain events, it was to be decided on the court's assessment of the facts materialising;
3. that where the defendant's negligence consisted of an omission, causation depended on the answer to the hypothetical question of what the claimant would have done if the defendant had not been guilty of an omission, which was a matter of inference to be determined from all the circumstances; and
4. that where the plaintiff's loss depended on the hypothetical action of a third party, the plaintiff was entitled to succeed, if he could show that there was a real and substantial, rather that a speculative, chance that the third party would have acted so as to confer the benefit or avoid the risk to the claimant.[77]

Stuart-Smith LJ referred to the House of Lords case of *Spring v Guardian Assurance*[78] where it was held that an employer who negligently gave a bad reference for the claimant, a former employee, owed a duty of care to the latter and was liable for any economic loss suffered by him, by reason of the reference being negligently prepared. The case was remitted to the Court of Appeal for the assessment of damages, the claimant's case being that he failed to obtain employment with the third party, because of the adverse reference. Lord Lowry expressed the opinion, *obiter*, that once the duty of care was held to exist, and the defendant's negligence was proved, the claimant only had to show that by reason of that negligence, he had lost a reasonable chance of employment, and had thereby sustained loss.[79] He did not need to prove that 'but for' the negligent reference, the third party would have employed him. In the instant case, Hobhouse LJ stated that the plaintiffs were not obliged to prove more than they had lost something of substance. They had done this by showing that they had a measurable chance of negotiating significantly better terms.[80] It was up to the trial judge to assess the value of the chance they had lost to negotiate better terms.

The learning in *Allied Maples* was applied in the Supreme Court case of *Perry v Raleys Solicitors*.[81] In that case, the claimant, a retired miner, instructed his solicitors

[77] See also *Assetco plc v Grant Thornton UK plc* [2020] EWCA Civ 1151; *McCrindle Group Ltd v McLay Murray and Spens* [2013] CSOH 72.

[78] [1994] 3 All ER 129.

[79] Ibid at 154.

[80] [1995] 1 WLR 1602 at 1621.

[81] [2020] AC 352.

in relation to his claim for an award, under a government scheme for compensating miners who had developed vibration white finger (VWF), which was a condition caused by the excessive use of vibratory tools. The scheme contemplated two types of award, namely, a general damages award, which depended on the level of severity of the claimant's VWF, and a services award, which depended on the claimant establishing that before developing VWF he had been able to undertake one or more of six routine domestic tasks, without assistance, that he could no longer undertake these tasks without assistance due to his VWF, and that he had received the necessary assistance with these tasks from others. The claimant settled his claim for payment of a general damages award only, without making a claim for a services award, within the available time frame. Some years later, he brought proceedings against the defendants for damages in negligence, claiming that due to their failure to give him appropriate advice, he had lost the opportunity to claim a services award. The trial judge dismissed the claim, on the grounds that the claimant had failed to prove that the defendants' admitted negligent advice had caused him any loss. The Court of Appeal allowed the claimant's appeal, holding that the judge had erred in conducting a trial within a trial, on the issue of whether the claimant needed assistance to perform these tasks, and in imposing on the claimant the burden of proving that fact on a balance of probabilities. The defendants appealed.

The Supreme Court held that the question whether the negligent advice had caused a claimant's loss depended on what the claimant would have done upon receipt of competent advice. This required to be proved by the claimant on a balance of probabilities. In short, the claimant was required to prove, on the balance of probabilities, that properly advised by the defendants, he would have made an honest claim to a services award, under the scheme, in time.[82] It had not been wrong in law or principle for the judge to have conducted a trial of that question. Lord Briggs stated that the instant case was a correct application of the dividing line, established in *Allied Maples*, between those matters which required to be proved by the client on the balance of probabilities and those to be addressed by reference to the value of a lost opportunity.[83]

In the above cases, where the defendant's negligence had deprived the pursuer of a chance, the court was essentially required to answer the question whether, if he had not been so deprived, the pursuer would have been able to take action to avoid harm (physical or financial) or to gain a financial advantage. In short, there was a causal link between the negligent act on the part of the defender and the pursuer's loss. However, in the House of Lords case of *Gregg v Scott*,[84] the House of Lords was required to decide whether the mere reduction of a chance of avoiding harm could rank as a freestanding right of action. In *Gregg* the claimant visited the defendant doctor, because the former had a lump under his arm. The doctor negligently misdiagnosed

[82] See also *Moda International Brands Ltd v Gately LLP* [2019] EWHC 1326; *Prime London Residential Development Jersey Master Holding Ltd v Withers LLP* [2021] EWHC 2401; *Score Draw Ltd v PNH International Ltd* [2021] EWHC 756; *Coote v Ullstein* [2022] EWHC 607; *Kirkton Investments Ltd v VMH LLP* [2011] CSOH 200.

[83] Ibid at 364. See also *McCann v Harper Macleod* 2025 CSOH 27.

[84] [2005] 2 AC 176.

the claimant's condition as benign. A year later another general practitioner referred the claimant to hospital, for an examination. It was discovered that the claimant had cancer of the lymph gland. By the time that the diagnosis was made the tumour had spread to the claimant's chest. He was left with poor prospects of survival. The trial judge held that on the expert evidence, the delay in diagnosis had reduced the claimant's chance of survival for more than ten years (which was considered a cure) from 42 to 25 per cent. The judge, therefore, dismissed the claimant's action on the basis that the delay had not deprived the claimant of a prospect of a cure (meaning surviving more than ten years) because at the time of his misdiagnosis, the claimant had less than a 50 per cent chance of surviving more than ten years anyway. The Court of Appeal dismissed the claimant's appeal. The claimant appealed, claiming, *inter alia*, that the reduction of his chances of survival was itself a compensatable head of damage. By a bare majority, the House of Lords held that in accordance with the general rules of causation, a claimant was required to prove that the defendant's negligence caused the harm in question. There could be no remedy in tort, simply for a reduction in the chance of recovery from illness.[85]

[85] See also *JD v Mather* [2012] EWHC 3063; *Oliver v Williams* [2013] EWHC 600. For a discussion of *Gregg* see J Stapleton 'Loss of the Chance of Cure from Cancer' (2005) 68 MLR 996; K B Lockhart, 'Loss of a Chance in Medical Negligence: *Gregg v Scott*' (2005) 17 SLT 93.

Chapter 7

Legal Causation

Whereas the defender's negligent conduct may have caused harm to the pursuer, in a factual sense, the law will not permit the latter to recover if the loss is deemed to be too remote. In ascertaining whether the harm which the pursuer has sustained is too remote, the law in effect adopts a practical approach. Such an approach is well illustrated in the Inner House case of ***Blaikie v British Transport Commission***.[1] In that case, the deceased was an engine driver. The pursuers, namely, his widow and children, claimed that as a result of the negligence, on the part of an engine fitter, there was a serious danger of the boiler on the engine, which the deceased was driving, exploding, the upshot of which was that it was necessary for the deceased, and his fireman, to extinguish the fire. Shortly after making strenuous efforts to extinguish the fire, he collapsed and died. The pursuers claimed that the driver's death was due to a coronary thrombosis, which was precipitated by the strain and exertion which the pursuer incurred while extinguishing the fire. However, the Inner House held that the deceased's injury was too remote to allow the pursuer to recover. The Lord Justice Clerk stated:

> The law has always had to come to some sort of compromise with the doctrine of causation. The problem is a practical, rather than an intellectual one. It is easy and usual to bedevil it with subtleties, but the attitude of the law is that expediency, and good sense, dictate that, for practical purposes, a line has to be drawn somewhere, and that in drawing it, the Court is to be guided by the practical experience of the reasonable man, rather than by the theoretical speculations of the philosopher.[2]

There are two competing tests which are employed by the courts in order to address this issue, namely:

1. the 'directness' test; and
2. the 'foreseeability' test.

---

[1] 1961 SC 44.
[2] Ibid at 49.

THE 'DIRECTNESS' TEST

The leading case on the directness test is the Court of Appeal case of *Re Polemis*.[3] In that case, a chartered vessel was unloading in Casablanca. During the voyage of the ship, benzene (or petrol) had leaked from tins. As a consequence, there was a considerable amount of petrol vapour in the hold of the ship. The servants of the defendant charterers negligently let a plank of wood fall into the hold. The fall of the plank caused a spark, which in turn caused the petrol to explode. The ship was completely destroyed. The charterers were held liable for the damage which had been caused, on the basis that such loss was the direct consequence of the defendant's negligence. It was irrelevant that the type of damage caused was not reasonably foreseeable.[4]

THE 'FORESEEABILITY' TEST

The competing test, as far as legal causation is concerned, is found in the Privy Council case of *Overseas Tankship (UK) Ltd v Morts Dock and Engineering Co Ltd (The Wagon Mound)*.[5] In that case, OT Ltd were charterers of a ship, which was known as the *Wagon Mound*. It was moored in a wharf in Sydney Harbour. OT's servants negligently allowed a large quantity of oil to be spilled. The oil spread to another wharf, where another ship was under repair. Sparks from the welding operations, which were taking place in that part of the harbour, fell onto the water. Either rags or cotton waste, which were floating on the water, caught fire. The wharf and the equipment on it caught fire and were damaged. The Privy Council held that while the damage in question was the direct cause of the spillage, it was, at the same time, unforeseeable. The damage in question was not that which a reasonable man would have foreseen.[6] Therefore, the defendants were not liable.[7]

A good illustration of the application of the foreseeability test is seen in *Bradford v Robinson Rentals Ltd*.[8] In that case, the plaintiff had been sent by his employers on a lengthy journey, in very cold weather, in a van which had no heating. The plaintiff suffered frostbite, as a consequence. It was held that the employers owed him a duty of care which had been breached. Furthermore, the harm which he had sustained was foreseeable in nature. The employers were, therefore, held liable.

Currently, it is the rule in the *Wagon Mound*, in contrast to that in *Re Polemis*, which finds favour with the courts, in determining whether the harm which has been caused by the defendant's negligent act is too remote to allow the pursuer to recover. The foresight of the hypothetical reasonable man in the position of the defender determines whether the latter is liable.[9]

---

3 [1921] 3 KB 560.
4 Ibid at 572 (per Bankes LJ).
5 [1961] AC 388.
6 Ibid at 426 (per Viscount Simonds).
7 See also *Agouman v Leigh Day* [2016] EWHC 1324; *Conarken Group Ltd v Network Rail Infrastructure Ltd* [2011] EWCA Civ 644.
8 [1967] 1 WLR 337.
9 *Simmons v British Steel plc* 2004 SC (HL) 94 at 100 (per Lord Hope).

What needs to be foreseen?

The defender need not actually foresee the occurrence of the accident which injures the pursuer. Rather, it suffices that the defender can foresee that the relevant harm would occur *if* the accident did take place. This point was decided in the House of Lords case of *Galashiels Gas Co Ltd v O'Donnell*.[10] In that case, the defenders occupied a lift at their gasworks. The lift was ostensibly in safe working order. However, on one occasion, something went wrong. The gates allowing access to the lift were left open. If the lift system was operating efficiently, the gates should not have been capable of being opened. The lift cage had ascended from the level where the deceased was standing. Therefore, the deceased should not have been able to access the lift shaft. After the lift cage had ascended, the deceased entered the shaft with the bogie which he had been pushing. He fell to the bottom of the shaft and was killed. Since the occurrence of the accident, no satisfactory explanation of the accident had been found. However, the House held that the defenders were liable, since it was foreseeable that the deceased would be killed if the accident did take place, notwithstanding the fact that occurrence of the accident was not.

Whereas the type of harm which the pursuer sustains requires to be foreseeable, at the time the accident takes place, the precise series of events which occurs as a result of the defender's negligence does not. This particular point was established in the House of Lords case of *Hughes v Lord Advocate*.[11] In that case, the pursuer, aged eight, and his uncle, aged ten, were playing on a public road. Their attention was drawn to an unattended canvas shelter, which was situated over an uncovered manhole, which had been left temporarily unattended by Post Office workers. The workers were at fault by leaving the manhole in that state. Warning paraffin lamps had been placed around the tent. The boys entered the tent and decided to explore the manhole. They enlisted the aid of a ladder and a paraffin lamp. The pursuer tripped against the lamp, which fell into the manhole. The paraffin, which had leaked from the lamp, on its coming into contact with the bottom of the manhole, vapourised with the heat of the lamp. There was an explosion. The pursuer lost his balance and fell into the manhole. He sustained serious injury. The House held that the defender (who was representing the Postmaster General) was liable for the harm which the pursuer had sustained, since, notwithstanding the fact that the precise concatenation of events which had taken place was not reasonably foreseeable, the *type* of harm (that is, harm by burning) which the pursuer had sustained was foreseeable. Lord Morris stated:[12]

> The circumstances that an explosion as such could not have been contemplated does not alter the fact that it could reasonably have been foreseen that a boy, who played in and about the canvas shelter, and played with things that were thereabouts, might get hurt, and might in some way burn himself. That is just what happened. The pursuer did burn himself, though his burns were graver than would have been expected. The fact that the features or

---

[10] [1949] AC 275. The case was decided in terms of liability for breach of statutory duty (see Ch. 10).

[11] [1963] SC (HL) 31.

[12] Ibid at 43–4. See also *Galbraith's Curator v Stewart* (No2) 1998 SLT 1305.

developments of an accident may not reasonably have been foreseen, does not mean that the accident itself was not foreseeable.[13]

Degree of foreseeability required

The question which falls to be answered now is what degree of foreseeability is required of the defender, before he can be liable for the harm which he has caused? In the first instance case of *Tremain v Pike*,[14] the plaintiff was employed by the defendant as a herdsman. He contracted Weil's disease (leptospirosis) from rats' urine, because the defendant had allowed the rat population in his farm to become too large. It was held that the harm suffered by the plaintiff was too remote to allow him to recover, since, while some form of injury from rat bites, or food poisoning, by the consumption of food or drink, which was contaminated by rats, was foreseeable, it was not reasonably foreseeable that the claimant would develop Weil's disease.

Tremain sets a high ceiling, as it were, for the degree of foreseeability required of the defender for liability to lie. However, the author would argue that that threshold is too high. Indeed, *Tremain* sits uncomfortably with the decision of the House of Lords in *Page v Smith*, which has already been discussed.[15] It is difficult to predict the outcome of a particular case, as far as this area of law is concerned.

For example, in the Court of Appeal case of *Lamb v Camden LBC*[16] a local authority and their contractors, who were replacing a sewer under a road, broke a water main. Water escaped and undermined the foundations of the plaintiffs' house, which was situated nearby. The house had been let furnished to a tenant. However, the house required to be vacated, because it was unsafe. The house became a sitting target for squatters, who soon moved into the house. They were ultimately ejected but, by then, had inflicted serious damage to the premises. The plaintiffs sued the local authority to recover the costs of repairing the premises. However, the Court of Appeal held that the damage which had been done by the squatters was too remote to allow the plaintiffs to recover.

In referring to remoteness of damage, Watkins LJ stated:

> A robust and sensible approach to this very important area of law of the study of remoteness will, more often than not, produce, I think, an instinctive feeling that the event or act, being weighed in the balance, is too remote to sound in damages for the plaintiff. I do not pretend that in all cases the answer will come easily to the inquirer. But that the question must be asked and answered in all these cases I have no doubt ... To return to the present case, I have the instinctive feeling that the squatters' damage is too remote.[17]

---

13 See also *Armstead v Royal and Sun Alliance Insurance Co Ltd* [2024] UKSC 6; *Jolley v Sutton LBC* [2000] 1 WLR 1082; *Wisniewski v Central Manchester Health Authority* [1998] PIQR P324; *Corr v IBC Vehicles Ltd* [2008] 1 AC 884; *Hadlow v Peterborough City Council* [2011] EWCA Civ 1329; and *Conarken Group Ltd v Network Rail Infrastructure Ltd* [2011] EWCA Civ 644. See also *Lear v Hickstead Ltd* [2016] 4 WLR 73; *Stewart v West African Terminals Ltd.* [1964] 2 Lloyds Rep 371 at 375.

14 [1969] 1 WLR 1556.

15 See p.110.

16 [1981] QB 625.

17 Ibid at 647.

Lamb should be contrasted with *Ward v Cannock Chase District Council*.[18] There, the defendant local authority owned a number of cottages, which were situated in an area which was zoned for industrial development. As the cottages became vacant, the local authority had boarded them up. With the passage of time, the cottages were falling into disrepair and were being damaged by vandals. The plaintiff had purchased two cottages at the end of a terrace. The local authority had ceased to maintain the other houses in the terrace as they became vacant. Vandals removed tiles, bricks and timbers from the buildings, the upshot of which was that one night, part of the terrace which adjoined the claimant's house collapsed, bringing down part of the gable wall and the roof of the claimant's cottage. The claimant obtained a court order requiring the local authority to repair his premises. While his premises were vacant, vandals removed a water tank and did further damage. Subsequently, vandals again broke into his property and stole, *inter alia*, machinery and livestock. The plaintiff sued the local authority.

At first instance, it was held that the local authority was liable for the damage caused to the plaintiff's premises by the collapse of the adjoining premises. The local authority was also liable for the damage to the plaintiff's premises caused by the acts of the vandals, since such acts were foreseeable. However, the loss caused by the damage to and theft of the plaintiff's chattels was not recoverable, in that the loss was not a reasonably foreseeable consequence of the local authority's breach of duty, on the basis that one would have expected the plaintiff to have taken measures to secure his chattels against such damage.[19]

Serious manifestation of event foreseen

If the type of harm which the pursuer sustains is foreseeable, the defender whose negligent act caused the harm will remain liable, notwithstanding the fact that the extent of the harm is much greater than could reasonably have been foreseen. For example, in *Vacwell Engineering Co Ltd v BDH Chemicals Ltd*[20] the defendants, who were manufacturers and distributors of chemicals, sold a chemical to the plaintiffs, who made plant and equipment for transistor devices. The defendants were unaware that the chemical which had been sold to the plaintiffs was of an explosive character when the chemical came into contact with water. The plaintiffs were similarly unaware of the qualities of the chemical. In order to prepare it for use in their manufacturing process, it was necessary to wash the labels off the ampoules (which contained the chemical) in sinks containing water and detergent. Several ampoules were accidentally dropped into the sink. The ampoules shattered, thereby releasing the chemical in the water. There was a violent reaction, the upshot of which was that the remaining ampoules shattered and caused an explosion. One scientist was killed and another was seriously injured. Property was also seriously damaged. It was held that, notwithstanding the fact that the magnitude of the explosion was not reasonably foreseeable, an explosion

[18] [1986] Ch 546.
[19] Ibid at 572.
[20] [1971] 1 QB 88.

of a minor nature was foreseeable. The damage was, therefore, not too remote to preclude recovery in negligence.

However, *Vacwell* should be contrasted with the Court of Appeal case of *Doughty v Turner*.[21] In that case, the plaintiff, who was employed at the defendants' factory, was injured when another workman inadvertently knocked an asbestos cover into a cauldron of very hot molten liquid. The extreme heat caused the cover to undergo a chemical change. Water was released. The water turned into steam. Several minutes later there was an eruption of molten liquid from the cauldron. The plaintiff was injured. However, the court held that the plaintiff could not recover damages from the defendants, since the eruption of the liquid could not be described as a variant of the dangers which could arise from splashing. In the last analysis, the type of harm which the plaintiff had sustained was not reasonably foreseeable.

However, in the author's view, *Doughty* does not sit comfortably with *Hughes v Lord Advocate*,[22] which was distinguished. It could be forcefully argued that the injury which had been sustained by the plaintiff in *Doughty*, which had been caused by the liquid coming into contact with him, was a foreseeable consequence of the lid being dropped into the cauldron. In other words, the injury which the plaintiff had sustained emanated from a known source of danger: namely, a cauldron which contained molten liquid. The precise concatenation of events by means of which the injury occurred (that is, the way in which the liquid came to be splashed on to the plaintiff) was, in the light of the reasoning in *Hughes*, irrelevant. Indeed, *Doughty* illustrates the difficulty of ascertaining whether one form of harm which the pursuer sustains differs in nature from another. This difficulty was identified in the Privy Council case of *AG of the British Virgin Islands v Hartwell*.[23] Lord Nicholl's stated:

> [There] are no hard-and-fast rules applicable when distinguishing one description of damage, which was reasonably foreseeable, and in respect of which a duty of care arose, from another description of damage, which was not reasonably foreseeable, and in respect of which there was no duty of care ... Whether, for identifying the scope of a duty of care, one kind of damage is relevantly different from another, depends upon the degree of generality applicable in the particular case. That in turn, depends upon what is fair and reasonable in the circumstances.

'THIN SKULL' RULE

Whilst in order to recover damages, the pursuer is required to establish that the harm which he has sustained, by reason of the negligence of the defender, is foreseeable, it may happen that the *extent* of the injury is graver, owing to the personal characteristics of the pursuer. For example, the pursuer is running along a road and a cyclist negligently collides with him, the result of which is that the pursuer receives head injuries, which normally would have proved minor in nature. However, the pursuer has an abnormally thin skull. The upshot of this is that the extent of his injuries is much more serious. In such circumstances, the application of the thin skull rule

[21] [1964] 1 All ER 98.

[22] 1963 SC (HL) 31 (see above p.165).

[23] [2004] 1 WLR 1273 at 1280–1.

would allow him to recover, on the grounds that the defender is required to 'take' his victim as he finds him. In other words, in the aforementioned scenario, the thin skull rule would allow the pursuer to recover from the defender in respect of the full extent of his injuries, which directly derived from a state of affairs (or type of harm) that was reasonably foreseeable.

A good illustration of the application of the 'thin skull' rule is seen in *Smith v Leech Brain and Co*.[24] In that case, the plaintiff was a galvaniser who worked at the defendants' factory. He suffered a burn on his lip from molten metal. The defendant was negligent in failing to ensure that the plaintiff was adequately protected. The burn caused the plaintiff to contract cancer, since the tissues on his lips were in a pre-malignant state. He died within three years of the accident. The defendants argued that they were not responsible for his death, since it could not have been foreseen that the burn would cause cancer and death. In holding the defendants liable for the plaintiff's death, the court held that a burn to the plaintiff's lips was foreseeable. Therefore, under the thin skull rule, the defendants were required to 'take the plaintiff as they found him'. They were, therefore, liable for the full extent of the harm which the plaintiff had sustained.

Again, in the Court of Appeal case of *Robinson v Post Office*[25] the claimant was employed by the defendants. When descending from a tower wagon, he slipped, because of oil which had been deposited on the ladder. He sustained a wound on his leg. A doctor gave him an anti-tetanus injection. The plaintiff developed encephalitis as a result of an allergy. The court held the defendants liable. It was foreseeable that if oil were negligently allowed to escape on to a ladder, a workman was liable to slip and sustain a wound, which might require medical treatment. It was also foreseeable that an anti-tetanus prophylactic would be deemed necessary. The defendants were required to take the plaintiff as they found him, that is, with an allergy to the injection. They were, therefore, liable for the full extent of the harm the plaintiff had suffered.[26]

More recently, in the House of Lords case of *Simmons v British Steel plc*[27] the pursuer was injured at work on account of the defenders' negligence. He sustained a severe blow to the head. After the accident the pursuer experienced an exacerbation of a pre-existing skin condition. He also developed a change in his personality which resulted in severe depressive illness. The House held that the defenders were required to take the pursuer as they found him. Since the harm which the pursuer had sustained was reasonably foreseeable, the defenders were liable for any personal injury (physical or psychiatric) which the pursuer had suffered, notwithstanding the fact the extent of his injury was more severe because of his personal characteristics.

[24] [1962] 2 QB 405.

[25] [1974] 1 WLR 1176.

[26] See also *Brice v Brown* [1984] 1 All ER 997. See also *Sayers v Perrin* [1966] Qd.R 89. As a result of the defendant's negligence, the plaintiff suffered an electric shock. At the time of the accident, a poliomyelitis virus was already present in his body. He developed poliomyelitis. It was held that the defendant was liable for this illness, since it was the direct result of a state of affairs which was foreseeable.

[27] 2004 SC (HL) 94.

'THIN SKULL' RULE AND IMPECUNIOSITY

Some people have limited financial means. It is, therefore, foreseeable that such individuals can be seriously impacted by damage which has been inflicted on their property by the defender's negligence. For example, the pursuer may cycle to work. After his bike is damaged beyond repair, by the negligence of the defender, the pursuer is obliged to take public transport, since he cannot afford to buy another bike. To what extent, if any, can the pursuer's impecuniosity be considered, when one is considering if the harm in question is too remote to allow him to recover damages, in the form of transport costs?

Traditionally, the law adopted a bold stance to impecuniosity, in that the courts would not allow the pursuer to recover for loss which directly derived from his own poverty. In *Liesbosch (Dredger) v SS Edison*[28] the plaintiffs were under contract to complete a piece of work within a given time. Their dredger was sunk by the negligence of the defendants. However, the plaintiffs were too poor to buy a substitute dredger. The plaintiffs were put to much greater expense in fulfilling their contact because, *inter alia*, they were required to hire a substitute dredger at an exorbitant rate. The substitute dredger was also much more expensive to work than the *Liesbosch*.

The House of Lords held that the plaintiffs were entitled to recover:

1. the market price of a substitute dredger, comparable to the *Liesbosch*;
2. the cost of adaptation, transport and insurance of the substitute vessel; and
3. compensation for the loss on the contract, for the period between the sinking of the *Liesbosch* and the time when a substitute dredger could have been available.

The claim for extra expenses, due to the poverty of the plaintiffs, was rejected, on the grounds that this was an extraneous matter and, therefore, too remote to warrant recovery.

However, the courts have not felt particularly comfortable with the decision in *Liesbosch* and have been inclined to distinguish it. For example in the Court of Appeal case of *Martindale v Duncan*[29] the plaintiff's vehicle was damaged by the negligence of the defendant. The plaintiff was unable to bear the cost of repairs himself. His car was off the road for a period of fourteen weeks, which included the period in which he had waited for the defendant's insurers to agree to pay for the relevant repairs. The defendant contended that the claimant should have had the repairs carried out immediately, and, therefore, on the authority of *Liesbosch*, claimed that they were liable to pay only the cost of hiring a substitute vehicle during the period when the car could have been taken to a garage for repairs, and for the likely time it would have taken until the completion of such repairs. However the court, in distinguishing *Liesbosch*, held that the defendant was liable for the cost of hire during the entire fourteen-week period.

[28] [1933] AC 449.

[29] [1973] 1 WLR 574.

Again, in *Mattocks v Mann*[30] the plaintiff's vehicle was damaged by the defendant. The plaintiff was required to hire a replacement vehicle. The repairers refused to release her own vehicle until she had met the cost of repair. However, she had insufficient resources to do so. She, therefore, continued to hire a car until she had received payment from the defendant's insurers. The Court of Appeal held that the claimant was entitled to recover the additional cost of hiring a replacement vehicle, including the cost of hire during the period between the date on which her vehicle had been repaired and the date on which her vehicle had been released by the repairer.

The decision in *Liesbosch* came under further scrutiny in the House of Lords case of *Langden v O'Connor*.[31] In that case, the claimant's car was damaged as a result of the defendant's negligence. The car was required to be repaired at a garage. However, the claimant was unemployed, and could not afford to pay for the hire of a replacement car while his own car was off the road. He, therefore, signed an agreement with a credit hire company, whereby it provided a hire car at no cost to him, by way of the provision of a twenty-six-week credit facility, in order to allow the company to recover its charges from the negligent driver's insurers. The agreement also included an insurance policy to provide payment, in the event of non-recovery within that period. These fees were much higher than the equivalent rates which were charged by traditional car hire firms. The defendant admitted liability. However, he disputed the claim for damages, which included a sum of money that formed part of the credit hire company's charges. The House of Lords held that, in determining the question of damages payable to an injured party, whose expenditure had been augmented by his impecuniosity, the court was not precluded from considering the injured party's lack of means. In short, the defendant was required to take the claimant as he found him. Therefore, the former had to bear the consequences, if it was reasonably foreseeable that the claimant would require to borrow money or incur some other expenditure to mitigate his damages. By a majority, the House held that the claimant was entitled to recover the whole cost of hiring the car. In coming to that decision, the majority rejected the learning in *Liesbosch*.[32]

Goldkamp and Nolan argue that subsequent decisions concerning motor insurance claims have treated loss deriving from the impecuniosity of the pursuer as a question of mitigation, rather than in terms of foreseeable loss which was occasioned by the impecuniosity of the pursuer.[33] In other words, the impecuniosity of the pursuer falls to be considered by the court, in assessing the pursuer's damages. However, at the same time, the pursuer is under a duty to mitigate his losses.[34]

By way of conclusion, the author is of the view that firstly, *Liesbosch* no longer represents good law, and secondly, the thin skull rule, in terms of impecuniosity on the part of the pursuer, is not confined to motor insurance cases.[35]

---

[30] [1993] RTR 13.

[31] [2004] 1 AC 1067.

[32] Ibid at 1073 (per Lord Nicholls).

[33] Goudkamp and Nolan in *Winfield and Jolowicz on Tort* (20th edn) at 7-070.

[34] See for example *Dimond v Lovell* [2002] 1 AC 384 at 486–7 (per Lord Hobhouse); *Alcoa Minerals of Jamaica Inc v Broderick* [2002] 1 AC 371.

[35] See for example *Haxton v Philips Electronics UK Ltd* [2014] 1 WLR 2721.

BREAKING THE CHAIN OF CAUSATION

It may happen that an event occurs between the defender's negligent act and the pursuer's sustaining harm. The intervening act may, in the eye of the law, break the link or chain of causation between the negligent act and the subsequent harm which has been sustained by the pursuer. The effect of this is to negate, or eclipse, the defender's liability for his conduct. In such circumstances, the intervening act is said to be a *novus actus interveniens*.

What is a *novus actus interveniens*?

We now discuss how the courts decide whether an intervening act ranks as a *novus actus interveniens*, or alternatively, as a *causa causans*, that is to say, an act which is not independent of the original act of negligence, and thereby simply acts as a causative link between the act and the subsequent harm. The courts have never enunciated a general formula to assist one in distinguishing between a *causa causans* and a *novus actus interveniens*. It remains a grey and untidy area of law, with the courts simply prepared to address the issue on a case-by-case basis. Judges approach the issue intuitively. Indeed, there is no precise test for establishing whether the chain of causation has been broken, in any particular case. The issue is determined by the application of common sense.[36]

'Natural and reasonable' intervening acts

In some cases the courts have employed the concept of 'natural and reasonable' to determine whether an intervening act breaks the chain of causation between the defender's negligent act and the harm which the pursuer sustains. In *The Oropesa*[37] two vessels (the *Manchester Regiment* and the *Oropesa*) collided, owing partly to the negligence of the defendant, the *Oropesa*. After about ninety minutes, the captain of the *Manchester Regiment* decided to discuss salvage arrangements with the captain of the *Oropesa*. He embarked in a lifeboat with some of his crew, including the son of the claimants. However, the boat capsized in the heavy sea after half an hour. The son was drowned. It was held that the action of the captain did not constitute a *novus actus interveniens*. According to Lord Wright:

> [T]he hand of casualty lay heavily on [the *Oropesa*] and the conduct both of the master and of the deceased was directly caused by and flowed from it. There was an unbroken sequence of cause and effect between the negligence which caused the *Oropesa* to collide with the *Manchester Regiment*, and their action, which was dictated by the exigencies of the position.

[36] *Crown River Cruises Ltd v Kimbolton Fireworks Ltd* [1996] CLC 1214 at 1226 (per Potter J). See also *James v White Lion Hotel* [2020] PIQR P10 at [100]–[105] incl. (Approved on appeal: [2021] EWCA Civ 31) where Judge Cotter QC applied the concepts of both foreseeability and reasonableness (discussed below) to determine whether the chain of causation had been broken by the claimant's conduct. For a discussion of *James*, see 152 Rep.B 5 and (2020) 3 J.PI. C 139.

[37] [1943] P 32.

His Lordship continued:[38]

> To break the chain of causation it must be shown that there is something which I will call ultroneous, something unwarrantable, a new cause which disturbs the sequence of events, something which can be described as either unreasonable or extraneous or extrinsic … When a collision takes place by the fault of the defending ship in an action for damages, the damage is recoverable if it is the natural and reasonable result of the negligent act, and it will assume this character if it can be shown to be such a consequence as in the ordinary course of things would flow from the situation which the offending ship had created.

In other words, according to Lord Wright, if the intervening act was the natural and reasonable result of the original act of negligence, it fell to be categorised as a *causa causans* and therefore did not break the chain of causation. Otherwise such an act ranked as a *novus actus interveniens*.[39]

Intervening act 'reasonably likely' and 'natural' and 'probable'

On some occasions, the courts have employed the concept of 'reasonably likely' to ascertain if the relevant intervening act has broken the chain of causation between the negligent act of the defender and the harm which the pursuer sustains. For example, in *Rouse v Squires*,[40] one winter's evening, an articulated lorry, which was being negligently driven by the first defendant, skidded into a jack-knife position, and came to rest on the slow and centre lanes of a motorway. A car, which was being driven by the husband of the claimant, collided with the lorry. A lorry which was being driven by the second defendant then negligently collided with the parked lorry. That lorry was knocked forward by the impact of the collision and killed the claimant's husband, who was assisting at the scene of the accident. The Court of Appeal held that the first defendant was liable for the subsequent damage, since the intervening act of the second defendant did not break the chain of causation between the first and the harm which had been caused by the second negligent acts. The intervening act (that is, the second defendant's negligent act) was, as a consequence of the original act of negligence, reasonably likely to occur.[41]

Again, in *Knightly v Johns*[42] the first defendant was involved in a serious road accident, in a tunnel. The fourth defendant, who was a police inspector, ordered the plaintiff, who was a police constable, to close the tunnel entrance to oncoming traffic. In order to do this, the plaintiff was required to drive against the flow of traffic. In the course of his journey, he collided with a vehicle which was being driven by the second defendant. He sued the second defendant for causing him serious injuries. He also sued the police inspector (the fourth defendant) and the Chief Constable of the West Midlands (the third defendant) as the inspector's superior officer, for the inspector's negligence, in instructing (or at least permitting) him to ride the wrong way. However, the plaintiff alleged that the first defendant was first and foremost

[38] Ibid at 39.
[39] See also *Sayers v Harlow Urban DC* [1958] 1 WLR 623.
[40] [1973] QB 889.
[41] Ibid at 901 (per Buckley LJ). See also *Newby v General Lighterage Co Ltd* [1955] 1 Lloyds Rep 273.
[42] [1982] 1 WLR 349.

responsible for the accident and injuries, since it was his negligence which was the cause of his injury.

However, the Court of Appeal held that the police inspector's (that is, the fourth defendant) unreasonable instructions to the plaintiff, to drive against the flow of the traffic, broke the chain of causation between the first defendant's act of negligence and the subsequent injury which the plaintiff had sustained. The court, in reaching that decision, held that one was required to ascertain if the whole sequence of events was a natural and probable consequence of the first defendant's negligence, and a reasonably foreseeable result of it.[43]

'Unreasonable' intervening acts

An intervening act which ranks as unreasonable can break the chain of causation. For example, in *McKew v Holland, Hannen an Cubitts (Scotland) Ltd*[44] the pursuer was injured in an accident which had been caused by the defenders' negligence. As a result, the pursuer's leg became numb. The leg tended to give way without warning. One day, when he was descending stairs, he felt his leg give way. The pursuer jumped to the bottom of the stair and sustained further injury. The House of Lords held that the pursuer could not recover for this further loss, since he had acted unreasonably in placing himself in such a position that he could do little to save himself if his leg did give way. Furthermore, such unreasonable conduct constituted a *novus actus interveniens* and, therefore, broke the chain of causation between the defender's negligent act and the injury which the pursuer had sustained by jumping down the stairs.

However, what ranks as unreasonable conduct, in terms of a given intervening act, is sometimes difficult to predict, such difficulty arising from the fact that the word 'unreasonable' is semantically imprecise. Indeed, the word 'unreasonable' has been judicially described as 'a protean adjective' whose 'nuances run from irrationality to simple incaution or unwisdom'.[45] For example, in the Court of Appeal case of *Philco Radio and Television Corporation of Great Britain v J Spurling Ltd*[46] the defendants negligently delivered parcels of flammable film scrap to the plaintiff's premises. No warning had been given by the defendants of the fact that the contents of the parcel were flammable. A typist, who was employed at the premises, touched some of the scrap with a lighted cigarette. There was a violent explosion which seriously damaged the plaintiff's premises. It was held that the typist's conduct was not so unreasonable as to break the chain of causation between the defendant's original act of negligence and the subsequent damage which the plaintiffs had sustained. The defendants, therefore, remained liable for the damage to the plaintiffs' premises. Interestingly, Tucker LJ, after describing questions of causation and of *novus actus interveniens* as 'always difficult', stated that the instant case was 'on the borderline'.[47]

[43] Per Stephenson LJ at 865. See also *Scott's Trustees v Moss* (1889) 17 R 32. See also *Hyett v Great Western Railway Co* [1948] 1 KB 345.

[44] 1970 SC (HL) 20.

[45] *Scott v Gavigan* [2016] EWCA Civ 544 at [11] (per Christopher Clarke LJ).

[46] [1949] 2 All ER 882.

[47] Ibid at 885.

The application of the concept of unreasonableness in relation to a *novus actus interveniens* was also seen in the Court of Appeal case of *Spencer v Wincanton Holdings Ltd*.[48] In that case, the claimant was employed by the defendant. The former was injured due to the latter's negligence. He lost part of his left leg as a result of the injury. He was required to wear a prosthesis in order to walk. However, he could not wear it while driving. One day, he attempted to fill his car with petrol without his prothesis or using his sticks. He tripped and fell and sustained further injury. The court held that the defendant was liable for this injury. In the last analysis, the fall in the petrol station was reasonably foreseeable at the time of the original accident. Furthermore, the claimant's conduct was not so unreasonable as to constitute a *novus actus interveniens*.[49]

However, in the Court of Appeal case of *Clay v TUI UK Ltd*[50] a holidaymaker fell from an ornamental balcony and fractured his skull after he had become trapped on the balcony as a result of a defect in the locking mechanism on the balcony door for which the defendant company was liable. By a majority, the court held that the conduct of the claimant was so unreasonable that it broke the chain of causation.

Foreseeable intervening acts

The concept of foreseeability is sometimes used by the courts to determine whether the chain of causation has been broken between the defender's negligence and the subsequent harm which the pursuer sustains. For example, in *Donaghy v National Coal Board*[51] a young miner sued his employers under common law and also for breach of statutory duty, in respect of injuries which he had received when a detonator, which had been left in the pursuer's workplace, in breach of the relevant legislation, exploded when he hit it with a hammer. However, the Inner House held that the act of the pursuer constituted a *novus actus interveniens* since his act was not reasonably foreseeable.

Similarly, in *Wieland v Cyril Lord Carpets Ltd*[52] the plaintiff suffered a neck injury due to the defendant's negligence. The injury made it difficult for her to see properly through her bi-focals. As a result, after attending hospital, she fell while descending stairs. As a consequence, she sustained further injuries. It was held that the defendant was responsible for these subsequent injuries, since the accident was the foreseeable consequence of the defendant's original negligent act.

---

48 [2010] PIQR P8.

49 See also the Court of Appeal case of *Emeh v Kensington and Chelsea and Westminster Area Health Authority* [1985] QB 1012. The claimant underwent a sterilisation operation in the defendants' hospital. However, the operation was performed negligently. She became pregnant. She refused to have an abortion to terminate the pregnancy. She subsequently gave birth to a child who had severe congenital deformities. It was held that the refusal on the part of the claimant to have an abortion was not so unreasonable as to eclipse the defendants' wrongdoing. Therefore, the claimant was entitled to recover damages for the financial loss which accrued from the sterilisation operation. See also *Sparrow v Andre* [2016] EWHC 739.

50 [2018] EWCA Civ 177.

51 1957 SLT (N) 35.

52 [1969] 3 All ER 1006.

An interesting example of the application of foreseeability in relation to the concept *novus actus interveniens* is seen in *Crown River Cruises Ltd v Kimbolton Fireworks Ltd*.[53] In that case, the claimants operated pleasure barges on the River Thames. The first defendants provided a firework display to commemorate the Battle of Britain. One of the plaintiff's vessels was set alight by a firework. The second defendants, a fire authority, were called. They attended the blaze and then left. However, the fire recurred. It also spread to a second barge (the *Suerita*) which was damaged. It was held, in effect, that since it was reasonably foreseeable that the fire would spread, the conduct of the second defendants did not break the chain of causation between the original act of negligence by the first defendants and the subsequent damage to the *Suerita*. In short, it was reasonably foreseeable that the second defendants would negligently omit to extinguish the fire. The first defendants' negligence remained the effective cause of the damage.[54]

The defendant remains liable for a foreseeable act by a third party, notwithstanding the fact that such an act is both deliberate and unlawful.[55] In other words, such conduct does not rank as a *novus actus interveniens*. For example, in *Hosie v Arbroath Football Club Ltd*[56] the pursuer, who was attending a football match at the defenders' stadium, was seriously injured when a group of unruly fans who wished to enter the stadium forced an exit gate (which had not been properly maintained by the defenders) which fell on him. It was held that the conduct of the unruly fans did not constitute a *novus actus interveniens*. The defenders were held liable for the harm caused to the pursuer.[57]

Acts carried out in 'agony of moment'

The law will not normally regard the automatic reaction to a dangerous situation which has been created by the negligence of the defender as a *novus actus interveniens*. The leading case is *Scott v Shepherd*.[58] In that case, the defendant tossed a lighted squib among a group of people. One of the group threw away the squib. It hit the

[53] [1996] CLC 1214.

[54] See also *Humber Oil Terminal Trustee Ltd v Owners of Ship Sivand* [1998] CLC 751.

[55] For example, in *Stansbie v Troman* [1948] 2 KB 48 a decorator was left alone in the plaintiff's house. He left the house with the external door unlocked to buy a roll of wallpaper. A thief entered and stole valuables. The Court of Appeal held that the decorator remained liable for theft. See also the Court of Appeal case of *Davies v Liverpool Corp* [1949] 2 All ER 175. A tram conductor failed to take adequate precautions to ensure that passengers could board the tram with safety. An unauthorised person rang the 'stop/start' bell. The tram started to move as the plaintiff was attempting to board it. She fell and was injured. It was held that the act of the third party did not break the chain of causation between the negligence of the conductor and the plaintiff's injury since such conduct was reasonably foreseeable. See also *Newby v General Lighterage Co Ltd* [1955] 1 Lloyds Rep 273. A barge had been properly tied up at a wharf on the Thames where it was known that children and youths were wont to interfere with the barges. Some unknown persons untied it. It collided with a rowing boat and damaged it. The barge owners were held liable for not fastening it more securely. They could not escape liability by showing that the damage was caused by wrongful interference by a third party. See also *Farah v Abdullahi* [2020] EWHC 825.

[56] 1978 SLT 122.

[57] See also *Cunningham v Reading FC* [1992] PIQR P141.

[58] [1773] 3 Wils 403.

plaintiff and injured him. It was held that the throwing away of the squib did not amount to a *novus actus interveniens*. Therefore, the defendant remained liable for the harm caused.

Again, in *Brandon v Osborne, Garrett and Co Ltd*[59] a skylight (which was broken due to the negligence of contractors, who were engaged in repairing the roof) fell from the roof of a shop, where the plaintiff was standing with her husband. She injured her leg in trying to pull him out of danger. It was held at first instance that she could recover for the injury which she had sustained.

Resuers' actions and breaking chain of causation

For policy reasons, the courts are not willing to regard any reasonable attempt which the pursuer makes to rescue a third party or property belonging to a third party[60] from danger, which has been caused by the negligence of the defender (and the pursuer is injured in that attempt), as breaking the chain of causation between the defender's act and the harm caused. For example, in the leading case of *Baker v T.E. Hopkins*[61] the defendant company was employed to clean out a contaminated well on a farm. It was decided to use a pump, powered by a petrol engine, for this purpose. The pump was placed inside the well. Two employees went down the well and were overcome by carbon monoxide fumes, which had built up in the well. A medical practitioner, who had been called to the well, descended the well, in order to give the men first aid. He, himself, was overcome by the fumes and died. The Court of Appeal held that, since the doctor's act of rescue was reasonable, it did not amount to a *novus actus interveniens*. The defendants were, therefore, liable for the practitioner's death, as well as for the deaths of the workers.

Suicide as a *novus actus interveniens*

Victims of physical injury can suffer long-term effects. Severe depression is not uncommon. Occasionally, such depression can lead to suicide. The question which falls to be answered in the context of the present discussion is whether suicide which has resulted from depression, which had been brought about by the defender's negligence, ranks as a *novus actus interveniens*. The leading case is the House of Lords case of *Corr v IBC Vehicles Ltd*.[62] In that case, the claimant's husband was employed by the defendant as a maintenance engineer. He sustained serious head injuries caused by malfunctioning machinery in the defendant's factory. He became depressed and committed suicide. The claimant sued the defendant for her husband's death. The House held that the depressive illness from which the deceased had suffered had been the direct and foreseeable consequence of the accident, for which the defendant had been responsible. Furthermore, his suicide, although a deliberate and conscious act on the part of the deceased, had been the direct result of that depressive illness, at a time when his capacity to make reasoned and informed judgements about his future

---

59 [1924] 1 KB 548.

60 *Hyett v Great Western Railway Co* [1948] 1 KB 345.

61 [1959] 1 WLR 966.

62 [2008] 1 AC 884.

had been impaired by that illness. The chain of causal consequences for which the defendant was liable had not been broken by the deceased's suicide. In short, the suicide did not rank as a *novus actus interveniens*. The defendant was, therefore, liable for the deceased's death. According to Lord Bingham, the principle of *novus actus interveniens* rested on fairness.[63] It was not fair to hold a tortfeasor liable, however gross his breach of duty was, for damage which had been caused by some independent supervening cause, for which the tortfeasor was not responsible. The judge approved decisions which had been taken by the courts, to the effect that the informed conscious decision by a person who was not suffering from a depressive illness ranked as a *novus actus interveniens*.[64]

Lord Scott was prepared to employ the 'thin skull' rule in deciding that the chain of causation had not been broken between the defendant's act of negligence and the claimant's death.[65] According to the judge, the claimant's depressive disorder was a result of the defendant's negligent act. By the application of the learning in *Page v Smith* no distinction fell to be drawn between physical and psychiatric injury in terms of the harm which the claimant had sustained. The defendant was required to take the claimant 'as he found him'. In short, the claimant's act of suicide did not break the chain of causation.

[63] Ibid at 903.

[64] Ibid at 904. See also *Dalling v R J Heale and Co Ltd* [2011] EWCA Civ. 365.

[65] [2008] 1 AC 884 at 908–9.

Chapter 8

Defences

We now consider the main defences which apply in negligence.

The defences which are discussed apply generally in delict, but have specific relevance in a negligence action.

CONTRIBUTORY NEGLIGENCE

At common law, contributory negligence was a complete defence in an action for damages.[1] That is to say, that if the pursuer contributed to his own loss he was regarded as the sole author of his misfortune, irrespective of his degree of fault. However, the law became very complicated as a result of this rule. Judges began to develop various rules in an attempt to circumvent the harshness of the rule. One such rule was the last opportunity rule. For example, in *Davies v Mann*[2] the plaintiff negligently left his ass on a highway. The defendant was driving too fast and negligently collided with and killed the ass. The plaintiff was allowed to recover since the defendant had the last opportunity of avoiding the accident.[3] However, the last opportunity rule was also open to criticism, since it resulted in the person whose negligence came last being held wholly responsible for the damage.

Sometimes, rather than focussing on the chronological sequence of events, the courts would attempt to isolate what was the 'decisive and immediate' cause of the pursuer's loss. In the House of Lords case of *Taylor v Dumbarton Tramways Co*[4] a two-year-old child who was playing on a roadway suffered injury when a tram drove off, without it first being established that there was no child to the south side of the tram-car. The pursuer was allowed to recover damages. Lord Chancellor Finlay stated:[5]

Even granting that there was some negligence in leaving a child of such tender years in the street without more efficient guidance, yet that negligence was not part of the transaction itself in which the accident occurred. Historically, it led up to it, but the accident was really ... entirely caused by the omission of those in charge of the car to

---

1 *Butterfield v Forrester* (1809) 11 East 70, 103 ER 926; *Cayzer Irvine and Co. v Carron Co* (1884) 9 App Cas 873; *Commissioner of Police v Reeves* [2000] 1 AC 360 at 371 (per Lord Hoffman).

2 (1842) 10 M & W 546; 152 ER 588.

3 See also *Carse v NB Steam Packet Co* (1895) 22 R 475.

4 1918 SC (HL) 96.

5 Ibid at 103.

look out to see whether there was any child about on the south side of the car as well as the north side of the car. In turn, Viscount Haldane stated:[6]

> [In] order that contributory negligence may be an answer to the plaintiff's action, the negligence which contributed must have been shown to be negligence which actually and directly led in itself to the accident; it must not be a negligence, independent of the act which caused the accident. The question always is, Which was the decisive and immediate cause? and, if the decisive and immediate cause was the negligence of the defender, then it does not matter that there was negligence on the part of the pursuer apart from which he would not have been in a position which brought about the injury by the accident.

The common law rule precluding liability if the pursuer was contributorily negligent generated a degree of artifice on the part of judges as they attempted to avoid finding a small degree of contributory negligence, given that such a finding would defeat the claim entirely. However, the common law was altered by the Law Reform (Contributory Negligence) Act 1945 which introduced a fairer and more realistic approach.[7]

LAW REFORM (CONTRIBUTORY NEGLIGENCE) ACT 1945

Section 1(1) of the Law Reform (Contributory Negligence) Act 1945 (the 'Act') provides:

> Where a person suffers damage as the result partly of his own fault and partly of the fault of any other person, or persons, a claim in respect of that damage shall not be defeated by reason of the fault of the person suffering the damage, but the damages recoverable in respect thereof shall be reduced to such extent as the court thinks just and equitable having regard to the claimant's share in the responsibility for the damage.

Under s4 of the Act '"damage" includes loss of life and personal injury'. The expression 'damage' would probably also cover damage to property. The Act also covers economic loss.[8] 'Fault' is defined, as far as Scotland is concerned, in s5(a) as 'a wrongful act, breach of statutory duty, or negligent act or omission which gives rise to liability in damages, or would apart from this Act, give rise to the defence of contributory negligence'. 'Fault' would also cover deliberate acts on the part of the pursuer.[9]

---

6 Ibid at 105–6.

7 In *Stapley v Gypsum Mines Ltd* [1953] AC 663 at 677 Lord Porter stated that: 'It [the 1945 Act] enables the court ... to seek less strenuously to find some ground for holding the plaintiff free from blame.' Again, in *Suhib Foods Ltd v Paskin Kryriakides Sands* [2003] PNLR 30 at [72] Bowsher J stated that the purpose of the 1945 Act was to do away with the injustices of the 'last opportunity rule'.

8 See for example *Platform Home Loans Ltd v Oyston Shipways Ltd* [2000] 2 AC 190.

9 For example, in *Reeves v Commissioner of Police of the Metropolis* [2000] 1 AC 360 a prisoner committed suicide by hanging himself while in prison custody. The defendant was under a duty to prevent deliberate self-harm by the prisoner. Responsibility for the suicide was apportioned equally between the deceased and the defendant. Lord Hoffman stated at 370, 'Because the police were under a duty to take reasonable care not to give [the deceased] the opportunity to kill himself, the common sense answer to the question whether their carelessness caused his death is "Yes". Because [the deceased] also had responsibility for his own life, the common-sense answer to the question whether he caused his own death is "Yes". Therefore, both causes contributed to his death and the Act of 1945 provides the means

However, the Act is inapplicable in relation to actions based on dishonesty.[10]

The pursuer's blameworthiness in relation to which damages fall to be reduced need not be associated with the defender's breach of duty. For example, in the Court of Appeal case of *Blackmore v Dept of Communities and Local Government*[11] a former employee of the defendant died as a result of lung cancer. The deceased had been exposed to asbestos during the period in which he worked for the defender. The deceased had not been provided with protective equipment. The deceased had smoked from the age of fourteen until his death at the age of seventy-four. Claims in terms of both negligence and breach of statutory duty were brought by his estate against the defendant. The defendant conceded liability. The sole issue before the court was the apportionment of damages, if any, based on the deceased's smoking. The court held that in determining the issue of apportionment under the 1945 Act, no distinction fell to be made between a claimant who contributed to his injury by conduct which was related to his work and a claimant who contributed to his injury by conduct which was not.[12] The concept of responsibility and blameworthiness under s1 was broad enough to cover both situations.

There are no clearly defined rules as to what conduct on the part of the pursuer ranks as 'just and equitable'. In the Court of Appeal case of *Quintas v National Smelting Co*[13] Sellers LJ stated:

> [T]he respective responsibilities of the parties and what is just and equitable having regard thereto, can only properly be assessed when it has been found what the plaintiff in fact did and what the defendants failed in their duty to do.

The court determines what the total amount of damages would have been if the pursuer had not been at fault, and then apportions liability, as a percentage of the total. If there is more than one defender, liability will be apportioned between them depending on their respective blameworthiness. For example, in the Court of Appeal case of *Davies v Swan Motor Company (Swansea) LD*[14] a bus ran into a lorry. Davies was killed. Both the bus driver and the lorry driver were at fault. Davies himself had been partly to blame for his injury, in that when the accident had taken place, he had been standing on the lorry sidestep, contrary to instructions. It was held that Davies's own negligence had contributed to his death. Damages were therefore reduced by one-fifth. The bus driver was held responsible for two-thirds of the remainder, and the lorry driver was held responsible for the remaining one-third.

Appellate courts are generally reluctant to overturn a trial judge's decision as to how liability should be apportioned.[15] However, the Supreme Court case of *Jackson*

of reflecting this division of responsibility in the award of damages ...' See also the Court of Appeal case of *Murphy v Culhane* [1977] QB 94 where the Court of Appeal held that the defence of contributory negligence could be successfully invoked in relation to an assault which had been perpetrated by the plaintiff's husband.

[10] *Corporation Nationale Del Cobre de Chile v Sogemin Metals Ltd* [1997] 1 WLR 1396.

[11] [2018] 2 WLR 139.

[12] Ibid at 147.

[13] [1961] 1 WLR 401 at 408.

[14] [1949] 2 KB 291.

[15] See for example the Inner House case of *Porter v Strathclyde Regional Council* 1991 SLT 446.

v Murray[16] provides a good example that, in certain circumstances, an appellate court is prepared to do so. In that case, the pursuer raised an action for damages in respect of injuries which she had received as a result of being struck by a motor vehicle which was being driven by the defender, after the pursuer had alighted from a school bus. The Lord Ordinary found the defender liable in negligence. However, he found that the pursuer had been contributorily negligent and reduced damages by 90 per cent. The pursuer reclaimed against the decision to the Inner House which reduced the assessment of contributory negligence to 70 per cent. The pursuer then appealed to the Supreme Court, which decided that the appellant be awarded 50 per cent damages.

Pursuer required to contribute to damage

For the defence of contributory negligence to apply, it is essential that the pursuer's conduct contributes to the damage which he sustains, for example, where a motorcyclist fails to wear a crash helmet[17] or where a car passenger fails to wear his seat belt.[18]

The pursuer need not owe the defender a duty of care, for the defence of contributory negligence to succeed.[19] However, for the defence to apply, the pursuer ought to have foreseen the consequences of his failure to take the relevant prophylactic action. For example, in *Jones v Livox Quarries Ltd*[20] the plaintiff was riding on the tow bar of a traxcavator (a vehicle which is used to carry stones). There was, of course, an obvious danger of his being thrown off the vehicle. However, he was hit by a vehicle which approached from behind him. He was injured. It was claimed on his behalf that he had not contributed to his injury. However, the Court of Appeal held that the damages which were awarded to him fell to be reduced under the Act, on account of his contributory negligence, on the basis that the plaintiff ought to reasonably have foreseen that if he did not act as a reasonably prudent man, he might be hurt.[21] The plaintiff was also required to foresee that others might be careless.

Standard of care

The standard of care which applies to the defence of contributory negligence is the same as that applying generally in the law of negligence, namely an objective standard.[22]

However, the courts are prepared to take into account the personal idiosyncrasies of the pursuer. For example, in *Condon v Condon*[23] the plaintiff, who was a passenger in the front seat of a car which was being driven by the defendant, refused to wear a seat belt because she had a phobia, which made the wearing of a seat belt unbearable

16 2015 SC (UKSC) 105.
17 *O'Connell v Jackson* [1972] 1 QB 270.
18 *Froom v Butcher* [1976] QB 286.
19 *Davies* n13.
20 [1952] 2 QB 608.
21 Ibid at 615 (per Denning LJ).
22 *A C Billings and Sons Ltd v Riden* [1958] AC 240. See also *Porter v Strathclyde Regional Council* 1991 SLT 446; *Campbell v Advantage Insurance Co* [2022] QB 354.
23 [1978] RTR 483.

because she had a fear about being trapped in the event of an accident. The car was being driven negligently by the defendant and was involved in an accident. The plaintiff suffered an eye injury caused by a piece of glass, broken from the car windscreen or window. In an action for damages for personal injuries caused by the defendant's negligence, the defendant claimed that the plaintiff had been contributorily negligent. However, it was held that the plaintiff had not been contributorily negligent. In short, the court could take into account the plaintiff's phobia. Again, in *Mackay v Borthwick*[24] the pursuer was a passenger in a car. She was injured in an accident. Liability was admitted. However, the defender claimed that the pursuer had been contributorily negligent in failing to wear a seat belt. P gave evidence to the court that she did not wear a seat belt because she found that uncomfortable, on account of a hiatus hernia. After stating that it was an exceptional case, the court held that the failure of the pursuer to wear a seat belt did not amount to contributory negligence.

As far as children are concerned, children can be held to be contributorily negligent. However, there are no hard and fast rules as to the age at which a child can be held to be contributorily negligent.[25] For example, in *McKinnel v White*[26] a five-year-old ran across a road and was injured by a passing vehicle. It was held that the damages which were awarded to him fell to be reduced on account of his contributory negligence.[27] However, concessions are made in respect of children. In determining whether the pursuer has been contributorily negligent, the court adopts an objective standard and takes into account how a child of a similar age would be expected to act in the circumstances. The age, intelligence and experience of a child of the age of the pursuer are considered.[28] For example, in the Privy Council case of *Yachuk v Oliver*

[24] 1982 SLT 265.

[25] *Ellis v Kelly* [2018] 4 WLR 124 at [48] (per Yip J).

[26] 1971 SLT (Notes) 61.

[27] See also the Inner House case of *Campbell v Ord and Maddison* (1873) 1 R 149 at 153 (per Lord Justice Clerk) in which it was held that a child of four could be contributorily negligent. In the Inner House case of *Cass v Edinburgh and District Tramways Co Ltd* 1909 SC 1068 a child aged 4½ was held capable of contributory negligence. See also *Harvey v Cairns* 1989 SLT 107 in which a six-year-old child was held contributorily negligent to the extent of two-thirds, when she stepped from a pavement into the path of an oncoming vehicle which was being driven at an excessive speed. In *Banner's Tutor v Kennedy's Trs* 1978 SLT (Notes) 83 a girl aged five alighted from the rear of a minibus and ran into a lorry. She was found to be of average intelligence and had been warned by her parents of the danger of heavy traffic. She had some experience of heavy traffic. Furthermore, an express warning had been given by the driver of the minibus. She was held to be one-fifth responsible and her damages were reduced accordingly. In *O'Connor v Matthews* 1996 SLT 408 a twelve-year-old boy suffered severe brain injury when he was knocked down by a van in a road accident. He raised an action for damages against the driver of the vehicle and his employer. It was held that the pursuer and the driver were equally to blame for the accident. Therefore, the damages which were awarded to him fell to be reduced by 50 per cent on account of his contributory negligence. In *Dawson v Scottish Power plc* 1999 SLT 672 a boy who was almost eleven was injured while climbing over a steel fence (which had spikes on top) surrounding an electricity sub-station, in order to retrieve a football. He was held to be one-third contributorily negligent. In the Inner House case of *McCluskey v Wallace* 1998 SLT 711 a four-year-old child was held to be 20 per cent contributorily negligent when she was knocked off her bicycle by a car driven by the defender.

[28] *Ellis* n22 at [48]. See also *Owens v Lewis* [2024] EWHC 609.

Blais Co Ltd[29] the defendants negligently supplied the plaintiff (aged nine) with petrol. The latter used the petrol to play a game. He was badly burned. It was held that there had been no contributory negligence on the part of the plaintiff, since a normal child of his age could not be expected to know the properties of petrol. Again, in the Court of Appeal case of *Gough v Thorne*[30] a girl aged thirteen was beckoned to cross a road by a lorry driver who had stopped his vehicle. She was hit by a lorry which had overtaken the lorry on the inside of the road. The court held that she had not been contributorily negligent, in that she had behaved as any other child of her age would have done in the circumstances.[31]

However, a child will not necessarily be contributorily negligent if the adult accompanying the child is negligent. In *Oliver v Birmingham and Midlands Omnibus Ltd*[32] a child was struck by an omnibus and injured while crossing a road with his grandfather. The grandfather had been negligent in letting go of the child's hand. However, the child's claim was not reduced. Similarly, in *Brogan's Tutors v Glasgow District Council*[33] a two-year-old child was left on his own for a short time while his mother ran his bath. There was an electric fire in the room in which the child had been left. It had been switched on. It had a guard over it. However, the guard over it had missing retaining screws. When the child's mother investigated noise in the room, she discovered the child being thrown backwards and forwards. The child had succeeded in gripping the uppermost of two elements, which was live at the time. When the child's mother switched the fire off, the child was thrown into the middle of the room. As a result, the child suffered burning injuries. The Lord Ordinary held that the guard had been insecure from installation by the defenders, who were the landlords. It was held that they were 20 per cent to blame. The remaining 80 per cent was apportioned to the child's mother, having regard to the fact that the fire had obviously been unsafe for some time. The judge rejected the defenders' argument to the effect that a doctrine of identification fell to be applied, with the effect of cutting down the child's right to damages.

Physically and mentally disabled

As far as the defence of contributory negligence is concerned, a person who is physically or mentally disabled will be judged by the standard of a person who has similar disabilities. In the Court of Appeal case of *Cork v Kirby Maclean Ltd*[34] the plaintiff, unknown to his employers, was subject to epilepsy and had been forbidden to work at heights. As a result of an epileptic fit, he fell from a platform, which should have had guardrails and toe-boards to comply with relevant legislation. Damages to his representatives were therefore reduced by 50 per cent.

29 [1949] AC 386.
30 [1966] 1 WLR 1387.
31 See also *Probert v Moore* [2012] EWHC 2324.
32 [1933] 1 KB 35.
33 1978 SLT (Notes) 47.
34 [1952] 2 All ER 402.

However, a person of unsound mind who is unable to appreciate the danger of a given course of action will not be contributorily negligent, on the grounds that it would not be just and equitable to attribute responsibility to such a person.[35]

CONTRIBUTORY NEGLIGENCE AND THE 'AGONY OF THE MOMENT' RULE

There is no contributory negligence on the part of the pursuer if the defender has put him in a dangerous situation, by virtue of the defender's negligence, and damage accrues to the pursuer because of his trying to extricate himself from that situation. For example, in *Jones v Boyce*[36] the plaintiff was a passenger in a coach which had just set off. The coupling rein, which was defective, broke. The coach was in danger of being overturned. The plaintiff jumped off the coach. He was injured. It was held that there was no contributory negligence on his part. In the House of Lords case of *Laird Line v United States Shipping Board*[37] Lord Dunedin stated that '[It] is not in the mouth of those who have created the danger of the situation to be minutely critical of what is done by those whom they by their fault, involved in the danger.'[38] However, if the pursuer is simply threatened with personal inconvenience of a trifling kind, he is not entitled to take unreasonable risks.[39]

CONTRIBUTORY NEGLIGENCE AND THE DILEMMA RULE

Another exception to the defence of contributory negligence is the so-called dilemma rule. That is to say, where the pursuer chooses the wrong course of action of two options which are open to him, in a situation created by negligence of the defender, and the former is injured, as a consequence, the pursuer will not be held to have been contributorily negligent. For example, in the Inner House case of *Wallace v Bergius*[40] a driver who was travelling on his own side of the road saw a vehicle approaching him on that side of the road. He swerved to the other side of the road, as did the driver of the other vehicle. The driver of the first vehicle was not held to be contributorily negligent in these circumstances.

CONTRIBUTORY NEGLIGENCE SPECIFIC SITUATIONS

Slipping/tripping cases

The defence of contributory negligence is often invoked in cases where the pursuer has either tripped or slipped. For example, in the Inner House case of *Porter v*

---

35 *Reeves v Commissioner of Police of the Metropolis* [2001] 1 AC 360 at 372 (per Lord Hoffman). See also *PPX v Aulakh* [2019] EWHC 717.

36 (1816) 1 Starkie 493; 171 ER 540.

37 1924 SC (HL) 37 at 40.

38 See also *Sayers v Harlow UDC* [1958] 1 WLR 623.

39 *Adams v Lancashire and Yorkshire Railway Co* (1868–9) LR 4 CP 739.

40 1915 SC 205.

Strathclyde Regional Council[41] a nursery assistant slipped on some food which had been spilled on the floor of a room where young children were eating. She sued her employers, claiming that they had failed to instruct and enforce a proper system for cleaning up pieces of food from the kitchen floor, and that they had failed to take reasonable care to ensure that children were adequately supervised, with a view to prevent food being discarded on the floor. However, the pursuer knew that food spillage was a common occurrence. Both parties were held equally to blame for the accident. In short, the pursuer was found to have been 50 per cent contributorily negligent, and her damages were reduced accordingly.[42]

Road traffic accident cases

The defence of contributory negligence is frequently invoked in road accident cases. In *Campbell v Gillespie*[43] the pursuer sought damages in respect of the death of her husband. The deceased was killed when he drove his car into the back of an unlit stationary lorry. The lorry had broken down and was being worked on by a mechanic (the third defender) who had disconnected the batteries of the lorry to change them, thus extinguishing the lorry's lights. A police warning sign had been placed at the side of the carriageway. The mechanic had parked his van, which was lit, in front of the lorry, rather than to its rear. It was claimed that if it was necessary to switch off the hazard lights, he had a duty to take reasonable steps to give an alternative warning, and had duty to switch on the hazard warning lights on the breakdown vehicle, and to park it at the rear of the lorry so that it could be seen by traffic travelling on the carriageway which was blocked by the lorry. The temporary judge, while accepting that the third defender was at fault, also concluded that the deceased was at fault. If he had been keeping a good lookout, he would have seen the police sign. He had also failed to observe the unlit rear of the lorry in time. The judge concluded:[44]

> The actings and omissions of the [deceased] and of the third defender are both causes of the accident. In my opinion the accident was due partly to the presence of an inadequately lit obstruction which was not sufficiently flagged, given the circumstances, and partly due to the deceased's failure to take reasonable care to keep a proper lookout and keep proper control as he proceeded along the roadway … It has been said more than once that these questions should be approached broadly and judged as a matter of common sense, looking at the whole circumstances. Every case depends on its own peculiar circumstances. I have

41 1991 SLT 446.

42 The court would have made a similar apportionment (that is, 50 per cent) in the Outer House case of *McClafferty v British Telecommunications plc* 1987 SLT 327 if liability had been established (a pedestrian tripped on a raised manhole cover). See also *McMillan v Lord Advocate* 1991 SLT 150; *Brown v City of Edinburgh Council* 1999 SLT (Sh Ct) 43; *Ellis v Bristol City Council* 2007 ICR 1614; *Porter v Scottish Borders Council* 2009 Rep.LR 46; *Cheung v Zhu (t/a Yang Sing Fish and Chip)* [2011] EWHC 2913; *Caerphilly CBC v Button* [2011] ICR D3; *Beaton v Ocean Terminal Ltd* 2018 CSOH 74; *Lowe v Cairnstar Ltd* 2020 SLT (Sh Ct) 151.

43 1996 SLT 503.

44 Ibid at 510.

> concluded that fault should be shared on the basis of 60 per cent fault to [the deceased] and 40 per cent to the third defender.[45]

In *Malcolm v Fair*[46] the pursuer, a pedestrian, who was under the influence of alcohol, started to cross a road without having observed an approaching car. He was struck by the car, the driver of which had failed to observe him. It was held that the pedestrian and the driver were equally to blame. The pursuer's damages were reduced by 50 per cent. Again, in *Buck v Ainsley*[47]the defender was driving her car on a road shortly after midnight. She collided with the pursuer who was wearing dark clothing at the time. The latter was injured. The pursuer's damages were reduced by 70 per cent.

Again, in *Blackhall v Macinnes*[48] the pursuer was struck by a car when, following a puncture, she was attempting to change the wheel at the side of a dual carriageway. At the time of the accident, daylight was fading, visibility was poor and traffic was relatively heavy. She was found to be contributorily negligent to the extent of 20 per cent. The Lord Ordinary stated that the course of action adopted by the pursuer, namely an attempt to change the offside wheel while on the carriageway, was particularly hazardous.[49]

The defence of contributory negligence has also been raised against passengers in cars which have been driven by intoxicated drivers. In *Owens v Brimmell*[50] the plaintiff, knowing that the defendant was under the influence of alcohol, took a lift from him. The plaintiff (who was not wearing a seat belt at the time) was injured when the car collided with a lamppost. He was held to be 20 per cent contributorily negligent for the injuries which he had sustained.[51]

The defence of contributory negligence has also been invoked against drivers or passengers who have failed to wear seat belts and have thus sustained more serious injury than otherwise would have been the case. It is now recognised by statute that it is an offence for those travelling in a car not to wear a seat belt.[52] As far as the law of delict is concerned, where injuries are either sustained or aggravated because of a failure to wear a seat belt, the award of damages will be reduced proportionately. This

---

45 See also the Court of Appeal case of *Dolby v Milner* 1996 CLY 4430. In that case, D had been turning right into a major road when he collided with M, a motorcyclist. M had been travelling at an excessive speed and had failed to take evasive action. D raised an action against the motorcyclist in respect of the damage to his car and the motorcyclist counterclaimed for personal injuries. The trial judge apportioned liability as 75 per cent against M and 25 per cent against D. M appealed. On appeal the court reversed the trial judge's apportionment. The court held that D was under a continuing obligation to give way. Although M was travelling in excess of the speed limit and had failed to take evasive action the motorcycle had been visible from 95 yards away. D ought to have seen it.

46 1993 SLT 342. See also *Kemp v Secretary of State for Scotland* 2000 SLT 471. In that case, the pursuer, who was under the influence of alcohol at the time, tripped and fell on a raised kerb at the edge of a footpath. He was found to be contributorily negligent. His damages were reduced by one-third.

47 [2017] CSOH 73.

48 1997 SLT 649.

49 At 650.

50 [1977] QB 859.

51 See also *Campbell v Advantage Insurance Co Ltd* [2021] EWCA Civ 1698. See also *Currie v Clamps Executor* 2002 SLT 196; *Gleeson v Court* [2007] EWHC 2397; *Sloan v Triplett* 1985 SLT 294; *McCaig v Langan* 1964 SLT 121; *Hill v Chivers* 1987 SLT 323.

52 Road Traffic Act 1988, s14(3) and associated regulations.

was the case even prior to the introduction of legislation requiring the wearing of seat belts. In the Court of Appeal case of *Froom v Butcher*[53] the claimant would not have suffered head and chest injuries had he been wearing his seat belt. However, the wearing of a seat belt would have made no difference to the broken finger which the claimant also sustained. Lord Denning MR suggested that the appropriate reduction was 25 per cent where the injuries would have been prevented altogether by wearing a seat belt, and 15 per cent where the injuries would have been less severe, had the seat belt been worn.[54] In *Froom*, the claimant's damages were reduced by 20 per cent.[55] In the Scottish case of *Mitchell v Swanson's Executor*[56] an eighteen-year-old man, who was a front-seat passenger in a car, sustained serious injuries which would have been lessened, but not avoided, had he been wearing a seat belt. It was observed that where damage would have been prevented by wearing a seat belt, the appropriate reduction was 20 per cent. However, in the instant case, damages fell to be reduced by 10 per cent.[57]

Workplace Accidents

Contributory negligence is often raised as a defence in actions related to the workplace. For example, in *Beggs v Motherwell Bridge Fabrication Ltd*[58] a factory worker was killed following an accident which occurred when he was driving a forklift truck along a road which was situated within factory grounds. Potholes had formed in the road and old railway lines protruded from the surface. The truck came to a sudden halt when the forks stuck in the road surface. The deceased was propelled forward. He sustained fatal injuries. His widow and children raised an action against his employer, claiming *inter alia* that the latter had breached their common law duty to take reasonable care for the safety of employees. The Lord Ordinary (Lord Eassie) held that the deceased was 20 per cent contributorily negligent for the accident on the grounds that he had failed to set the forks at a proper height.

In *McLellan v Dundee City Council*[59] the pursuer, who was employed as a gardener by the defenders, suffered significant injury to his right hand after attempting to clear a blockage in the central gutter of a triple mower he was using to cut grass. He raised

53 [1976] QB 286.

54 Ibid at 296.

55 See also *Campbell v Advantage Insurance Co Ltd* [2020] EWHC 2210.

56 1980 SLT (Notes) 41.

57 See also *Hanlon v Cuthbertson* 1981 SLT (Notes) 57 (10 per cent reduction); *Sloan v Triplett* 1985 SLT 294 (20 per cent reduction suggested); *Hill v Chivers* 1987 SLT 323 (33 per cent deduction. However, that related to both the pursuer's failure to wear a seat belt and the pursuer's allowing himself to be driven by an intoxicated driver). In *Taylor v Leslie* 1998 SLT 1248 a passenger in a car was killed in the Orkney island of Shapinsay. He was being driven by an underaged, unlicensed and uninsured driver at the time. The car had been on a grass farm track which led down to a road. The driver was revving the engine so that the wheels of the car began to spin. The deceased opened the front passenger door in order to observe the spinning wheels. He was not wearing a seat belt and had encouraged the driver to rev up the engine even more. The car sped on to the road and collided with another vehicle causing the deceased's death. The deceased was held to be 50 per cent contributorily negligent in the circumstances.

58 1998 SLT 1215.

59 [2009] CSOH 9.

an action against the defender, claiming *inter alia* that it had breached its common law duty of care to him. It was held that damages fell to be reduced by 20 per cent.

In *MacDonald v Wood Group Engineering (North Sea) Ltd*[60] the pursuer, an experienced deck crew rigger, was injured while transferring material and equipment from a supply vessel on to a platform on an oil rig. Whilst the defenders were held *inter alia* to have breached their common law duty of care to him, the pursuer was held to be 50 per cent contributorily negligent.

TWO OR MORE WRONGDOERS

It may happen that there are two or more defenders in cases where the defence of contributory negligence is raised. In such circumstances, how does the court apportion damages? This question fell to be answered in the House of Lords case of *Fitzgerald v Lane*.[61] The facts of the case were simple. The plaintiff was crossing a busy high street, at a pelican crossing which was showing green in the traffic's favour, when he was struck by a car driven by the first defendant. The plaintiff was propelled into the road where he was struck by another car which was driven by the second defendant. The plaintiff was seriously injured. The trial judge held that each party was a third to blame. On that basis judgment was entered against both defendants for two-thirds of the plaintiff's damages. The Court of Appeal upheld the judge's decision on causation and quantum, but allowed the defendants' appeal on apportionment, holding that judgment should be entered for the plaintiff against each defendant for half of his damages, with an order for contribution between the defendants on a fifty-fifty basis. The House of Lords, in upholding that decision, held that the trial judge had telescoped or elided two separate issues, namely whether the plaintiff was contributorily negligent, and to what extent damages should be reduced as a consequence, and secondly, the amount of contribution recoverable between the two defendants, having regard to the extent of their responsibility for the damage recovered by the plaintiff.[62] The House held that the plaintiff was substantially the author of his own misfortune and found him to be 50 per cent contributorily negligent. His damages were reduced by 50 per cent. Each defendant was therefore required to contribute equally to the remainder.

ILLEGALITY

If the pursuer participated in criminal activity at the time he sustained harm, by virtue of the conduct of the defender, he may be prevented from recovering damages, by operation of the defence of illegality. Thus, if two burglars, A and B, agree to open a safe by means of explosives, and A so negligently handles the explosive charge as to injure B, B might find some difficulty in maintaining an action for negligence against A.[63] In short, the pursuer should not be allowed to profit (in the broad sense) from his

60 [2010] CSOH 165.

61 [1989] AC 328.

62 Ibid at 339 (per Lord Akner).

63 See the dictum of Lord Asquith in *NCB v England* [1954] AC 403 at 429.

own wrong or turpitude.[64] The defence is based on public policy considerations.[65] The maxim *ex turpi causa non oritur actio* has its origins in the law of contract. In *Reeves v Commissioner of Police of the Metropolis*[66] Buxton LJ stated that 'the limits of this defence are very difficult to state or rationalise, it being recognised as sitting more easily in the law of contract than of tort'.[67] However, the courts have experienced difficulty in applying the defence in delict/tort cases. Indeed, the defence represents a grey area of the law of delict/tort. The defence was not recognised in England until *Ashton v Turner*.[68] The defence of illegality was a relative latecomer as far as the law of delict is concerned.

The defence operates as a complete defence. That is to say, that if the court accepts the defence, the pursuer is entitled to no remedy.

The relevant criminal act on the part of pursuer may be joint in nature.[69] However, the defence may be invoked against a pursuer who has acted alone in the course of criminal activity.[70]

It is only in cases of serious crime that the defence is likely to succeed.[71] For example, over the years, many people have recovered damages in respect of injuries which have been sustained in motor accidents, notwithstanding that they have been exceeding the speed limit at the time.

Duncan v Ross Harper and Murphy[72] illustrates the operation of the defence. There, a nineteen-year-old man was injured while he was a passenger in a negligently driven Ford Escort. He had participated in the theft of the vehicle. The action raised by the pursuer was not against the driver of the car, but rather against the solicitors whom he had instructed to deal with his personal injury claim. The solicitors had failed to raise the action for personal injuries against the driver within the statutory limitation period. The pursuer, therefore, sought to recover damages from his solicitors in

64 In *Clunis v Camden and Islington Health Authority* [1998] QB 978 at 990 Beldam LJ stated that the court ought not allow itself to be made an instrument to enforce obligations alleged to arise out of the plaintiff's own criminal act.

65 See for example *Lewis-Ranwell v G4S Health Services* (UK) Ltd [2024] EWCA Civ 138. In *Hewison v Meridan Shipping* n65 Ward LJ stated at 793 that it was an inherent aspect of the public policy which informs the whole doctrine.

66 [1999] QB 169 at 184.

67 In *Hewison v Meridan Shipping plc Ltd* [2003] ICR 766 at 787 Ward LJ stated that the search for principle was elusive.

68 [1981] QB 137 per C Whitting (ed) *Street on Torts* (16th edn) (OUP, 2020) at 215, fn 124.

69 See for example *Lindsay v Poole* 1984 SLT 269; *Pitts v Hunt* [1991] 1 QB 24; *Sloan v Triplett* 1985 SLT 294; *Ashcroft's Curator Bonis v Stewart* 1988 SLT 163; *Wilson v Price* 1989 SLT 484; *Weir v Wyper* 1992 SLT 579; *Taylor v Leslie* 1998 SLT 1248; *Currie v Clamps Exr* 2002 SLT 196; *Anderson v Hameed* 2010 Rep LR 132; *Beaumont v Ferrier* [2014] EWHC 2398.

70 See for example *Revill v Newberry* [1996] QB 567; *Clunis v Camden and Islington Health Authority* [1998] QB 978; *Gray v Thames Trains Ltd* [2009] 1 AC 1339; *Henderson v Dorset Heathcare University NHS Foundation Trust* [2018] 3 WLR 1651; *Lewis-Ranwell v G4S Health Services (UK) Ltd* [2024] EWCA Civ 138.

71 In the Supreme Court case of *Les Laboratoires Servier v Apotex Inc* [2015] AC 430 at 447 Lord Sumption was of the opinion that 'turpitude' in terms of the defence of illegality was confined to criminal and quasi criminal acts because only acts in these categories engaged public interest, which was the foundation of the illegality defence.

72 1993 SLT 105.

respect of professional negligence. The Lord Ordinary (Lord Kirkwood) held that the solicitors had been negligent. However, he assoilzied the defenders on the basis that, even if the personal injuries action had been raised timeously, the defence of illegality would have prevented the pursuer from recovering any damages against his fellow wrongdoer. The pursuer had been involved in the theft of the car and, accordingly, was not entitled to recover damages from his co-participant in crime.

Duncan should be contrasted with two English cases.

The first case is the Court of Appeal case of *Day v Womble Bond Dickinson (UK) Ltd*.[73] In that case, Day ('D') had been convicted (in a case which had been brought by Natural England) for cutting down trees in a site of special scientific interest (SSSI). D then brought a claim for breach of contract and/or damages against his solicitors – namely, Womble Bond Dickenson (WBD) – on the basis that D would have been acquitted of a criminal offence, if his criminal trial had been properly defended. WBD claimed, by way of a defence, that the action against them was bound to fail, *inter alia*, by reason of the doctrine of illegality. At first instance, the trial judge struck out the claimants' claim. In the Court of Appeal, Coulson LJ stated[74] that it was a rule of law, as well as a manifestation of public policy, that a civil court would not award damages to compensate a claimant for a disadvantage which the criminal courts had imposed on him or her, by way of punishment for a criminal act for which he or she was responsible. The judge concluded by deciding that D's claim failed.[75]

The second case was the Supreme Court case of *Stoffel v Grondona*[76] in which the defendant, G, agreed with M to take part in a mortgage fraud, whereby G would use her good credit history to obtain a mortgage advance. It was agreed that M, who was thereby able to raise capital finance he would not have been able to raise otherwise, would retain control of the property, making mortgage repayments, and receiving any rental income, but that G would recover 50 per cent of the proceeds of sale, if it was later sold. G obtained the mortgage advance, without disclosing to the lenders any details of her arrangement with M. However, following completion, G's solicitors ('S') failed to register at the Land Registry the transfer to her of the property, or the new legal charge in favour of her lender. Subsequently, the mortgage repayments fell into arrears. Being unable to enforce its security over the property, G's lenders brought proceedings against her, to obtain a money judgment. In turn, G brought a claim against S, seeking damages for breach of duty and breach of contract. S admitted negligence and breach of contract but contended that since the purpose of instructing them was to further a mortgage fraud, the claim should be dismissed under the common doctrine of illegality. The trial judge and the Court of Appeal allowed G's claim against S. S appealed. The Supreme Court dismissed S's appeal.

Lord Lloyd-Jones (with whom the remainder of the court agreed) stated that the defence of illegality had been significantly developed by the Supreme Court case of *Patel v Mirza*[77] where a majority of the court had rejected the reliance principle,

[73] [2020] EWCA Civ 447.

[74] Ibid at [28].

[75] D's appeal succeeded, to a limited extent, on other grounds. See (2020) 156 RepB 7.

[76] [2021] AC 540.

[77] [2017] AC 467.

whereby relief was refused to parties who had to rely on their own illegality in order to establish their case. In its place, the court adopted a more flexible approach which addressed underlying policy considerations, and also permitted account to be taken of the proportionality of the outcome.[78] In determining whether a claim was barred by the defence of illegality, by virtue of being contrary to the public interest (because it would be harmful to the integrity of the legal system) one was required to take three factors into consideration.[79] The first consideration was the underlying purpose of the prohibition which had been transgressed. The second consideration was whether there were any other relevant public policies which could be rendered ineffective, or less effective, by the denial of the claim. The third was proportionality, that was to say, whether denial of the claim would be a proportionate response to the illegality.

As far as the application of the first factor was concerned, Lord Lloyd-Jones stated that the background to G's claim against S was a serious fraud.[80] The judge stated that deterrence was one underlying policy of the law against fraud. However, he doubted whether permitting a civil remedy to persons such as G would undermine that policy to any considerable extent. The risk that they might be left without a remedy if their solicitor should prove negligent in registering a transaction was unlikely to feature in their thinking. A further underlying purpose of the prohibition against mortgage fraud was the protection of the public and, in particular, mortgagees from suffering loss. However, refusing G a remedy against S for failing to register the transaction would not enhance that protection, simply because registration of the transaction could only take place *after* the completion of the conveyance. By the time of S's negligent breach of duty, the loan had already been advanced by the lender. The registration was not a necessary step in perpetrating the fraud. By the time the negligent act had taken place, the fraud was complete.[81] Therefore, denying a remedy to G against S would not afford any protection to the lender.

As far as the second consideration was concerned, in relation to public policy, conveyancing solicitors should perform their duties diligently and without negligence.[82] In the event of a negligent breach of duty, those who use their services should be entitled to seek a civil remedy for the loss which they had suffered. To permit solicitors to escape liability for negligence in the conduct of their clients' affairs, when they discover, after the event, that a misrepresentation had been made to a mortgagee, would run counter to these policies. To deny G a remedy would also be a disincentive to the diligent performance of solicitors of their duties.[83]

As far as the third factor was concerned, the court observed that the mortgage fraud simply provided a background to the claim by G against S, in respect of their negligence in registering the title.[84] The way in which G had procured finance to obtain that title was irrelevant to S's obligation to register the title. By the time S was

[78] Ibid at 547.
[79] Ibid at 553.
[80] Ibid at 555.
[81] Ibid at 556.
[82] Ibid at 556.
[83] Ibid at 558.
[84] Ibid at 559.

required to register the title, the defrauding of the lender has already taken place. G's claim for breach of duty against S was conceptually entirely separate from her fraud of the mortgagee.[85]

However, in *Duncan* the very fact that the pursuer had flouted the criminal law automatically deprived him of a remedy, in terms of the law of delict. In other words, it was quite irrelevant that the pursuer's prior criminal conduct was quite unrelated to the defender's professional negligence. It simply sufficed that the pursuer did not come before the court with 'clean hands'. It will be interesting to see whether the Scottish courts follow *Stoffel*.

In determining whether the defence of illegality is applicable, the court takes into account the degree of moral turpitude which is associated with the pursuer's conduct. However, this is a rough and ready exercise and underscores the general point that the defence of illegality represents a grey area of the law of delict. The courts seem to approach each case intuitively.[86]

For example, in *Weir v Wyper*[87] a sixteen-year-old girl went on a trip with another girl and two men. One of the men and the other girl left the car. Thus the girl was left with the defender in the car in the dark, and in an unfamiliar place. She knew that the defender only held a provisional licence but nevertheless asked him for a lift home. The defender began to drive at high speed, breaking violently when he required to stop. The car left the road and overturned, and the pursuer was injured. Lord Coulsfield concluded that the defence of illegality should not apply in these circumstances. His Lordship was of the view that each case had to be decided on its own merits. In the instant case, the pursuer was not participating in any significant criminal activity.[88]

Again, in *Buckett v Staffordshire CC*[89] the claimant, who was sixteen when the accident took place, was trespassing on the roof of a school building one weekend.

---

85 Ibid at 561.

86 In the Supreme Court case of *Les Laboratoires Servier v Apotex Inc* [2015] AC 430 at 440, Lord Sumption stated that the application of the defence of illegality called for a value judgment about the significance of the illegality and the injustice of barring the claimant's claim on account of it.

87 1992 SLT 579.

88 Ibid at 583. See also *Currie v Clump's Executor* 2002 SLT 196. The degree of criminality, being a minor statutory breach, was not serious enough to disable the injured party from recovering. The pursuer had allowed himself to be carried in a car which had been taken without the owner's consent. Lord Clarke expressed the view (ibid at 200) that even if there had been a breach of s178(1) of the Road Traffic Act 1998 it could not be considered a serious breach. The courts adopted a pragmatic approach as to whether participation in criminal conduct disabled an injured party from recovering damages; *Toms v Royal Mail Group plc* 2006 SLT 431. A man was killed when he fell asleep at the wheel of a lorry which he was driving for the Post Office. It was alleged that the deceased's driving hours exceeded those permitted by statute. The defender argued that the pursuer's action was defeated by the defence of *ex turpi causa*. Lord Glennie stated (at para. 38) that even if it was shown that the deceased was in breach of the legal limit in the hours driven or worked, and even if he was aware of such contravention of the law, such illegality was collateral to the pursuer's claim, and was insufficient to defeat the claim; *Taylor v Leslie* 1998 SLT 1248 (the facts are discussed above, n 57, in relation to contributory negligence). The driver's illegal conduct would not have been considered particularly reprehensible on the Orkney island in question, and it would be wrong to deny recovery on the grounds that the deceased was engaged in the course of a common criminal enterprise with the defender.

89 [2015] 4 WLUK 121.

In the course of so doing, he fell through a fragile area of glass. He sustained serious injury as a result of the fall. He sued the defendant, claiming that the latter, as occupier of the school, had breached its statutory duty to him in terms of the Occupier Liability Acts 1957 and 1984. In turn, the defendant invoked the defence of illegality, asserting that up to the time of his fall, the claimant, with others, was engaged in a course of conduct which the defendant alleged amounted, *inter alia*, to wanton vandalism and criminal damage. Judge Main QC stated[90] that if the claimant had fallen through the skylight while committing criminal damage to the sunlight glass, then the defence of illegality would have succeeded. However, at the time the accident took place, the claimant had ceased engaging in acts of criminal damage and dishonesty. He was merely trespassing on the school roof. The tort of trespass did not offend any public interest. However, the claimant failed in his action, since the judge held that the defendant had not breached its statutory duty to him.[91]

In *Ashmore v Rock Steady Security Ltd*[92] a nightclub doorman punched the pursuer causing him to fall backwards and strike his head on the pavement. In a subsequent action, it was held that the pursuer's persistent annoyance and verbal abuse of the doorman did not operate to defeat his claim, on the basis of *ex turpi causa non oritur actio*. Indeed, the pursuer stood exonerated of any unlawful act.

Again, in the Court of Appeal case of *Kirkham v Chief Constable of the Greater Manchester Police*[93] the police knew that a prisoner was a suicide risk but failed to pass on this information to the prison authorities. The prisoner, who was suffering from clinical depression, committed suicide. The plaintiff, as administratrix of her husband's estate, brought an action in negligence against the chief constable. The defendant argued *inter alia* that the defence of *ex turpi causa non oritur actio* was applicable. However, the court held that since suicide was no longer an offence, and that allowing the defence of illegality to succeed would not affront the public conscience, the defence did not succeed.[94]

However, the illegality defence was successfully invoked in the Court of Appeal case of *Pitts v Hunt*.[95] In that case, the plaintiff and his friend were at a disco, drinking. They set off home on Hunt's motorcycle. The plaintiff was aware that Hunt was neither licensed nor insured to drive. The plaintiff rode pillion on the way home and actively encouraged Hunt to drive in a fast, reckless manner, deliberately intended to frighten other members of the public using the highway. The motorcycle collided with a car. The plaintiff was seriously injured, and Hunt was killed. Hunt's blood alcohol level was found to have been twice over the legal limit. It was held that the plaintiff had encouraged Hunt to commit offences. Therefore on the grounds of public policy the plaintiff was precluded from recovering compensation for his injuries.[96]

---

90 Ibid at para. 185.

91 Ibid at para. 202.

92 2006 SLT 207.

93 [1990] 2 QB 283.

94 Ibid at 291 (per Lloyd LJ).

95 [1991] 1 QB 24.

96 Ibid at 46 (per Beldam LJ). *Pitts* should be contrasted with *Dormer v Wilson Green Realisations 123 Ltd* [2025] EWHC 523. In that case, the claimant had sustained brain injury as a pillion passenger on a motorcycle which was being driven dangerously by the defendant. The defence of illegality failed in

The Court of Appeal had the opportunity to discuss the relevance of turpitude in relation to the defence of illegality in *Lewis-Ranwell v G4S Health Services Ltd*.[97] Lewis-Ranwell ('L') was diagnosed with schizophrenia in his mid-twenties. He had spells of intensive psychiatric care in 2016 and 2017. In 2019 L attacked and killed three elderly men in their homes, in the delusional belief that they were paedophiles. L was charged with murder, but following a trial in Exeter Crown Court, he was found not guilty by reason of insanity. That meant, because of his mental illness, he did not know at the time of the killings that what he was doing was wrong. In the two days before the killings, L had been arrested by the police for burglary and detained at a police station before being released. He then committed an assault on an elderly man and was arrested again. He was released on bail the following day. During his periods of detention L had behaved violently and erratically and was apparently mentally very unwell. L was seen or spoken to by health professionals employed by G4S Health Services (UK) Ltd ('G4S') and Devon Partnership NHS Trust ('the Trust').

In February 2020 L commenced proceedings in the High Court against G4S, the police, the Trust and the local authority, seeking damages for personal injury, loss of liberty, loss of reputation and pecuniary loss. In general terms, L claimed that it should have been obvious to all concerned, during both detentions, that if he were released, there was a real danger that he would injure other people, and that the necessary steps should have been taken to keep him in detention, until it was safe for him to be released.

The defendants issued an application that the claim should be struck out, on the basis that the defendants could rely on the defence of illegality, since L's claim was based on three unlawful homicides. At first instance, the applications were dismissed, on the basis that because the verdict not guilty by reason of insanity meant he did not know what he was doing was wrong, L's conduct did not have the necessary element of turpitude. The defendants appealed.

In the Court of Appeal Underhill LJ reviewed the case law concerning circumstances where the claimant was mentally ill. He concluded that there was no binding authority on the question whether the defence of illegality applied where the unlawful act in question was done when the claimant was insane.[98] Addressing the instant case, the judge stated that L had suffered serious injury (in the technical sense) from the failure of others who had owed him a duty to protect him from harm of the kind he in fact suffered.[99] It was clearly the public policy of the law that people in that position should be compensated for the loss which they had suffered. The question which the court was required to answer was whether that public policy should be outweighed by the other consideration of the public policy relied on by the defendants. For Underhill LJ public policy assumed two forms, namely, (1) the consistency principle and (2) the public confidence principle.

---

terms of the claimant's having participated in the joint enterprise of dangerous driving, since the claimant neither encouraged it nor intended to do so (ibid at [58]).

97 [2024] EWCA Civ 138. See (2024) 179 Rep.Bul.6; [2024] CLJ 429.

98 Ibid at [85].

99 Ibid at [90].

As far as (1) was concerned, there was no inconsistency with the criminal law in allowing L to recover, on the grounds that he bore no criminal responsibility for the acts which he had committed. He had been acquitted in the criminal court, by reason of insanity.[100] As far as consistency with the civil law was concerned, the judge stated that insanity was no defence to an action in tort.[101] That was to say, that if L's victims' estates had chosen to sue him for their deaths, he would have been liable, notwithstanding the fact that he acted while insane. The defendants claimed that it would be incoherent if the law took a different approach to his responsibility for his acts, in the context of a claim brought by him for damages against a third party. However, the judge was of the view that allowing L to recover was not inconsistent with the rule that insanity did not preclude liability to his victims.[102]

As far as (2) was concerned, Underhill LJ was of the view that allowing L to recover did not flout the values of society.[103] Whereas those who were killed or injured were always required to be treated as primary victims, the killer might also be a victim if he was suffering from serious mental illness, and had been let down by those responsible for his care. The judge then addressed other public policy considerations. As far as the impact on NHS funding by allowing claims similar to those of L to succeed was concerned, the number of such cases was tiny.[104] He was also of the view that denial of compensation to claimants who committed homicide while insane was unlikely to have any deterrent effect.[105]

The appeal, therefore, fell to be dismissed.[106]

The defence of *ex turpi causa* was recently invoked by the defendants in the Court of Appeal case of *Ali v Logistica Polska Sp*.[107] The facts of the case were simple and straightforward. The defendant B's lorry negligently drove into A's car when it was parked and unattended. The accident caused damage to A's car which rendered it undrivable. A had been using his car regularly for both work, social, domestic and pleasure purposes. A had need for a replacement of his car. However, A did not have an alternative vehicle which was available to him that would have been reasonable for him to use while his vehicle was being repaired. While A's car was being repaired, he hired a replacement vehicle on credit hire terms. The period of hire was thirty-six days. The total hire charges were £21,558.72. There was no evidence that prior to the accident A's car was in any way unroadworthy. However, A's Ministry of Transport (MOT) certificate for the car had expired 4½ months before the accident. The hire charges were claimed as special damages, as were the modest cost of repairs to A's car and recovery of the car to the garage.

B argued, *inter alia*, that since A did not have a valid MOT certificate, the defence of *ex turpi causa* applied. However, the Court of Appeal held that the defence was

100 Ibid at [92].
101 Ibid at [100].
102 Ibid at [101].
103 Ibid at [104].
104 Ibid at [114].
105 Ibid at [115].
106 Ibid at [118].
107 [2024] EWCA Civ 1479.

inapplicable. Stuart-Smith LJ stated that the criminal offence of failing to obtain an MOT was a relatively minor offence when considering proportionality.[108] The judge went on to state that allowing recovery for hire charges did not undermine the effectiveness of the criminal law.[109] However, denying recovery might amount in substance to an additional penalty which was disproportionate to the nature and seriousness of the wrongdoing. The judge went on to hold that A's claim was not barred by the doctrine of *ex turpi causa*.[110] It would be disproportionate to bar the claim on that basis.

By way of conclusion on the defence of illegality, in *Les Laboratoires Servier v Apotex Inc*[111] Lord Toulson stated that the case law relating to the defence was notoriously untidy. Again, in *Jetivia SA v Bilta (UK) Ltd*[112] Lord Sumption was of the view that the defence had generated a perplexing mass of case law. The Law Commission for England and Wales was unwilling to advocate legislative intervention, suggesting that the courts should develop the law by making it more transparent and less arbitrary, and by doing more to articulate the policy rationales that underlie their decisions.[113] The defence of illegality has not been examined thus far by the Scottish Law Commission.

Volenti non fit injuria

The defence of *volenti non fit injuria* simply means that a wrongful act is not done to one who is willing. It is sometimes referred to as the pursuer's voluntary assumption of risk.[114] The defence is one of considerable antiquity and its origins can be traced back to the time of Aristotle.[115] Essentially, what the defence means is that where a person consents to run the risk of injury (without compensation) which has been caused by another, the former cannot, thereafter, claim damages in respect of an injury caused by the risk which they had accepted.[116] According to Lord Herschell, 'The maxim is founded on good sense and justice. One who has invited or assented to an act being done towards him cannot, when he suffers from it, complain of it as a wrong.'[117]

108 Ibid at [49].

109 Ibid at [50].

110 Ibid at [53].

111 [2015] AC 430 at 453.

112 [2016] AC 1 at 25.

113 Law Commission, *The Illegality Defence*. Law Com. No. 320 at para. 1.6 (16 March 2010).

114 See the discussion by Lord Nimmo Smith in *McTear v Imperial Tobacco Ltd* 2005 2 SC 1 as the various ways in which the defence might be articulated (at para. 7.205).

115 See T Ingham, 'A History of the Defence of *Volenti Non Fit Injuria*' 1981 JR 1 at 1. In the Court of Appeal case of *Wooldridge v Sumner* [1963] 2 QB 43 at 69 Diplock LJ (as he then was) stated that the maxim *volenti non fit injuria* stated the principle of estoppel applicable originally to a Roman citizen who consented to being sold as a slave.

116 In *Frost v E.K. Cole Ltd* 1949 SLT (Notes) 41 Lord Guthrie observed (at 41) that 'The maxim is appropriate to a case where he suffers by the act of another but is held to have voluntarily accepted the risk of that act.'

117 [1891] AC 325 at 360.

Volenti operates as a complete defence to an action.[118] The onus of proving that the pursuer was *volenti* rests on the defender.[119] The defence must be specifically pled if it is to be relied on at proof.

In *Morris v Murray*[120] the plaintiff had spent the afternoon drinking with the defendant. The defendant had a pilot's licence. Following the drinking session, both men went for a flight in the defendant's light aircraft. The aircraft crashed soon after take-off, and the pilot was killed. The plaintiff was injured. He raised an action against the pilot's representatives. They successfully relied on the defence of *volenti*. The Court of Appeal held that the plaintiff had willingly boarded the aircraft, in the knowledge that the pilot was drunk, and also that the plaintiff was not so drunk as to be incapable of appreciating the nature and extent of the risk involved in the expedition.

For the defence to apply, the defender requires to show that the pursuer, with full knowledge of the nature and extent of the risk which he ran, freely and voluntarily agreed to incur it. Furthermore, the pursuer must be both *sciens* and *volens*. That is to say, that there must be full knowledge of the risk and evidence of the pursuer's acceptance of the risk.[121] Thus, in *White v Blackmore and Ors*[122] an action in respect of the death of a spectator at a 'jalopy' (that is, old car) racing event (who had been killed after a car which was taking part in the race got out of control) was not defeated by the defence of *volenti*. The deceased had no knowledge of the risk which had been caused by the defendants' failure to take proper precautions at the event, by virtue of the fact that the ropes surrounding the track had not been properly arranged.

It is not enough that the pursuer ought to have known of the risk to which he was exposing himself. Whilst the pursuer's consent can either be express or inferred from the whole circumstances,[123] it requires to be real and freely given. Therefore, consent which has been extracted by violence, or threats thereof, is not real consent.

The agreement of the pursuer to run the risk is construed narrowly against the defender. The Court of Appeal case of *Slater v Clay Cross Co Ltd*[124] illustrates this point. In that case, a woman was struck by a train while walking along a narrow railway tunnel. She and other villagers had been in the habit of using the tunnel as a shortcut. The train driver was found to have been negligent in failing to sound the train's whistle and slow down, when entering the tunnel. The woman was found to have been contributorily negligent. However, she was not found to have been *volens*. Denning LJ (as he then was) stated:

118 *ICI Ltd v Shatwell* [1965] AC 325.

119 See for example *McTear v Imperial Tobacco Ltd* 2005 2 SC 1 at para. 7.204 (per Lord Nimmo Smith).

120 [1991] 2 WLR 195.

121 *Toms v Royal Mail Group plc* 2006 SLT 431 at 439 (per Lord Glennie). See also *Smith v Charles Baker and Sons* [1891] AC 325 at 338 (per Lord Halsbury).

122 [1972] 2 QB 651.

123 *Imperial Chemical Industries Ltd v Shatwell* [1965] AC 656. See also *McTear v Imperial Tobacco Ltd* 2005 2 SC 1 at para. 7.205.

124 [1956] 2 QB 264.

> It seems to me that when this lady walked in the tunnel, although it may be said that she voluntarily took the risk of danger from the running of the railway in the ordinary and accustomed way, nevertheless she did not take the risk of negligence by the driver.[125]

The basis of the defence is that the pursuer waives his right to an action in negligence against the defender.[126] Lord Denning MR stated in *Nettleship v Weston*:[127]

> Knowledge of the risk of injury is not enough. Nor is a willingness to take the risk of injury. Nothing will suffice short of an agreement to waive any claim for negligence. The plaintiff must agree either expressly or impliedly,[128] to waive any claim for injury that may befall him due to lack of reasonable care by the defendant, or more accurately, due to the failure of the defendant to measure up to the standard of care that the law requires of him.

In *Nettleship* the defendant had been receiving driving lessons from the claimant and, on one occasion, the claimant was injured when the defendant struck a lamppost. The instructor sued his pupil. However, the defence of *volenti* was unsuccessful. The claimant had asked for, and had been given an assurance that there was a policy of insurance in force, which covered injury to a passenger. By checking his position, in terms of the car insurance, before agreeing to instruct the defendant, the claimant had shown expressly that he had not consented to run the risk of injury.

The consent, whether express or inferred, requires to be to the particular risk involved in the relevant accident.[129] This point is illustrated in *Fowler v Tierney*.[130] A girl was injured in a collision with a motor car, while riding pillion on a motor scooter which was being driven by the defender. The accident was caused by the negligence of the defender. It was established that the defender had been initially unwilling to give the pursuer a lift, because he was only a provisional licence holder, and as such was not permitted to take pillion passengers. The court held that the pursuer was willing to take the risk of trouble with the police, but was not waiving her rights with regard to injury caused by driver's negligence. Therefore, the defence of *volenti* did not succeed.

The defence of *volenti* can be excluded by statute. Thus, s149 of the Road Traffic Act 1988 excludes the defence of *volenti* in an action brought by a passenger in a negligently driven vehicle in circumstances where insurance is necessary by law. This provision is designed to prevent passengers being denied the benefits of third-party insurance which users of motor vehicles are obliged to hold.[131] The statutory exclusion

---

[125] [1956] 2 QB 264 at 271.

[126] *Bankhead* v *McCarthy* 1963 SC 263 at 265 per Lord Walker under reference to *Stewart's Exrx v Clyde Navigation Trs.* 1946 SC 317.

[127] [1971] 2 QB 691 at 701.

[128] *Smith v Baker and Sons* [1891] AC 325 at 336 (per Lord Halsbury).

[129] D M Walker *The Law of Delict in Scotland* (W Green, 1981) at 347. See *Gleghorn v Oldham* (1927) 43 TLR 465 (plaintiff hit by companion's golf club while on a golf course); *Gillmore v LCC* [1938] 4 All ER 331 (plaintiff injured by falling on a slippery floor while participating in a PT class). See also *Lewis v Buckpool Golf Club* 1993 SLT (ShCt) 43.

[130] 1974 SLT (Notes) 23.

[131] At one time, the defence could succeed in these circumstances. See the observations of Lord Kilbrandon in *McCaig v Langan* 1964 SLT 121 at 124.

of the defence is illustrated in the Inner House decision of *Winnick v Dick*.[132] In that case, which was decided under the analogous provision in the earlier Road Traffic Act 1972, the parties to the action had been drinking together in a public house. The pursuer then took a lift in the defender's car and was injured. The defender attempted to rely on the defence of *volenti*. However, the defence was barred by statute.[133]

The defence of *volenti* is applicable only to a case of future negligence on the part of the defender. Where the act of negligence has already occurred, and the pursuer steps into the situation created thereby, with his eyes open, the proper analysis may not be *volenti* but *novus actus interveniens*.[134] For example, in *Sabri-Tabrizi v Lothian Health Board*[135] the pursuer underwent a sterilisation procedure. However, as a result of negligence, it failed, and the pursuer subsequently became pregnant. Following a termination, she became pregnant again and gave birth to a stillborn child. She sought damages from the Health Board. The Board argued that the real cause of the pursuer's pregnancy was her decision to have intercourse in the knowledge that the sterilisation procedure had failed. Such action, the Board argued, amounted to a *novus actus interveniens*. The Lord Ordinary (Lord Nimmo Smith) accepted that argument. The Health Board also argued that the pursuer had taken the risk of pregnancy on herself, and that the maxim *volenti non fit injuria* applied. The Lord Ordinary held, however, that acceptance of risk necessary for the application of the maxim must occur either before or at the same time as the negligent act or omission. That was clearly not so in the instant case, in that the pursuer had not accepted the risk of possible failure of the sterilisation operation before it was carried out.[136]

We now consider the application of the defence in particular areas of activity.

OCCUPIERS

The defence of *volenti* may be available to the occupier of premises on which the pursuer is injured. In *Titchener v British Railways Board*[137] a railway line was bordered by a dilapidated fence. The pursuer who was aged fifteen went through one of the gaps in the fence in order to cross the railway line. She was struck by a train and severely injured as a result. She sued the defenders, averring that they were in breach of their duty to take reasonable care in terms of the Occupiers (Scotland) Liability Act 1960. The girl had admitted that she was aware of the line's existence, and also of the danger of going on to it. In these circumstances, had a breach of duty been made out (which

132 1984 SLT 185.

133 *Winnick* was subsequently approved and applied in *Pitts v Hunt* [1991] 1 QB 24 at 48 (per Beldam LJ) (discussed above) where the court took the view that the defence would have applied on the facts of the case, had it not been for the statutory exclusion in the Road Traffic Act 1972.

134 *Toms v Royal Mail Group plc* 2006 SLT 431 at 440 (per Lord Glennie). See also *McTear v Imperial Tobacco Ltd* 2005 2 SC 1 at 7.206 (per Lord Nimmo Smith).

135 1998 SC 373.

136 Ibid at 377.

137 1984 SC (HL) 34.

it was not), the House of Lords held that the defence of *volenti* would have applied, as the pursuer had willingly accepted the risk of walking on the line.[138]

Titchener can be contrasted with *McGlone v British Railways Board.*[139] In that case, a twelve-year-old boy suffered injury when he climbed a transformer which was situated on premises which was occupied by the defenders. The transformer was surrounded on three sides by a strongly constructed mesh fence. There was no fence on the side nearest the railway line. Warning notices bearing the words 'Danger-Overhead live wires' had been attached to the fence. The boy, having got through some barbed wire, and having climbed the transformer, sustained severe burning from electric shock when his arm came into contact with the live wires. His father raised an action against the defenders under the Occupiers Liability (Scotland) Act 1960. The defenders sought to rely on the defence of *volenti non fit injuria*. However, the House of Lords took the view that the defence did not succeed on the grounds that the boy did not have a proper appreciation of the risk from live wires.[140] (In the event, the defenders were found not to have been in breach of duty.)

LANDLORDS

Where a tenant continues in occupation of property, in the knowledge of a specific risk, such continued occupation does not demonstrate that the tenant willingly accepts that risk. For example, in *Hughes Tutrix v Glasgow District Council*[141] a tenant raised an action as tutrix of a child who had been injured when she caught her hand on a broken toilet bowl. The action was raised against the landlords, it being averred that they were in breach of s3(1) of the Occupiers Liability (Scotland) Act 1960 in respect of their failure to repair the bowl, despite several complaints having been made to them in respect of the bowl's condition. The defender pled *volenti* contending that, by continuing to reside in the premises, while aware of the condition of the toilet bowl, the pursuer had accepted the danger and was therefore barred from

138 Specific provision is made for the defence of *volenti* under s2(3) of the Occupiers Liability (Scotland) Act 1960. See also *Devlin v Strathclyde RC* 1993 SLT 699. Lord Coulsfield held that had there been a breach of duty (which there was not), the defence of *volenti* would have applied against a fourteen-year-old boy who was killed when he fell through a skylight on a school roof. The deceased had jumped on to the skylight during a game of tig, whereupon the skylight shattered and he fell to his death. Lord Coulsfield expressed his agreement (at 703) with Lord Hailsham in *Titchener*, to the effect that the different pleas of sole fault and *volenti* may involve 'little more than different ways of formulating the same result'. See also *Ratcliff v McConnell and Ors* [1999] 1 WLR 670 (a nineteen-year-old college student was aware of, and had accepted the risk of diving into an open air college swimming pool and sustained serious injuries when he hit his head on the bottom). See also *Tomlinson v Congleton BC* [2004] 1 AC 46; *James v White Lion Hotel* [2021] QB 1153; see (2020) 152 Rep.B 5.

139 1966 SC (HL) 1.

140 Ibid at 13 (per Lord Reid). See also the observations of Lord Pearce at 18: 'Had the intruder been a young man of, (say) 18 years, such an inference [of acceptance of the risk] would have been wholly justified on the facts of this case ... If an invader with appreciation of the possible consequences defies the exclusion and the warning, the reasonable inference is that he is accepting the risk and taking the consequences on his own head. But since this was a boy of twelve years, who was believed when he said that he did not appreciate the danger, it was, in my opinion, right to reject the inference.'

141 1982 SLT (Sh Ct) 70.

asserting her claim. The sheriff held that the defender had failed to demonstrate that the pursuer had 'willingly' accepted the danger, and even if the defender had shown willing acceptance on the pursuer's part, it was impossible to suggest that the child herself had willingly accepted the state of the bowl. Accordingly, the defender's plea of *volenti* was rejected.

SPORTING EVENTS

The plea of *volenti* is often raised successfully where injury occurs to a spectator at a sporting event.[142] By attending, the pursuer takes the risk of an error of judgement by a participant but does not consent to a reckless disregard for his own safety. This is illustrated in the Court of Appeal case of *Wooldridge v Sumner*.[143] In that case, there was a competition at a horse show. A horse rounded a bend at considerable speed. The horse became temporarily out of control. A photographer, in fright, fell into the horse's path and was injured. Diplock LJ concluded that the defendant was guilty of an error or errors of judgement or a lapse of skill.[144] In short, the defendant had not been negligent. As far as the application of the *volenti* defence was concerned the judge stated:

> A person attending a game or competition takes the risk of any damage caused to him by any act of a participant, done in the course of and for the purposes of the game or competition, notwithstanding that such an act may involve an error of judgement or lapse of skill, unless the participants conduct is such as to evince a reckless disregard of the spectator's safety.[145]

Participants

Where, in a sporting activity, an injury is inflicted by one participant on another, the availability of the defence of *volenti* will depend on the particular circumstances. Participants are deemed to consent impliedly to the risk of injury which is incidental to the sport in question.[146] They are not considered to have consented to the use of unnecessary force.[147] In the Court of Appeal case of *Smolden v Whitworth*[148] the claimant was seriously injured when his neck was broken after a scrum collapsed during a rugby match. It was held that the referee had failed to ensure that the standard sequence of engagement was used by the players, and that the standard of refereeing had fallen below an acceptable standard. The referee was not entitled to argue that the

142 See, generally, B Gardiner 'Liability for Sporting Injuries' 2008 JPIL 16.

143 [1963] 2 QB 43.

144 Ibid at 72.

145 Ibid at 68. Sellers LJ was of the view (at 56) that the defence of *volenti* was normally inapplicable where a spectator or a competitor was injured during a competition or a game, provided that the competition or the game is being performed within the rules and the requirement of the sport and by persons of adequate skill and competence.

146 *Smolden v Whitworth* [1997] PIQR P133 at P147 (per Cornhill CJ).

147 For an interesting discussion, see A Duff, 'Civil Actions and Sporting Injuries Sustained by Professional Footballers' 1994 SLT (Sh Ct) 43.

148 n 141 above.

claimant had consented to the risk of injury by participating voluntarily in the scrum. While the claimant might have consented to the ordinary risks of the game, he could not be said to have agreed to the referee's breach of duty in failing to apply the rules which were intended to protect players from injury.

In *Czernuszka v King*[149] the claimant was a member of a rugby team. Many members of both sides were novice players. The opposing team included the defendant who attempted to dominate the play and use her weight and greater experience (as well as her language) to intimidate the claimant's team. Towards the end of the match, the defendant tackled the claimant but was winded in her own tackle. Shortly thereafter a ruck was formed, after which the claimant, while acting as scrum half, bent down to pick up the ball. Before the ball was in the claimant's possession, the defendant launched herself at the claimant, while the latter was bending over in a highly vulnerable position and landed on her with her full weight in a belly flop position, on top of the claimant's neck and back, with her hands on the claimant's legs. The claimant sustained serious injuries. She brought an action against the defendant, claiming that the latter had breached her duty of care by failing to exercise such a degree of care which was appropriate in all the circumstances. However, the defendant resisted the claim arguing that in a sporting context, liability could only be established if the defendant was shown to have been reckless, or to have demonstrated a very high degree of carelessness. In allowing the claim with damages to be assessed, the court held that there was no rule or principle that in a sporting context, the conduct in question required to be reckless, or that a very high degree of carelessness had to be demonstrated, in order for liability to be established. The defendant had failed to exercise a degree of care that was appropriate in the circumstances.[150]

EMPLOYMENT SITUATIONS

In an employment situation the defence of *volenti* rarely succeeds.[151] This is simply because it is difficult to establish that an employee has any real freedom of choice in relation to the acceptance of the risk of injury, since he works under economic pressure. In the Court of Appeal case of *Bowater v Rowley Regis Corporation*[152] Goddard LJ stated that in an employment context, the courts should apply the defence of *volenti* with extreme caution. In turn, Scott LJ doubted whether the defence of *volenti* could very often apply in circumstances of an injury to a servant by the negligence of his master.[153]

In the House of Lords case of *Smith v Baker and Sons*[154] the plaintiff was employed by the defendant to drill holes in rocks. The plaintiff was aware that a crane regularly swung loads of stones over his head. A stone fell and injured him. The employer

149 [2023] 4 WLR 26.

150 See also *Condon v Basi* [1985] 1 WLR 866.

151 *Baddely v Earl Granville* (1887) 19 QBD 423; *Wheeler v New Merton Board Mills Ltd* [1933] 2 KB 669. *Morris v Murray* [1991] 2 QB 6 at 17 (per Fox LJ).

152 [1944] KB 476 at 480.

153 Ibid at 479. See also *Christmas v General Cleaning Contractors Ltd* [1952] 1 KB 141.

154 [1891] AC 325.

defendant relied on the defence of *volenti*, to the effect that the plaintiff had consented to run the risk of injury from falling stones. The House held that whereas the plaintiff had continued to work knowing the risk, he had not voluntarily *accepted* the risk. Indeed, several complaints had been made to management, raising concerns about danger. The plaintiff may have been *sciens* (knowing). However, he was not *volens* (willing). That is to say, that his continuing to work did not indicate that the plaintiff was *volens*.[155]

The reluctance of the courts to hold an employee to be *volens* is also illustrated in the Court of Appeal case of *Monaghan v WH Rhodes and Son*.[156] There, iron ladders, which were normally used when loading a ship, were blocked. The plaintiff, therefore, attempted to use a Jacobs ladder (a type of rope ladder) which was fastened at the top to the coamings of the hatch and swung loose some feet from the bottom of the hold. The plaintiff was going up the ladder when it swung and caught his hand between the ladder and the coamings, and in trying to free himself, the plaintiff fell to the foot of the hold and was severely injured. He was held not to be *volens*, there being no sufficient evidence that he undertook the risk of the dangerous ladder.[157]

If, in an employment context, there is an express contract term to the effect that an employee will accept a certain risk of injury, that will be governed by the Unfair Contract Terms Act 1977. A contractual term which attempts to exclude or limit liability for death or personal injury arising from breach of duty in the course of any business is void.[158]

RESCUERS

A person will not be considered to be *volens* if he is trying to save life or rescue valuable property. This is because they are not held to have freely and voluntarily assumed the risk of injury where they are acting under a social or moral duty. The reasons for this are found in public policy. The law does not wish to discourage people from rescuing others. The leading case is *Baker v T E Hopkins and Son Ltd*.[159] The defendants operated a petrol-driven pump to clear out a well. The pump released carbon monoxide fumes. Realising the danger, the employer instructed his employees not to go down the well until he arrived. However, two employees did go down the well and were overcome by fumes. A doctor was summoned to the scene. He was urged not to go down the well. However, in an effort to save the two men who were in difficulty, the doctor tied a rope around himself and then went down the well, leaving instructions that he should be hauled up if he got into difficulty. He descended the well. However, he discovered that nothing could be done for the men. The doctor started to ascend the well. However, he collapsed, and his full weight came onto the rope. Those on the surface started to haul him to the surface. The rope became caught in

155 See also *Stewarts Exrs v Clyde Navigation Tr* 1946 SC 317.

156 [1920] 1 KB 487.

157 Ibid at 499 (per Atkin LJ) as he then was.

158 Unfair Contact Terms Act 1977, s16, as amended by the Law Reform (Miscellaneous Provisions) (Scotland) Act 1990, s68.

159 [1959] 1 WLR 966.

a pipe or cross member of the well and he could not be hauled up any further. Soon afterwards the fire brigade brought him to the surface. He was by then unconscious. He died before reaching hospital. The other two men were dead when they were brought up. The executors of the doctor sued the defendants. It was held that the defendants owed the doctor a duty of care. The court rejected the defence that the doctor had been *volens*.[160]

However, in the Court of Appeal case of *Cutler v United Dairies (London) Ltd*[161] the defence of *volenti* served to defeat the claim of the plaintiff, who was injured while attempting to restrain a horse which had bolted. Slesser LJ stated:[162]

> The appellants can ... properly say that the respondent agreed to accept freely and voluntarily with full knowledge of the risk he ran, the chances of the injury which he suffered. The case is one where the maxim *volenti non fit injuria* applies.

SELF-HARM

To what extent, if any, is the defence of *volenti* relevant to circumstances in which a person commits suicide as a result of the defender's negligence? In the House of Lords case of *Reeves v Commissioner of Police for the Metropolis*[163] a prisoner who was in police custody committed suicide by hanging by using his shirt as a ligature. He was able to do this because a hatch on his cell door had been left open. The police had owed the deceased a duty to prevent him from hanging himself. It was held that the defence of *volenti* could not be relied on where the act of suicide was the very act which the defendant had a duty to prevent. The very existence of the duty foreclosed the *volenti* argument. Lord Jauncey rationalised the decision as follows:[164] 'If the defence were available in circumstances such as the present, where the deceased was known to have suicidal tendencies, it would effectively negative the effect of any duty of care in respect of such suicide ...'[165]

RES JUDICATA

The defence of *res judicata* is to the effect that the issue has already been litigated between the same parties and has been determined by a competent court. It is a complete defence and has long been recognised as such.

---

160 Ibid at 984 (per Willmer LJ).

161 [1933] 2 KB 297.

162 Ibid at 306.

163 [2000] 1 AC 431.

164 Ibid at 375.

165 See also *Kirkham v Chief Constable of the Greater Manchester Police* [1990] 2 QB 283. The defence of *volenti* in respect of an act of suicide was inappropriate where the act of the deceased relied on is the very act which the duty cast upon the defendant required him to prevent (per Farquarson LJ at 295). See also *Corr v IBC Vehicles Ltd* [2008] 1 AC 884. A worker who committed suicide while in a state of depression which was induced by an industrial accident was not *volens*. Lord Bingham stated (at 905): '[His suicide] was not something to which [the deceased] had consented voluntarily and with his eyes open but an act performed because of the psychological condition which the employer's breach of duty had induced.'

> It has been accepted for good reason that in individual disputes a single action and one final judgement is sufficient, lest otherwise the ambit of suits be greatly increased and cause very great and insurmountable difficulty, especially if different judgements are pronounced.[166]

In *Graham v Secretary of State for Scotland*[167] Lord President Cooper stated that the plea of *res judicata* is:

> common to most legal systems and is based upon considerations of public policy, equity and common sense which will not tolerate that the same issue should be litigated repeatedly between the same parties on substantially the same basis.

A plea of *res judicata* will be upheld where there is identity as to the following matters:

1. The parties

In *RG v Glasgow City Council*[168] Lord Carloway stated that reference to the same parties should not be construed too strictly. It sufficed if the interest of the parties in the first and second action was the same.[169]

2. The subject matter

In *Graham* Lord President Cooper stated that the key question which the court was required to answer was what was litigated and what was decided?[170] The court is not tied to the parties' precise formulations in their pleadings; it may look at the substance of the matters pleaded, especially if the pleadings fail to focus on, or if they mask, the issues which were in dispute and were determined in the previous action.[171]

3. The *media concludendi*

The two suits must present one and the same ground of action, so that the specific point raised in the second suit must have been directly raised and concluded by the judgment of the first.[172]

---

166 Digest, 44, 2. 6.

167 1951 SC 368 at 387.

168 2020 SC 1 at 9.

169 See also *McCluskey v Scott Wilson Scotland Ltd.* 2024 SCLR 183; *Primary Health Care Centres (Bradford) Ltd v Ravangave* 2009 SLT 673.

170 1951 SC 368 at 387. See also *Smith v Sabre Insurance Co Ltd* 2013 SC 569.

171 *Primary Health Care Centres (Bradford) Ltd* n166 at 679.

172 *McCluskey* n168. See also *North British Railway Co v Lanarkshire and Dumbartonshire Railway Co* (1897) 24 R 564; *Edinburgh and District Water Trustees v Clippens Oil Co.* (1889) 1 F 899; *Glen v Dunlop* (1906) 13 SLT 898; *Matuszczyk v National Coal Board* 1955 SC 418; *Smith v Sabre Insurance Co Ltd* n167.

Index

References to footnotes are represented as page number followed by note number (eg 3n15).

EU Authorised Representative:
Easy Access System Europe Mustamäe tee 50, 10621 Tallinn, Estonia
gpsr.requests@easproject.com

Printed and bound by CPI Group (UK) Ltd, Croydon, CR0 4YY
17/08/2026
02198008-0003